THE TWO TELUGU STATES AFTER DEMERGER

DIFFERENT POLITICAL
&
ECONOMIC CONTOURS

Janardhan Reddy Janumpalli

Chennai • Bangalore

CLEVER FOX PUBLISHING
Chennai, India

Published by CLEVER FOX PUBLISHING 2023
Copyright © Janardhan Reddy Janumpalli 2023

All Rights Reserved.
ISBN: 978-93-56486-32-4

This book has been published with all reasonable efforts taken to make the material error-free after the consent of the author. No part of this book shall be used, reproduced in any manner whatsoever without written permission from the author, except in the case of brief quotations embodied in critical articles and reviews.

The Author of this book is solely responsible and liable for its content including but not limited to the views, representations, descriptions, statements, information, opinions and references ["Content"]. The Content of this book shall not constitute or be construed or deemed to reflect the opinion or expression of the Publisher or Editor. Neither the Publisher nor Editor endorse or approve the Content of this book or guarantee the reliability, accuracy or completeness of the Content published herein and do not make any representations or warranties of any kind, express or implied, including but not limited to the implied warranties of merchantability, fitness for a particular purpose. The Publisher and Editor shall not be liable whatsoever for any errors, omissions, whether such errors or omissions result from negligence, accident, or any other cause or claims for loss or damages of any kind, including without limitation, indirect or consequential loss or damage arising out of use, inability to use, or about the reliability, accuracy or sufficiency of the information contained in this book.

PREFACE

The book is a collection of articles written periodically, from 2014 on wards by the author after the demerger of two Telugu states. The articles cover the run up to the formation of the new states and the post demerger political and economic journey of them from 2014 – 2023 in them. It is a follow up to the book 'Mission Telangana' which covered the Telangana state struggle from 2010 to 2015. The main objective of the book is to know the impact of state division on the two resultant states. Also to know the veracity of the claims and counter claims of the people of two regions on the state division and its after effects. Few articles from 'Mission Telangana' are included in this book to make the thread contiguous from the passing of the Telangana state Bill in 2014 to the present in 2023. There is also some over lapping of information in a few articles to keep the context and continuity of the subject, as the articles were written separately.

The skepticism of anti Telangana state elements in the viability of the new state has created an anxious curiosity in the progress of Telangana state. All Andhras and some other state analysts were predicting a difficult journey for the state, with out knowing or assessing the antecedents of the two merged regions. A few of Telangana 'intellectuals' were also prophesying bad days to Telangana. It was all because of the continuous build up of a false narrative and working on it of the Andhra elite against the political, economic and social credentials of Telangana region. The Andhra literati, media, political leadership and the civil society in unison have created a myth of Andhra superiority in the united Andhra Pradesh.

And with their majority of 175 against 119 legislators in the Assembly and the cultivated political leverage with the Center have helped to dominate the ruling of the united state. They were successful in showing Telangana as second class to Andhra. Facts were deliberately submerged under a motivated fiction.

It took 58 years, many campaigns and loss of hundreds of lives, to come out of that dominance and win the separate state. It is now a history and an unique one at that in the annals of independent India. Telangana state can be termed as a hard earned 'political freedom inside a democracy'. After the demerger, in the lost 10 years the real facts have started emerging distinctly debunking the myth. The two Telugu states have taken different paths and have shown their widely varying political and economic contours, depending on their inherent differences. In the process, the apprehensions of State Reorganization Commission(SRC), the reluctance of Telangana people in 1956 and the claims of Telangana state activists later, on merger proved to be more than right.

Once the division has taken place the comparative financial position of the two states has come in to aclear cut juxtaposition. Andhra ended up with heavy revenue deficit, a recurrence of the before 1956 position. Telangana has shown revenue surplus like in 1956 residual Hyderabad state. In the very first year 2014-15, A.P. has claimed a big revenue deficit grant from the Center and got about Rs.12000 cr. In addition to that 14 and 15 Finance Commissions were influenced to get Rs.52,000 cr deficit grant for A. P. averaging about Rs.5000-6000 cr per year. It was the highest deficit grant to any new state created in independent India. Yet, the gap between revenue income and revenue expenditure of A. P. was not bridged in the last 10 years.

It is not the case with Telangana, which had revenue surplus before merger. In the new state after demerger also it has registered surplus and maintained it till the advent of Covid virus, in which time all the states in the country have gone in to deficit budget. T.S. has recovered from it and is making a prudential budget management with in the stipulated norms of the RBI. A.P. could not do it. That is a tell-tale story of the comparative financial strengths of the two regions from before the merger. Finally, the truth has come out clearly, erasing the made up false narrative.

Telangana was always having higher percentage of per capita revenue than Andhra region. Periodical official figures are available to corroborate it. Dhar commission 41.59%(1945-48); SRC 42.89%(1956); Two states audited budgets 43.54% (2014-15) and 59.16 % 2020-21). This is the recorded chronicle of excess revenue of Telangana over Andhra. One more important economic parameter is percentage of state owned tax revenue (SOTR) in the total revenue of the state. The total revenue of a state comprises of SOTR, central tax devolution and central grants. Higher percentage of SOTR leverages the state to manage its budget better. It can borrow more, service the debt better and increase its revenue with more capital investment. It helps the state register better growth year after year.

The financially leading states in the country like Hariyana, Maharashtra, Tamilnadu and Karnataka have higher SOTR. As per the RBI statement for the years from 2015 to 2021, these states have more than 65 % SOTR. TS with 72 -75 % is in the second highest place. AP's SOTR is 51% and all states average is 46 %. That broadly defines the comparative financial variation of A P and Telangana states. But the myth created before the demerger was that Andhra financial position is better than Telangana and with out A.P.'s economic support Telangana would be in a problem. But it proved to be totally incorrect and the credentials are reversed between the two.

In fact, it was all there to see from the very beginning. But the aggressive Andhra majority ensemble has succeeded gradually in creating a false narrative of Andhra hand holding Telangana. But it was totally a wrong premise. If Andhra was so comfortable with its finances in 1956, there was no need for asking for it to force merge with Telangana. There was no need to give several assurances to Telangana in the name of gentle men's agreement. It was a dire necessity for A. P. to merge with Telangana for economic viability and for a ready made first class capital in Hyderabad. It was totally unnecessary for Telangana, which ingenuous act has proved to be very costly for the region, as the history proved it.

In the united Andhra Pradesh approximately 50% of revenue income used to come from 10 districts of Telangna with a popluation of 3.52 cr, as against the population of 4.94 cr from Andhra's 13 districts.The revenue expenditure on an average used to be 35-38% in Telangana and 62-65% in Andhra. Even after the merger, there was no attempt to match the revenue income and expenditure in Andhra region. Instead the deficit was made good with a part of the revenue from Telangana continuously year after year. The Kumar Lalith and Bhargava committes in 1969-1970 have vouchsafed this. It continued all the 58 years. And the post merger budget figures have confirmed the fact. In the light of it,the Andhra government and its civil society needs to draw suitable inference from it and try to correct their state's financial inequity, instead of repeating the false narrative. There is no point in camouflaging its inherent financial weaknesses and blame the demerger. Now it has become a dire necessity for them to balance revenue income and expenditure, to make steady incremental progress.

The political development also in the two states, has taken different paths. Andhra embroiled it self in the false premises of victim hood,world class antics and caste politics. The maiden government which focused on world class capital, with out regard to its small economy and irrelevance of it has landed the state in deep trouble .The issue has become a rolling stone around the neck of the state . The people have realized it and gave a referendum like verdict against TDP government. But,the YSRCP govt. is bogged down with the impossible Amaravati capital and its own equivocal 3 capital alternative. Leaving aside the ailing economy, the government is indulging in heavy welfare administration. The excessive dependence on the Center's devolution and grants, makes the state over reliant on Center and runs the risk of joining the so called BIMARU states. The caste polarization politics and lack of understanding of the needs of the big deficit budget economy and the lack of proper perspective for the reconstruction of the state has forced the state to take a low contour of economic progress.

In contrast Telangana though it was given a bare state after a prolonged struggle, with out any substantial sops, has stuck earnestly to the reconstruction of the state, which was kept stagnant in the united state. The people have given a measured verdict in 2014 giving just enough majority to TRS to govern the new state. The TRS government has undertaken a premeditated and strategic reconstruction plan with out help from the Center. Making use of its own resources, refurbished by the availability of the share of its revenue which was spent on Andhra, in the united state has gone forward with relative ease. And has implemented a prudential budget of capital investment mixed with innovative welfare schemes and established its self reliant economy firmly. TRS was reelected with a massive majority in 2018. With a renewed political energy has completed many big ticket projects in Power, irrigation, industry, construction etc. and has joined the motley club of economically leading states in the country in a short time. It reached to a point of highest per capita income in the country. And is riding on an ever rising wave of economic development. It proves beyond doubt that it's merger with Andhra was a historic blunder.

Thus the two Telugu states have undertaken different political and economic journey, after demerger, resulting in a development on different contours both in politics and state economies. It makes an intersting study of facts and fiction in the A P state reorganization of 2014, vindicating the claims, hopes and aspirations of Telangana people.

Janardhan Reddy Janumpalli

Dedication

This book is dedicated to the memory of my beloved maternal grand mother Smt. Y. Janamma who made my education possible.

Janardhan Reddy Janumpalli

Gopaldinne (Village)

Veepangandla (Mandalam)

Wanaparthy (District)

TELANGANA

ACKNOWLEDGEMENTS

The book 'The Two Telugu states after demerger' is a compendium of articles written by me and published in different online/print media from 2014 to 2023. It is a follow up to my earlier book 'Mission Telangana', published on 15 February, 2023 by Clever Fox Publishing, Chennai. Mission Telangana covered the Telangana state struggle from 2010 to 2014.This book tries to present the political and economic journey of the two Telugu states after the division of the erstwhile Andhra Pradesh state. It is not a premeditated journalistic write-up. It is a spontaneous expression of views on the developments and the progress of the two states, after such a prolonged and poignant struggle. Particularly because of the curious anxiety created on the future of the Telangana state, as many learned people expressed skepticism on its success. Fortunately, their antipathy did not prove correct.

My thanks to Missiontelangna.com, website and The Hans India and Telangana Today News Papers for publishing my articles, which formed the content of this book, with spontaneous response. Without which I could not have compiled this book. My heartfelt thanks to Dileep Konatham, the young comrade in arms in Telangana state struggle and now Digital media director, in Telangana state government. He was the force behind Missiontelangna.com and ran a relentless campaign for Telangana state through the website with his dedicated team.

Acknowledgements

My special thanks and gratitude to Sri K Srinivas Reddy, The Editor, Telangana Today, who is doing an yeoman service to Telangana state with his esteemed News Paper. He gave me his unstinted support to my writings in Telangana Today and helped me to become a considerable journalist. My articles in Telangana Today form major part of this book.

My gratitude to Sri Manchreddi Janardhan Reddy, ardent Telangana state activist, who followed my writings, discussed, appreciated and encouraged me to write the book. He helped launch my earlier book 'Mission Telangana' in a memorable literary function with other better known authors.

My grateful thanks to Dr. G.R.Reddy, the advisor (Finance) to Govt. of Telangana, who has graciously agreed and wrote a very appreciative 'Foreword' to my book. He is the architect of the very prudential financial management of the new state.

My thanks are due to many of my friends and acquaintances who read my articles, encouraged my writings with their meaningful reviews.

I am thankful to my family members putting up with my journalistic shenanigans. Especially my wife Nirmala, a stickler with time table to put up my irregular time table because of my writings. She also yet times helped me in moderating my harsh comments in my writings. Rest of the family gave me an implicit support in my writings and encouraged to publish the books.

Last but not the least, my big thanks to my Publisher, Clever Fox Publishing Chennai and its associates, Sri.Sreevas Munnoolam, his team and M.Vinoda, who helped me bringing out this book so beautifully.

Janardhan Reddy Janumpalli

FOREWORD

This book, a collection of 63 articles written by Mr. Janumpalli, presents meticulous analysis of the events and issues since the enactment of Andhra Pradesh Reorganization Act (APRA) in 2014 resulting in the formation of Telangana State to September 2023. I compliment the author for his unwavering interest in the developments in Telangana and vividly presenting them to the reader in an engaging and objective manner. One comes across rarely a collection of articles by the same author covering the developments in Telangana on an ongoing basis. Mr. Janumpalli's writings filled with commitment, realism and emotions easily connect with the reader.

Telangana's neglect and step-motherly treatment did not end with the enactment of APRA. Many provisions in the Act are detrimental to the interests of Telangana and framed treating Telangana as a beneficiary in the combined State ignoring the fact that it was an oppressed region. In the combined State, many opportunities were lost and problems accumulated as a result of deliberate neglect of Telangana.

The situation at the time of formation of Telangana State was very bleak and challenging. Nine out of the then ten districts were categorized as backward and covered under Backward Regions Grant Fund. There were acute power shortages resulting in unscheduled power cuts and industrial units working only for a few days and that too in shifts. The agriculture and allied sectors, which support nearly 50 per cent of the population was in distress driving them to suicides. The growth of GSDP was at a lower level as compared with the all-India average. The challenging task before the Government was to address the long standing unfulfilled basic needs of the poor. Without brooding over the past neglect, the State Government took it as a challenge and went into a mission mode to reinvent Telangana. Telangana Government did not let the crisis go waste. Taking the crisis as an opportunity, the Government took up a number of first of its kind developmental and welfare programmes.

The results of these initiatives have borne fruit and are visible to the entire Country. Telangana has emerged as one of the fastest growing States in the entire Country after its formation as a separate State. This was commended by the NITI Aayog as well as International Agencies. It is no mean achievement that Telangana, the youngest State of the Indian Union has become a trailblazer and a role model for the entire Country.

All these developments have been vividly captured in the articles written by Mr.Janumpalli. For any reader interested in the developments in Telangana since its formation as a separate State, this book will undoubtedly serve as a very useful reference.

Dr. G. R. Reddy

Dr.G.R.Reddy

Dr. G. R. Reddy is a PhD in Economics and presently Advisor to the Government of Telangana (Finance) in the rank of a Cabinet Minister. He was Advisor to Government of Andhra Pradesh (Finance) during 2012-14. He was also Honorary Fellow at Centre for Economic and Social Studies between 2005 and 2010. He worked as Advisor to the Thirteenth Finance Commission, and as World Bank Consultant for some countries. His areas of interest are Public Finance Management, Center-State Fiscal Relations, and Economic Planning, Monitoring and Evaluation. He has many important publications in EPW, Financial Express, and Economic Times. He Co-authored a book on "Indian Fiscal Federalism" with Dr. Y V Reddy in 2019; he also Co-authored a book on "Center-State Financial Relations: A Study in Levels of Development of States" with M L Shastri, in 1988.

CONTENTS

Preface .... *iii*
Acknowledgements .... *ix*
Foreword .... *xi*

1. Shackles to Telangana & Sops to Seemandhra 1
2. Telangana cause cannot be a casualty of power politics 8
3. What combination is good for Telangana in the elections ? 12
4. Vote for a government 'of Telangana, by Telangana, for Telangana' 16
5. Telangana politics in a spin on a turning wicket 21
6. An Altruistic Telangana Political Identity 25
7. Telangana State – 'Freedom' inside a Democracy 29
8. Is KCR a 'fresher' in a College? 36
9. Polavaram Amendment – Are Bhadrachalam Tribals sacrificial goats !... 40
10. Andhra Capital Conundrum 44
11. KCR's Comments on Press - Times Now TV live debate 48
12. TV Channels ban in Telangana: Press is not God 52
13. TRS government under siege of 'power' 55
14. Center often dangles 'Governorgiri' to browbeat TS 60
15. Is Telangana a rich State ! 65
16. Andhra's budget deficit is the legacy of their own making 69

17. A.P. govt. 'in exile' in TS - a solution or a problem ! 75
18. 'Amaravati' capital ecologically challenged 81
19. Wither Scientific State Bifurcation !... 86
20. A reply to Kanche Ilaiah 92
21. Why Hyderabad people need to vote for TRS in
    GHMC Elections ?.. 96
22. NGRI report on Mission Kakatiya in Telangana: A comment 99
23. Telangana vindicates its statehood 103
24. Kaleshwaram Project : Springboard for State's growth............. 107
25. Facts and fiction on division 112
26. Kaleshwaram deserves national status 117
27. Discuss technicalities with experts 121
28. Benefits dwarf costs of Kaleshwaram 126
29. Undoing the spirit of Telangana 131
30. Telangana reasserts its identity.. 135
31. Avoid hostilities between two Telugu States 139
32. Mare's Nest In Andhra Pradesh.. 143
33. Elections a referendum on TDP government......................... 148
34. Capital dilemma of Andhra Pradesh 152
35. Kaleshwaram Project benefits beyond Agriculture................. 156
36. Do not belittle Telangana State formation 161
37. Making regulated farming work 166
38. BJP's daydreams will not come true....................................... 171
39. Regional parties suit new States 175
40. New Secretariat, new identity for Telangana 179
41. Sericulture as a money-spinner in Telugu states 184
42. If AP is right, why dodge the tribunal ! 189
43. Telangana on firm financial footing 194
44. Plugging chronic economic inequality 200
45. Divergent paths of Telugu States... 205

46. BJP's strange turf war in Telangana 210
47. Center needs treat Telangana with respect 214
48. G.O. on river water is anti-federal 220
49. Telangana scores a bull's eye 224
50. Telangana 8th Anniversary -The progress 229
51. National parties stoop low in State 234
52. Defeat of BJP's covert motives 238
53. Bharat Rashtra Samithi can be a game-changer for India 243
54. AP's capital dream keeps crashing 247
55. Munugode bypoll is a blot on democracy 252
56. Predatory politics of BJP exposed 256
57. Andhras' destabilizing politics 260
58. AP must shelve false complex 265
59. Chandrababu Naidu's 'Andhra chauvinism' ! 268
60. The 'crown' of Telangana 272
61. A decade of deeds, fulfillment 277
62. A unique tribute to Martyrs 283
63. PRLI - South Telangana's wellspring 288

1

SHACKLES TO TELANGANA & SOPS TO SEEMANDHRA

(Missiontelangana.com | 7 March, 2014)

Telangana State has arrived. It is coming into existence from 2nd June 2014, after a poignant struggle for decades. But, the tradeoff between the hegemony of seemandhra and the political freedom of Telangana brokered by Congress and BJP parties was equivocal in the end. It has ended up in a curiously lopsided situation. It has left Telangana in a feeling of 'pyrrhic achievement' and Seemandhra in a bonanza of packages, as if it was the underdog all along. Telangana government is kept on probation in Hyderabad city for 10 long years. It is a shackled state for Telangana and lavish sops to Seemandhra.

It can be seen clearly in the 13th schedule of the Act. Where in some national institutions are sanctioned/proposed for the two resultant states. The discrimination is quite clear.It is 20 for Andhra Pradesh and 6 for Telangana.Perhaps all the new states formed after independence together might not have got so many institutions/projects, as in case of residual A P . Even in their implementation there is also unmistakable discrimination.

The Congress Party had mismanaged the whole issue in the last four years and dragged it into a tight corner in the end. The Seemandhra politicians and media went into an overdrive of anti-Telangana propaganda. The BJP waiting in the wings was baiting Congress with a promise of full-fledged State. In the end BJP, also influenced by Seemandhra elements and seizing on the inevitability of its support has employed political coercion to broker a qualified Telangana State.

This has resulted in the bounty of packages, statuses and safeguards to Seemandhra, which are palpable political bribes. The irony is that the oppressor who had indulged in political despotism got all the concessions as if it was the aggrieved. The oppressed was given a bare state of their own with clipped wings. This is another episode of political gamesmanship, which Congress party was playing on Telangana, treating it as a political 'orphan' since it was liberated from Nizam in 1948. The statutory new Institutions/Projects,sanctioned/envisaged for the two states in the 13th Schedule are as follows.

A.P. Reorganization Act. The statutory new Institutions/Projects, sanctioned/envisaged for the two states in the 13th Schedule

Andhra Pradesh :
Sanctioned : IIT, NIT, IIM, IISER, CU, PU, AU, IIIT, AIIMS, TU (10)
1.National Institute of disaster management 2. Duggirajapatnam Port (2)
Examine the feasibility :
1. Steel Plant, Cuddapah
2. Crude oil and Petrochemical Refinery
3. Chennai – Vizag industrial corridor
4. Metro Rail VGTM
5. Metro Rail Vizag
6. Expanding Vizag, Vijayawada and Tirupati airports.
7. A railway Zone
8. Rapid rail and road connectivity from new capital to TS. (8)

Total = 10+2+8=20

Telangana State :
Sanctioned : TU and HU (2)

Examine the feasibility :
1. Steel Plant in Khammam
2. NTPC 4000 MW power Plant.
3. Road connectivity in the backward areas of TS
4. Rail Coach factory (4)

Total = 2+4=6

The A.P. Reorganization Bill proper itself1 is a departure from umpteen other such Bills enacted earlier, with several incongruities incorporated in it as political sops to seemandhra, impacting Telangana State adversely, in addition to the asymmetrical 13 th Schedule. Let us examine some of them.

1. The common capital: The status of Hyderabad as common capital and the 'governor giri' over it is a clear infringement on the autonomy of Telangana government. Its constitutional validity is questionable. The real purpose of this provision is to help the Seemandhra politico-corporate-czars. It is to continue their stranglehold on their lucre in Hyderabad city to manipulate and siphon it off under the protection of the Central government via the Governor. Because of this, they will not be very keen to complete the construction of their own capital in Seemandhra. They might like to use up all the 10 years' time. They may try to manipulate the things to continue their presence in Hyderabad city in one political form or another even after having their own capital. It is believed that a couple of lakhs of acres of prime land in and around Hyderabad is in the hands of Seemandhra carpetbaggers/political-corporate mafia . Telangana people feel that, if such unlawful gain made by Seemandhras in and around Hyderabad city is not accounted for, what is the use of getting a separate state after fighting such a tragic war.

2. Interstate water Boards: The interstate water boards proposed in the Bill are different from other such boards in the country. The other boards only regulate the water distribution, release of water and other related matters. But these water boards in the Bill are typically designed to safeguard the excessive use of water by Seemandhras. They are empowered to examine the new projects for their feasibility and accord permission before forwarding them to the Central Water Commission. Since seemandhra are already using excessive water in both the river basins of Godavari and Krishna, the Andhra counterpart in the Boards will be reluctant to accede to the upper riparian projects in Telangana. It makes the new projects in Telangana very difficult to come into execution.

Seemandhras can create endless hassles for taking up the irrigation projects of Telangana kept in pending deliberately in the united state for decades. The current Polavaram, Dummugudem and the Rayalaseema Projects are all heavily loaded against the interests of Telangana. Seemandhras will use their evident political clout with the center to complete them and harass initiation of new Telangana projects, using the interstate water boards. Polavaram Project which is included in the Reorganization Bill itself is against all norms and Congress Party's unscrupulous politics in case of

Bhadrachalam division is a clear example of this conspiracy. Telangana people want water boards like the interstate boards working elsewhere in the Country. Not these boards which will make Telangana projects to be at the mercy of Central and Seemandhra governments.

3. The Public debt on projects: In the Bill the public debt is proposed to be divided on population basis. It should be divided on the basis of where the money is spent. This will be a huge disadvantage to Telangana, as more debt is spent on Projects beneficial to seemandhra. This has to be examined in the light of similar problem in the earlier division of states and the numerous precedents.

4. Reservations In education & employment: It is an open secret that Seemandhras every year usurp a large no.of seats in educational institutions and jobs legitimately belonging to Telangana students/youth circumventing the rules in the united state. There is no such scope for Telangana youth in Seemandhra region. As per the Bill seemandhras continue their quotas in education & employment, in Hyderabad for next 10 years. This has to be analyzed institution wise in all the institutions listed in the Bill vis -a- vis the no.of seats available in education institutions in seemandhra area and an equitable distribution of seats is to be ensured. There should be separate entrance tests for Telangana and Seemandhra. As for the employment their quota has to be stopped forthwith as their usurpation in the matter had exceeded all the limits.

5. Allocation of employees & payment of their pension: This is another area where the allocation of employees and their pension payment is going to be against the interest of Telangana. It will heavily impact the financial commitment and the opportunities for employment in Telangana State. It is time to work out modalities to identify the jobs belonging to Telanganites and the usurpers there on. Allot them based on nativity and not based on their option and divide the employees between the two states. If the illegitimate employees are allotted to Telangana and their pensions are also to be paid by Telangana, it will be like adding insult to the injury. The legitimacy of the job has to be decided based on the rules on the date of appointment. If a seemandhra employee is appointed in a Telangana job he should be regarded as seemandhra based on his nativity and should be allotted to Seemandhra and his pension also has to be accounted for from seemandhra. Here it is needed to examine the details of all the employees and the irregularities identified. And rectify them to create much wanted employment to Telangana and avoid the draconian pension burden on Telangana.

6. Special packages for Rayalaseema and North coastal Andhra: All Telangana districts except Hyderabad district, Chittor, Cuddapah, Anantapur and Vizianagaram in seemandhra are the 13 districts of Andhra Pradesh that are identified by the Centre, for inclusion in the backward regions grant fund (BRGF). But the central government announced as part of the bifurcation of state a special package for all 4 Rayalaseema districts and 3 North coastal districts, but none in Telangana. If there is a need to provide a special package it should be given to all the backward districts on both sides of the divide. It is a superfluous award and is a clear case of political favoritism. The backwardness of these districts has nothing to do with the Telangana State and announcing this package in the context of division of state does not make any sense. There is a need to address the problems of backward areas everywhere in the country as a national policy not as part of state reorganization. Though Telangana people do not begrudge the special package for seemandhra districts, considering it as a quid pro quo for Telangana state neglecting all the Telangana districts identified as backward makes it a glaring injustice. It is going to create a very uneven playing field between the two states, because of economic concessions and tax benefits to these districts, affecting the economy of Telangana state.

7. Special financial status: Special financial status is given to economically unviable small states like NE region with certain specified criteria. But here it is being given for Seemandhra, bigger than Telangana and supposed to be a very resource rich region. The idea that Seemandhra is more deserved to have special status than Telangana is preposterous. If it is for Hyderabad revenue, the premise is already proved not correct. There are precedents like Madras and Bombay in earlier divisions. If special status is needed it should be given to Telangana which is smaller in size and was economically exploited by seemandhra for 58 years. It is a cockneyed concession and is given succumbing to the blackmail of BJP at the last minute. It is a brazen exhibition of political horse-trading. Bihar has already started its protest. There will be more. There is a need to demand and get the special status for Telangana state also.

8. Common Institutions: There is the issue of Common High Court, Public Service commission etc. Smaller states than Telangana have separate institutions. We must take all the measures to get the state level institutions separated statewise as soon as possible to avoid seemandhra pernicious interference.

There is a need to have discussions with subject matter specialists on all these matters and come up with clear cut solutions to act firmly to rectify them. There is a need to fight on all fronts to remove or reduce these restrictions at the earliest. For that there is a need to retain our Telangana regional character in the governance of Telangana State at least for the coming 10 years. The national parties will not help in this matter. They will be manipulated by seemandhras again as they are doing now. Therefore, TRS and TJAC on their own or in alliance with national parties have to play an important political role till Telangana state gets rid of these anomalies and ground a comprehensive state reconstruction plan, bridging the gaps created by Seemandhra administration.

2

TELANGANA CAUSE CANNOT BE A CASUALTY OF POWER POLITICS

(Missiontelangana.com | 22 March, 2014)

The forthcoming Telangana state has created some political convolutions in the region, ahead of general elections. All the political parties as their wont and as the need of their trade are playing power politics in the name of Telangana State. The people of Telangana, in the euphoria of getting the new state, are becoming complacent. They are in a vulnerable situation for diversion from the focus of Telangana cause to prosaic politics. It is a dodgy situation. Telangana State granted by UPA is full of fetters. To get an unencumbered state like other 28 states in the country there is a long way to go. To overcome those restrictions imposed on Telangana State perhaps they need an ardent struggle as the struggle for the state itself.

The parties like Congress and BJP and Seemandhra dominated local parties, if they have a say in the Telangana government they will gloss over those restrictions and use them for their political advantage. Therefore at least till they steer clear of these restrictions, Telangana people should focus unswervingly on Telangana political cause. They cannot succumb to half-truths of the power politics of those political parties. The Congress and BJP, who as national parties, are not particularly enamored of Telangana regional needs. These parties, if they are in power in Telangana, will sponsor Seemandhra influence on Telangana government directly or by proxy. Parties like TDP and YSRCP are confirmed adversaries to Telangana state. Their thriving in Telangana will be similar to the dangers of a Trojan horse.

Telangana people have experienced the malevolent tactics of these parties in 2004, 2009 general elections and during the long drawn tragic struggle since 9th, December 2009. They have to simply draw the inferences from those experiences and act wisely. Any ingenuous political preferences based on the motivated political propaganda of them this time around, will have a telling effect on the nascent state of Telangana in its efforts to come out of the probation imposed on it. All of them are claiming to have facilitated the award of Telangana state. But, if we examine the happenings in the last session of Parliament and the causes and effects of those happenings and the final outcome of T-Bill we will know who has done what.

People of Telangana are to be very critical and circumspect in choosing the political parties in these general elections. For Telangana, it is not a routine run of the mill general elections. The Party(s) which comes to power now will have to lay the foundation for the new state of Telangana. They have to get all the sanctions imposed on it by the central government in T-Bill removed. They have to keep the marauding Andhra dominated political parties, who are the antithesis of Telangana, out of Telangana. They have to estimate the backlog of backwardness forced on Telangana in the united state and usher in plans to rebuild Telangana with a careful identification, prioritization and execution of Projects that will meet the hopes of Telangana people in the new state. This cannot be done by the parties which have the remote control in Delhi or the administration which acts as proxy for Seemandhra interests. We all know by this time the Central government works for those who have more political clout with numbers or otherwise, or with a strong regional presence, commitment to the region and the ability to leverage their political strength.

Therefore, it is a litmus test for the commitment of Telangana people to the state of Telangana and their judgment. They cannot afford to fall prey to the litany of regular political commotion of caste, creed, class, persona etc. Those issues are very much there. They can be addressed at an appropriate time in an appropriate manner. But it is not the time to lend more credence to those things, which can dilute the process of consolidation of our new state of Telangana. They all should know that, though they are given a state of Telangana, it is not yet out of the woods.

Thus, Telangana cause cannot be a casualty of power politics. It is time for Telangana people to define their Telangana political ethos in clear terms and use it for taking the new state forward evading the diversions of banal politics.

3

WHAT COMBINATION IS GOOD FOR TELANGANA IN THE ELECTIONS ?

(Missiontelangna.com | 1 April, 2014)

Telangana has become an experimental ground for combinations of different political parties in the elections. There are several permutations and combinations with speculation, doing the round. Some of them are:

1. TRS alone
2. TRS, TJAC alliance
3. TRS, Congress alliance
4. TRS, BJP alliance
5. TRS, TJAC, T-Congress, CPI, ND alliance
6. TRS, TJAC, T-BJP, CPI, ND alliance
7. TRS, TJAC, T-Congress, T-BJP, CPI, ND alliance

What combination is good for Telangana in the elections ?

Some may appear possible; some desirable; some improbable. But Indian politics, especially A.P.state politics, thanks to Seemandhra political brand, will make some strange combinations possible in the hankering for political power. Here in this turmoil of political combinations in the nascent state of Telangana, the mute question is which is good for Telangana —- in the main a TRS truck with desultory Congress or reluctant BJP or going alone on its own. A great deal of discussion is taking place on the pros and cons of this issue.

A general debate in the public says that if TRS goes alone it can get around 50 MLA seats as a single largest party and has to depend on other parties for about 10-15 seats for forming a stable government. Congress is supposed to get 30-35 seats. BJP may get 8-10 seats. If TRS and congress make an alliance they can sweep the polls. But, the incompatibility between TRS and T-Congress is too obvious for this combination to work. The problem here is who should be the dominant partner and from which party the CM candidate should be? Sharing of seats has become a helluva problem between these two parties. The TDP and BJP imbroglio in Telangana also has the similar seat sharing hiatus.

A TRS, BJP, CPI and ND combination as partners of TJAC, should be a most desirable combination. But CPI wants the alliance along with Congress and is not comfortable with BJP. TRS and T-BJP also do not see eye to eye on this matter though they are lukewarm partners in TJAC. TRS and TJAC do not have such mutual relationship to each other to broker a workable arrangement. But, the said break in the alliance efforts of TDP and BJP, is bringing forth the speculation of possibility of TRS and T-BJP (BJP) coming together for the general elections in Telangana.

KCR move for tie-up with BJP

Primafacie, it appears to be a good proposition, because TRS and BJP combined, with their collective percentage of votes rather than their contesting separately, can win enough seats in the Assembly to form a stable government. BJP unlike Congress will not be in a position to dominate TRS in the government.

The T-BJP had participated in Telangana struggle with more commitment than T-Congress and played an important role in bringing around their wavering national executive to support T-Bill in the end. Unlike T-Congress, we can expect T-BJP playing a responsible complimentary role in Telangana government with TRS vis-à-vis their BJP national government in protecting the interests of Telangana, if BJP comes to power in the center, which appears to be more likely.

But, will the CBN and Modi honeymoon, which is primarily planned by CBN so painstakingly to spoil the sport for Telangana State, end so unceremoniously? Even if it ends, can TRS and BJP come together quickly and agree on an amicable seat sharing to form a durable alliance in the very few days remaining for such an eventful exercise? We will have to wait and see whether it can happen or any other permutation will take place. For Telangana State, the immediate need is to consolidate the new state into a self-governing, viable and vibrant state against the machinations of political parties, inimical to its interests.

At the end of the day it should be a combination which will form the government and augur well for the new state of Telangana to bring it out of its imposed probation, make it a full-fledged autonomous state like any other state in India, removing all the fetters fastened to it and lay the road for its rapid reconstruction. Maybe it would be a blessing in disguise for TRS if no alliance works out with any major party, to go alone with seat adjustments with its minor partners.

4

VOTE FOR A GOVERNMENT 'OF TELANGANA, BY TELANGANA, FOR TELANGANA'

(Missiontelangana.com | 25 April, 2015)

Telangana state is coming into existence on 2nd June. But it is not like other new states created earlier. The ruling Congress and opposition BJP tampered and tinkered with it to create a peculiar Telangana state with several unconstitutional restrictions outside the purview of article 3. The State is kept on probation for 10 long years with a common capital and 'governor giri' in the capital. Several issues, which have never formed part of state reorganization earlier, are incorporated into the Bill favoring Seemandhra. Thus, Telangana state is conditional and provisional. It will become autonomous, only when it comes out of the fetters imposed on it in the Act and has the political freedom like any other state in the country. Till that time it is a semi-self-governing state in the country and a kind of 'B' class state, while Seemandhra, the residual Andhra Pradesh is an 'A+'

class state without any conditions and some additional embellishments granted to it as part of the Act.

It now becomes the burden of Telangana state government to deal with those incongruous restrictions and the peculiar status of the state. The national parties and Seemandhra dominated other parties who are the reason for these restrictions will not be in a hurry to resolve these anomalies. Even the Telangana units of these parties will not have political freedom to act on this matter. And there is scope for further complicating and extending some of the restrictions, creating another chronic conflict, if these restrictions are not removed at the earliest. Therefore, the option for the fledgling T-state is to get a maiden government which is fully committed and has the political independence to fight to make the state full-fledged and self-governing like other states.

Now on the eve of general elections, every party is claiming to be instrumental in getting Telangana state and claiming their right to come into power. There is a plethora of manifestos on Telangana with usual promises of the moon. But the most relevant and immediate issue of importance for the Telangana government is its division blues. Some subjects of state and concurrent lists for Telangana are arbitrarily manipulated in the reorganization Act for obvious political reasons by Congress and BJP parties. They need amendments either by administrative or legal recourse. That can be a long drawn conflict with the center and the other residual state. In these circumstances, the ability and the commitment of the party or parties that are going to form the government in the new state, to deal with this cantankerous issue, become very important.

Congress, TDP-BJP combine and TRS are the principal parties that are fighting for control of the new Telangana state. We all know the shenanigans of Congress, BJP and TDP who are responsible for all the restrictions on Telangana State and their bias towards Seemandhra. CPI and T-BJP supported Telangana statehood with some commitment. But, their alliances with Congress and TDP respectively have diluted their ability to implement Telangana agenda for total political freedom in the new state. Therefore the need of the hour is a regional political party that is fully identified with the ethos of Telangana. It should have the ability to fight with the center and the political forces inimical to it in the state politically and constitutionally. And bring absolute political freedom to the state in the earliest possible time to make the creation of a new state meaningful. Such a party should be voted to power to form the maiden government of Telangana state.

Except TRS, we do not see any other political outfit in Telangana which has the concern, credentials and commitment to a full-fledged Telangana state. We wish we could have some more like it for a democratic option. In the circumstances we do not have any other alternative to

TRS. Therefore it becomes an imperative necessity for TRS to come to power on its own in the new state of Telangana to steer the state clear of Seemandhra and Central government influence on its governance and attain its full political freedom. But, the political forces opposing TRS are very formidable. They in addition to garnering many benefits in the equivocal division of the state, are scheming to entrench themselves in the new state of Telangana to continue their hegemony. Particularly the efforts of TDP and YSRCP are very disconcerting.

Over the years Telangana was pushed into a political subordination by Andhra Congress and TDP very calculatedly. We have seen its manifestation very clearly in the behavior of T-Congress and T-TDP during the last four years in the Telangana state struggle. Even T-BJP which has exhibited some Telangana spirit has succumbed to the machinations of Seemandhra influence on its national executive. There is a need to break this political stranglehold of Seemandhra and its nexus with the center in deciding the politics in Telangana. This general elections should be a watershed for such a break. Henceforth Telangana should have its own regional political identity to decide the destiny of its people in the new state. We see how regional parties are making a difference in favor of the local people in states like Tamilnadu, Bihar etc. Telangana at this stage imminently needs such a political dispensation, to cope up with the teething problems in the new state and make up its loss suffered in the united state.

It would have been comfortable for TRS if TJAC, its comrade in arms in Telangana udyamam is with it fully. But, it is very unfortunate that TJAC has taken a curious neutral stand. This ambiguity on the part of TJAC can lead to confusion among people, and can cause diversion of Telangana votes to other parties leading to a fractured verdict jeopardizing the formation of full-fledged Telangana state in near future. It can even lead to further complications in regard to Hyderabad city and other important issues like power and irrigation projects, division of employees and other assets in the division of the state affecting the interests of Telangana.

There is a need for all sections of Telangana society to coalesce into one and elect a political force to make the new found state to find its moorings and surge ahead with the rebuilding of Telangana. The need of the hour is to reject the political forces which are inimical to Telangana state unanimously without any confusion. Not to find faults in TRS or be judgmental on it with our likes and dislikes. Let us keep our predilections aside for once and support TRS to bring Telangana political ethos into power to lay the road for realization of the true purpose of our Telangana State. If TRS does not deliver the goods it will not survive for long. Some other regional political force shall enter into its shoes. But we cannot allow foes of Telangana to survive here to torment us any more, just because we have some reservations on TRS. We can't throw away the baby with the bath water as the saying goes.

Telangana needs its own political identity and governance. We need to have a state with all the self-governing rights like any other state in India. These general elections give us the chance to claim our rights. Settle the issue of our political freedom from Seemandhra once for all. Take the fight into the enemy's camp. A clear and stunning verdict of Telangana people for real political freedom is the only way. It will settle the T-State nice and easy on the rails for its run towards the progress.

5

TELANGANA POLITICS IN A SPIN ON A TURNING WICKET

(Missiontelangana.com | 15 May, 2014)

Telangana region has become a turning wicket for political parties. The municipal, local body and the general elections in tandem have created an ambience like the T-20, ODI and test matches of cricket played one after the other. As these three types of cricket lend different trajectory and turn to the bat and ball on the same wicket, the results of these elections in the same region coming one after the other are also providing a great deviation of spin and flight. The municipal elections turned in favor of Congress. The local body elections have provided a topsy-turvy tie-up like situation. We don't know what is in store for the test match like general elections. It is expected to spin prodigiously in favor of TRS, the party which made, 58 years elusive Telangana State,

Turning wicket

Generally for the elections conducted at shorter intervals the trends in the earlier elections will carry forward more or less similar turns into the elections followed. But, here in Telangana the situation is turning out to be different. Telangana State creation has given a different trajectory to the politics here. It has also affected Seemandhra region also, although the turn is not as much as in Telangana. Telangana has become a crucible of intense political reactions in the two regions of Andhra Pradesh. The congress party in seemandhra, TDP in Telangana are reaching their nadir. TDP had to bargain the alliance of BJP with it to survive in Telangana and to regain power in Seemandhra. BJP was forced to give up certain advantage in Telangana in exchange for the advantage of mor no. of MPs in Seemandhra with its tie up with TDP.

Though Congress was instrumental in granting Telangana statehood, its agonizingly long drawn dithering and its clumsy handling of T-Bill resulting in many unconstitutional restrictions on Telangana in the end have not endeared it much with Telangana people. Seemandhra people turned the table on it despite its extravagant freebies in the end as part of the division, because of its inability to control its own party in the region. And mismanaging the whole issue from the beginning, by dragging it to the fag end of the parliament without making any effort to remove the misapprehensions created in them by the motivated propaganda of Seemandhra congress and TDP.

Thus the fate of the political parties in A.P. are dictated by the long embroiled Telangana struggle and the emerging new state of Telangana. The political careers of many Congress honchos are on the block, it will be more severe on the Andhra side. T-Congress leaders also cannot escape this nemesis. They will be paying for the fatuous politics played on the anguish of Telangana, despite their having many opportunities to come to the rescue of people and help their party and themselves also.

The prodigious change in the turn, swing and spin in municipal, local body and general elections is a corollary to the unfolding of permutations and combinations of political parties and the emergence of new vision on Telangana state on the eve of the general elections. When Municipal elections were held there was no clarity on the combinations of political parties. In the local body elections some outlines of permutations of political parties become visible. By the time of general elections the battle lines were clearly drawn. The BJP-TDP un-holy alliance, the T-Congress arrogant aversion to TRS association has made TRS to leave its ambivalence and go for the war on its own, with a fierce determination. It might prove to be a blessing in disguise.

Unleashing a no holds barred campaign by TRS playing on the minds of Telangana people with a clear cut constituency wise development plan in the new state as against the run of the mill manifestos of Congress and BJP-TDP combine and their lackadaisical commitment to future of Telangana state has caught the imagination of people. This is expected to create an unplayable spin on the prodigiously turning wicket of Telangana, if we have to believe many nonpartisan political analysts and almost all the exit polls. The score card of election results for Telangana on 16th promises to be a thrilling test match win after the tentative results of municipal and local body elections.

Thus these general elections in Telangana to choose a government for the new state of Telangana will be an epoch-making event and teach a few political lessons to other parts of the country. If Telangana succeeds in installing a government of Telangana in letter and spirit, as we hope it will be a win for the legitimacy of Telangana cause and the political awakening of Telangana people.

Let us hope and pray that 16th May will swing and spin us to our long cherished victory.

6

AN ALTRUISTIC TELANGANA POLITICAL IDENTITY

(Missiontelangana.com | 22 May, 2014)

Telangana region had a checkered history. Its liberation from Nizam by military action and its Communist background gave the Centre a certain element of condescension towards it. The discrimination is quite apparent in its long campaign for statehood. There were several agreements, plans and formulas modified at regular intervals. They were all flouted with disdain by the dominant Andhra administration. The Central government never bothered to oversee the implementation of any of them. Whenever there were protests, the Central government would support the Andhra government to suppress the agitations. About 1600 youth have laid down their lives for liberation from this majority tyranny.

Telangana Kakatiya Identity

In the present chapter, both Congress and BJP, have played their self-seeking politics with Telangana sentiment and had reneged on it many a time, provoking TRS to undertake an uncompromising agitation since 2001. The congress under duress declared Telangana state on 9 December 2009 in Parliament. But, again went back because of Andhra politicians' volte-face and tormented Telangana people for 4 long years.1200 of its youth have committed suicide for the non-implementation of the declaration. Congress gave a state of Telangana, at the fag-end of the Parliament session with several unconstitutional restrictions to it, while bestowing several excessive concessions to Seemandhra as if it is the underdog. The behavior of Congress and BJP in the final act of adopting the T-Bill in Parliament speaks volumes of their bias to Seemandhra.

That is the treatment of the Centre for Telangana whichever party is in power there. It cannot be different now. Therefore, getting a State is not the end of troubles for Telangana. The people have to survive the 10 year long joint- capital in the company of the seemandhras, who are scheming to stay – put in Hyderabad and play vexatious politics to make Hyderabad a 'UT'. There are several contentious issues in the reorganization Act in small print, detrimental to Telangana. There will be a war of attrition on them. The center as usual will be helping the profligate seemandhra. Telangana is only like a political orphan to it. For, it does not have the numbers or resources to please the behemoth at the Centre.

Now that Telangana has elected TRS with absolute majority, the government should work for the interest of Telangana people alone. It should be free from the suzerainty of any other political entity as in the past. It should challenge the restrictions in the Act – in the parliament or in the courts or with the Central government. And disentangle the fetters one by one to make the state full-fledged at the earliest possible. The setback in the merged state and the present needs of Telangana State should be identified fastidiously. A systematic development plan is to be prepared and grounded methodically and transparently. The most important aspects of rebuilding of the new state are Employment, Power, Irrigation and Industrialisation in which areas Telangana was deliberately pushed backwards.

The other areas such as social welfare, education, health and technological development should be promoted simultaneously. Whatever is done, it should be done, keeping the feet firmly on the ground. No grandiose visions which will end in disappointment. The State needs to be different to fulfill the aspirations of people, which were long suppressed and also those now stoked up. But, we cannot create an economic or political model radically different from other states. It should be within the framework of the larger political and economic system of the country and deliver the promised goods.

The need of the hour is an independent and altruistic Telangana political identity. The leadership of Telangana and the people, both should become tough, pragmatic and artful to realize the benefit of the new State, got after such an arduous struggle and with such heavy price. The long lost political freedom to decide their own destiny is back in their hands now. It is up to them to make the right use of it. The definite mandate to TRS in 2014 general elections should be the watershed for such momentous change. The electoral wins for BJP in the Centre and TDP in seemandhra might not bode well for Telangana State.

The alliance of the two parties, the nexus of wily 'Naidu duo', their influence in the Central government and also the perfunctory attitude of Modi towards Telangana make us worry. That makes Telangana government to be doubly cautious, determined and resourceful to challenge the machinations of these honchos in the coming days.

7

TELANGANA STATE – 'FREEDOM' INSIDE A DEMOCRACY

(Missiontelangana.com | 3 June, 2014)

Telangana region has become a state after a 6 decade long struggle against its merger with Andhra in 1956. The struggle for statehood had been very long, intense and poignant. Several new states were created in India after independence —- some of them on linguistic basis; some on tribal identities; some on geography and culture.

Andhra and Telangana were merged based on their language, Telugu. As part of this linguistic integration many regions were merged in different states like in Maharashtra, Karnataka, Madhya Pradesh, H.P. etc. By and large the states reorganized based on language had gelled together very well except in the case of Andhra Pradesh.

Osmania University decorated on
Telangana Formation Day

In Andhra Pradesh it was a case of an exaggerated feeling of superiority of majority Andhras over Telangana people, resulting in ethnic domination. It has inevitably escalated in to a campaign for political freedom from the majority dominance inside a democracy.

Though the language was one, the political, economic and cultural backgrounds of the two regions were different. The State Reorganization Commission (SRC), was very circumspect about it. It had recommended against the merger. Pandit Nehru also had his own reservations. There was strong opposition from the people of Telangana. But somehow Andhras managed to merge the regions by political manipulation.

There was a Gentlemen's agreement with several safeguards to Telangana. Some people on both sides, in good faith, have believed that the merger will bring emotional integration in Telugu people long separated by history. And cement their relations to enrich the Telugu culture. But, paradoxically it did not happen. The people of the two regions did not mingle like long lost siblings as in the case of other linguistically formed states. Both Andhra and Telangana cultures went in their own ways causing little influence on each other.

Andhras had experience in politics in the provincial self-government system of British India. Their participation in the independence movement with Congress and other political parties in the mainstream Indian politics gave them a distinct political advantage. It has helped to create a bias towards them in the Congress party.

In Andhra state the Krishna, Godavari and Tungabhadra canal systems for irrigation in agriculture have given them economic advantage. The surplus income from agriculture led to education, investment and entrepreneurial experience. Because of Urdu medium in Telangana, the importation of English knowing Andhra employees into the administration by the military and civilian governments, from 1948 to 1952 and after have placed Andhra people in the key positions of the administration. In contrast, Telangana region was in Nizam's feudal dominion outside the Indian mainstream political system. Though Hyderabad was made into a first class city for the prestige of rich Nizam, the entire hinterland of Telangana was backward economically with lack of irrigational facilities and less favorable agro climatic conditions. There was not much surplus income for education, investment and development of enterprise.

In Telugu, though the language was same the dialect was different. Andhra Telugu with a mixture of Sanskrit was felt superior to Telangana idiom. Because of their economic well being and language bias the culture of Telangana was looked down upon. It has developed a kind of superiority complex in them. The Andhras kept Telangana people at arm's length. They had started asserting themselves in politics, economics and culture in the state. With all this background the 175 (Andhra) versus 119 (Telangana) members in the Legislative Assembly have given them all the political advantage they needed to control Telangana. A systematic exploitation of Telangana resources by majority Andhra administration has begun and went on unabated despite the opposition to it.

Slowly and steadily all the conditions and safeguards in the Gentlemen's agreement were flouted. There erupted a severe backlash in 1969 against Andhras for usurping Telangana jobs and Telangana surplus revenue. It was brutally suppressed by killing 369 youth in police firing. Then an 8-point development program was devised. The Government promised to correct, the violation of the promises of the Gentleman's agreement in the areas of jobs, budget allocations, and educational facilities. P.V.Narasimha Rao was made CM in 1971. Then some attempt was made to implement 'mulki rules' and the 8 point program. Andhras went to court. The Supreme Court upheld 'mulki rules'.

As a protest against it Andhras undertook the 1972 'Jai Andhra' campaign. PV Narasimha Rao was made to resign and president rule was imposed. The constitution was amended to abrogate 'mulki rules'. A new 6-point formula was contrived in 1973. Like other formulas it was also kept on the backburner by the indifferent Andhra administration. When Telangana employees complained about the non-implementation of the six-point formula, the government issued a G.O. 610 in 1985. Since then, no serious attempt was made to implement the G.O. The central government never bothered to oversee the implementation of any of these agreements or formulas.

Meanwhile, the Andhra dominated government unleashed several programs to make Hyderabad as the preferred haven, a kind of 'El Dorado' for Andhras. The surplus revenue from Telangana was spent in Andhra and to develop infrastructure for enterprises and industries of Andhras in Hyderabad. Vast government and private lands in Telangana were appropriated to Andhra's in the name of corporate benefits and other facades. Both CBN and YSR have increased the raiding of Telangana resources in the garb of economic liberalization and creation of infrastructure. Whatever development took place in Hyderabad; its fruits were made to be enjoyed mostly by seemandhras. The colonization and exploitation of Telangana as foreseen by Justice Fazal Ali in the SRC report has vastly exceeded, vindicating the apprehension. This has once again ignited the simmering Telangana statehood desire in Telangana people.

In this backdrop, the Telangana Rashtra Samithi (TRS) was formed in 2001 to fight for separate Telangana. The trials and tribulations of this episode of Telangana udyamam spearheaded by TRS is a history now. Because of it Telangana state was formed. Though state is given, it is shackled with many restrictions. The center, as its wont, has always treated Telangana with condescension. After the inevitable 'police action', the Indian army undertook an elimination of Telangana armed rebels against Nizam in the name of containing communism; imposed military and civilian rule after the liberation. Both the military and civilian rule treated local people vey unfairly. Considering them as imbeciles they had imported the English educated seemandhras. The state administration was Andhraised even before the first elected government came into place, thus sowing the seeds for the hegemony of Seemandhra.

Both Congress and BJP, the national parties have played their self-seeking politics with Telangana people. BJP promised Telangana in 1999. Congress party had a truck with TRS in 2004 with an assurance of Telangana State. BJP, when it gave 3 new states in 2000, did not keep its promise of Telangana allegedly because of TDP. Congress after winning power with the help of TRS in 2004 went back on its assurance. TRS was forced to undertake a continuous and uncompromising agitation. Bowing to popular pressure arising from KCR's fast-unto-death, the Congress declared Telangana state on 9 December 2009 in Parliament. But, again went back because of andhra politicians volte-face and tormented Telangana people for five long years. About 1200 of its youth have committed suicide for the non-implementation of the declaration.

Telangana was proving disastrous for Congress in both the regions. In such tenuous circumstances congress gave a state of Telangana, with several restrictions making it a 'B' class state, while Seemandhra was made an 'A +' state with several excessive concessions to it. The behavior of Congress and BJP in the final act of adopting the T-Bill in Parliament speaks volumes of their bias to Seemandhra. That is the treatment of the center for Telangana whatever national party is in power in the Centre. It would be the same in future also. The true intentions of Congress and BJP were revealed in the rhetoric of 2014 election campaign on either side of the divide in Andhra Pradesh.

Therefore, getting a state after 60 years is not the end of troubles for Telangana. There is still a long way to go. The people have to survive the 10 year long joint capital in the company of the Seemandhras, who are scheming to stay – put in Hyderabad and play vexatious politics to make Hyderabad a 'UT'.

There are several contentious issues in the Reorganization Act in small print, detrimental to Telangana. There will be a war of attrition on those numerous discriminations and unconstitutional restrictions. The center as usual will be helping the profligate Seemandhra. Telangana is only like a political orphan to it. For, it does not have the numbers or resources to please the behemoths at the center. Telangana politicians in Congress and TDP were systematically subordinated by Andhra politicians. They have lost their Telangana ethos and cannot comprehend the aspirations of Telangana people. There is a need for a new potent breed of politicians with Telangana identity who can defy the condescension of the center and make them heed to the legitimate demands of Telangana.

Hence, now Telangana peoples' imperative necessity should be to have a government of Telangana in the letter and spirit of it, in the new state. The government should work for the interest of Telangana people alone. It should be free from the suzerainty of any other political entity. It should challenge the conditions and restrictions imposed on it unconstitutionally in the Act —- in the parliament or in the courts or with the central government. And disentangle the fetters one by one to make a full-fledged state.

The setback in the merged state and the present needs of Telangana state should be identified fastidiously. A systematic development plan is to be prepared and grounded methodically and transparently. The most important aspects of rebuilding of the new state are Power, Irrigation, Industrialization and employment in which areas Telangana was deliberately pushed backwards. The other areas such as social welfare, education, health and technological development should be promoted simultaneously.

Whatever is done, it should be done, keeping the feet firmly on the ground. No grandiose visions which will end in disappointment. The state needs to be different to fulfill the aspirations of people, which were long suppressed and also those now stoked up. But, we cannot create an economic or political model radically different from other states. The state needs to be different within the framework of the larger political and economic system of the country and deliver the promised goods.

The need of the hour is a strong Telangana political ethos. The leadership of Telangana should leave their subservience to the center behind. The people of Telangana also should eschew their naiveté of being easy going and accommodating. Both should become tough, pragmatic and self-interested to realize the benefit of the new state, after such an arduous struggle and with such heavy price. The long lost political freedom to decide their own destiny is back in their hands now. It is up to them to make the right use of it and restore Telangana state's rightful place in the comity of states in the country. The definite mandate to TRS in 2014 general elections should be the watershed for such momentous change.

8

IS KCR A 'FRESHER' IN A COLLEGE?

(Missiontelangana.com | 7 June, 2014)

This is a rebuttal to the article : "Is Telangana and AP going the India – Pakistan Way?" written by Lata Jain in The Hans India (See box below).

This M/S Lata Jain is doing a lot of 'tarafdari' to seemandhra. She has also appeared to be supporting 'UT 'or 2nd Indian capital for Hyderabad in her article 'Hyderabad Status' 22 May, 2014. In this she is virtually castigating KCR for not being nice to CBN. Looks like CBN's propaganda machinery is out like in the olden days to buy the support of journalists in his political gamesmanship. His shenanigans on his oath taking ceremony site, Camp office and the site for the new capital all are doing their rounds. His playacting of invitation to KCR, for his swearing in ceremony, smacks of his penchant for devious propaganda. We all know his antecedents. He cannot be different now. We will be seeing more of such political gimmicks in the coming days. But the point to ponder here is why these journalists are falling to it so glibly forgetting their professional propriety.

Is KCR a 'fresher' in a College?

The ceremony was held in Raj Bhavan in an austere atmosphere by the Governor's office, marking the momentous event. Personal invitations as ostentatious as planned in CBN's oath taking ceremony were not there. Anyway, it is the prerogative of KCR to invite CBN personally or not. The very CBN, Who has banned the word Telangana in the Assembly; who stopped Telangana for 4 years from 9, December 2009; made life miserable for 4 crore Telangana people in those 4 years; caused the death of 1200 martyrs for Telangana; threatening KCR to dethrone even before 2019; challenging KCR to provide governance like him (?). Why he, the very anathema of Telangana State, should be invited 'personally' to the state formation day of Telangana, when such courtesy was not extended to anybody else.

Just because he is playacting now on this issue, why should journalists take cudgels on his behalf? Instead they should, comment on his pompous oath taking ceremony. They can appreciate the simple and dignified ceremony of Telangana at Raj Bhavan without wasting much money on the pomp. On the other hand CBN who is crying that Andhra has deficit budget and collecting money privately for building the capital is wasting Rs.10 crores on his vainglorious oath taking and Rs.3 crores on renovation of his camp office in Hyderabad. If he respects democracy, he could have attended KCR's oath taking ceremony on the invitation of the Governor, without cribbing unsportingly and egotistically for personal invitation.

For it was the maiden Telangana State government oath taking, an historical event. As CM-designate of residuary A.P. He has the responsibility to be there for political decorum. As is their wont, they won't follow decorum but find fault with others even if there is not one. If he is inviting KCR now personally, with the ulterior motive of showing him in a bad light, it cannot make him a man of great etiquette and culture. Everybody knows his acerbic manners and unscrupulous political behavior. There is no need for the media to make such a brouhaha on this matter. On the contrary they could have found fault with him for not being politically correct.

But the point to remember here is the revival of his propaganda apparatus and the journalists falling for it. The Hans India for some time is showing its bias towards seemandhra. This M/S Lata Jain appears to have developed a myopic view on Telangana. Some journalists in other newspapers are also trying to teach lessons to KCR as to how to be good with A.P. State. As if he only needs to be good, not the other side. It looks like they have taken it for granted that Telangana state only needs to be good. As if KCR is a fresher at a college and needs to respect CBN the senior, despite his ragging.

We all know, just because Telangana people go out of their way to be nice to these guys, they are not going to do nice things to them. It is like trying to quench our thirst in 'mriga thrushna'. On the contrary they can take advantage of it and try to upstage Telangana. They did the same for the last 60 years. There is no need for KCR to go to CBN's oath taking, after all this. That would not be in the fitness of the things. As usual, there will be some wagging of tongues and heavens are not going to fall for it. We know we need to fight for every inch of our rightful share and they will not part with it easily, it would be a war of attrition and we need to get prepared for it. Nobody needs to teach us lessons in this matter. We had been overly friendly with them and paid dearly for it. It is like 'Arab, his tent and the Camel' story. We don't want to repeat it. We will certainly make friends with them. But, only on equal terms as per the exigency. There is no need for us to seek their friendship unilaterally, as the predisposed media wants it.

9

POLAVARAM AMENDMENT – ARE BHADRACHALAM TRIBALS SACRIFICIAL GOATS !

(Missiontelangana.com | 7 July, 2014)

The union government promulgated an ordinance annexing 7 mandals of Bhadrachalam division to Seemandhra. Now the ordinance is used to amend A.P.Reorganization Act 2014 in the present Parliament session. It is done to facilitate the construction of Polavaram, a very controversial project with a potential to create perhaps the biggest harm to the environment and human settlements in the country. It submerges 306 villages in Telangana, A.P, Chhattisgarh and Odisha states. Displaces about 4 lakh people — most of them aboriginal tribes.

In addition, the project in its present design is said to be a potential disaster to Seemandhra also. As river Godavari is prone to very high floods to the magnitude of 90 lakh cusecs and above, the present spillway design for 50 lakh cusecs is not adequate. There is every possibility of the rock filled earthen dam to break. This can result in a watery grave to 50 lakh people downstream with about twenty towns getting washed away.

There are a couple of alternative designs available; one from Sri Ch.Hanumnth Rao former Engineer -in -Chief, and the other from Sri M.Dharma Rao Chief Engineer (Retd.). Govt. of erstwhile A.P. The design from Sri Hanumantha Rao envisages construction of 3 barrages instead of one earthen dam at Polavaram including one at Polavaram and two upstream. Sri M.Dharma Rao's design proposes a barrage on Sabari, balancing reservoirs on its tributaries and using anicut at Dummugudem on Godavari.

The two designs provide answers to every problem in the official design. All the benefits of the present design are met —- irrigating 7.2 lakh acres, diversion of 80 tmc to Krishna basin, supply of 23 tmc for drinking and industrial purposes, generating 960 MW hydro powers etc. Of the two because all the three barrages are on Godavari, the former appears to be closer to the concept of Polavaram multi-purpose Project.

The design reduces the cost, reaps some additional benefits and can be completed fast without any hassles from any quarter. It reduces the submergence of villages from 306 to 70; saves one lakh acres of agricultural land belonging to tribals and provides irrigation to it; navigation of sea going vessels from SRSP becomes possible; geological and environmental destruction is made minimal. Most importantly it eliminates the danger of 'dam break' totally, because of the barrages in place of one earthen dam.

These alternative designs are in the know of erstwhile A.P. government and the Central government. Yet, they have not taken them into consideration. The official design has drawn flak from everywhere and is beset with several hindrances and dangers. The inclusion of such a controversial project in the reorganization Act itself is disputed. Then annexing the whole Bhadrachalam division of 7 Mandals to A.P by an ordinance on the heels of the Act passed in the Parliament is an undemocratic Act. It is done to enable the A.P. government to submerge the villages in the project and rehabilitate the displaced in other villages of the division, instead of in the developed ayacut of the Project in Seemandhra.

Those Mandals were in Seemandhra region before 1959. But, now the people of those Mandals vehemently oppose the annexation and want to be in Telangana. It may be technically right to claim those villages in the demerger. But, the purpose and the way the annexation is done outside the Parliament through an ordinance are highly reprehensible. If it is felt so apposite, it could have been discussed in Parliament as part of the Reorganization Act and resolved on its merits. It is felt that; here the tribals of Bhadrachalam are being used as 'sacrificial goats' to Polavaram project, to satisfy the political ego of Seemandhra, as a quid pro quo for Telangana State. The BJP government is assisting it, without regard to the merits of the matter.

This amendment by the new government on the specious argument of carrying on the previous government's promise is a political skullduggery. It will not enhance the prestige of the Government of India. It will be challenged in the Court of Law. The Project may not materialize in its present design. But the issue is likely to create an unending strife between the two states. Central government has a responsibility to avoid it, without being biased.

10

ANDHRA CAPITAL CONUNDRUM

(The Hans India | 10 September, 2014)

There are megacities like Mumbai, Kolkata, Madras, Bangalore and Hyderabad as capitals for the states in India. We do not know whether they can be called world class or not. The remaining 23 states have smaller cities as capitals. We definitely can say they are not world class. Yet, they have been functioning as capitals of the respective states for decades.

Andhra capital configuration

It is good for every state to have a city like our mega cities for prestige and for some inherent advantages. But, as history reveals, it is not possible to create mega cities with a predisposition and in a short span of time. Like humans, cities also have their stars for their prosperity and growth. All the 28 state capitals did not become Mumbai. The modern city capitals like Bhubaneswar, Chandigarh, and Gandhinagar planned to be capitals, but also did not graduate to mega cities in the last several decades.

For seemandhras to lose a city like Hyderabad in the demerger is a traumatic experience indeed. Their yearning for a city like it for their capital is understandable. But, their, at least their political leadership's fixation for a world class city like, Singapore, Putrajaya, Chicago etc. in its place is highly farfetched. It simply does not make sense. Prudence demands that we make our bread according to our dough. Gujarathis, just because they have lost Mumbai, they did not try to create another Mumbai in Gujarat. Gandhinagar as capital is serving their interests admirably well.

The residual Andhra Pradesh has a GDP of $89 Billion with about $1500 PCI; Singapore's GDP is $300 Billion with $55000 PCI; Malaysia's GDP is $312 Billion with $14,880 PCI. The economy of residual A.P. with around one lakh crores annual budget, 70% of which goes for establishment expenditure, does not support a 'world class' capital dream. Even if they are planning to do it with private investment and sharing it with the government in that bizarre land pooling style, it can be too big for the government to manage with its limited economic resources. It cannot be cost effective and financially feasible.

Even if that profligate real estate is created, there need to be the clientele to use it and pay for it. It can create a real estate cataclysm. Some sample of which is already being experienced in Hyderabad's demand and supply of real estate. There is no need to create such a superfluous white elephant, while other pragmatic alternatives are available. "The government has no job doing real estate business in the name of land pooling. Its business is to govern the state by making use of government lands." Said Prof Yellamanchili Shivaji, former MP and a noted environmentalist. Obviously there is something more than what meets the eye for the CM rooting for Chicago style capital city on both sides of Krishna river in the vicinity of Vijayawada. It is not very difficult to surmise the reasons. It is already being discussed everywhere.

Residual A.P. has three political regions North coastal; Central coastal and Rayalaseema with Nellore. In these three regions some social groups are predominant influencing the political dominance as is the case elsewhere in India. North coastal region predominates with some OBC castes, which are not as dominant as in other two regions individually to swing the political decisions in their favor. That is why though Vizag is the biggest city and has more merit to be the capital of the state, it is not being considered. The central coastal districts are dominated by Kammas. The Rayalaseema with Nellore district is a Reddy caste stronghold. The competition is between these two groups. Since the present government is headed by CBN a Kamma and is supported by his politico-corporate social group, he is pitching for Vijayawada the stronghold of Kamma community.

The Rayalaseema region which was demanding Kurnool the erstwhile capital of Andhra state is losing the game because of their not being in the ruling dispensation. The Sivaramakrishnan Committee has recommended Donakonda region in between the two political regions of coastal Andhra and Rayalaseema as a preferred place for the capital. It has better credentials both political and economical for a long lasting and developing capital city. But CBN's predilection and his political clout with the proximity to the Center is not making it possible. The government has bulldozed the opposition from Rayalaseema and has decided Vijayawada as capital even before the ink has dried on the committee's report or its contents have fully come out.

But this political equation can change.Rayalaseema region will not be happy with the capital being set up in Vijayawada with the political bullying of CBN and his cohorts. Though the region is subdued now the issue can snowball into a major controversy, reminiscent of forced merger of Andhra and Telangana without consensus in 1956. In this context the preference of the Sivaramakrishnan Committee for Donakonda region makes ample sense. For, the place is in Prakasam district which comprises parts from earlier Gunturu,Kurnool and Nellore districts and also represents the two politically dominant social groups in equal measure. There is every possibility of consensus on it from both the regions. In a way Donakonda divides the state into two, more or less equal political regions with neither of the social groups feeling left out.

Besides It is centrally located with rail, road and air connectivity with plenty of government land for spatial expansion transforming the place steadily, phase wise, in to a mega city of India class if not world class. It will also avoid causing much stress to state's exchequer or causing real estate disasters.It does not bode well for the future of the state if the CM with his personal agenda fires the Vijayawada Capital blunderbuss, aimlessly. History can repeat itself, if the people at the helm do not learn the lessons from it and behave responsibly.

Professor Shivaji in a TV discussion observed that CBN might have sown the seed for Separate Rayalaseema by his ham handed announcement of Vijayawada as Capital, without consensus.

11

KCR'S COMMENTS ON PRESS - TIMES NOW TV LIVE DEBATE

(The Hans India | 15 September, 2014)

This has reference to The News hour Debate: Telangana CM K Chandrasekhar Rao threatens media, of Times Now TV with TRS MP Vinod, on 10th September 2014. Whatever be the propriety of KCR's comments on journalists, the behavior of Arnab Goswami the Times Now anchor in the live debate towards Vinod Kumar, TRS MP was more deplorable than what he wanted to censure in it. It has exceeded all the limits of journalistic etiquette. He was accusing the MP and sentencing him in one breath. He has berated him without allowing him to speak.

He was ordering him to file a case against his state's CM as if he is delivering the judgment in the case. The behavior of Goswami is more dictatorial than his purported allegation of dictatorial attitude of KCR. Arnab Goswami cannot pass a judgment and insult his own invitee for the discussion, without giving him a chance to reply coherently. It looked like he has called Vinod Kumar for the discussion just to do the insulting act, with a predetermined intent.

Thus he has joined those two implicated TV channels (not all the journalists of India) on whom KCR was venting his ire, for insulting Telangana people, their State, Assembly, Legislators and the very ethos of Telangana, in most vulgar lingo in Telugu, which perhaps Goswami and other national media men can never know or cannot understand its true nuance even if translated in to English. It cannot be called a freedom of expression or championing for it if Goswami is bullying the MP without allowing him to speak and berating him with his vituperations. Telanganites including the daughter of KCR feel that KCR should not have used those words feeling that they can be misinterpreted. But for using those words on those two channels no Telanganite feel any regret.

He was advocating for the MP to register a case against KCR in a police station in Delhi. He could have done the same thing without raving about Vinod Kumar. Or he could have complained to the Press Council of India, if he is so fastidious to set things right, instead of calling the MP and insulting him without hearing him. If journalists can say anything, but, the people cannot say anything against them, is not the connotation of freedom of speech. The MSOs of Telangana as part of Telangana society were insulted by the two channels and have protested against it. The two TV channels were trying to sabotage Telangana state formation for several years and were like thorns in the flesh of Telangana. The particular video on Telangana maiden Assembly by TV9 was the last straw on the camel's back. The MSOs of Telangana as part of Telangana society were insulted by the two channels and have protested against it. The two TV channels were trying to sabotage Telangana state formation for several years and were like thorns in the flesh of Telangana. The particular video on Telangana maiden Assembly by TV9 was the last straw on the camel's back.

TV9's Anti-Telangana rant on maiden Telangana Assembly: (Translation from Telugu) "What would happen if you screen a Hollywood movie in a multiplex to someone who is habituated to watching old movies on a touring theater? Sample this! As our leaders saw the State Assembly for the first time from so close a distance, they got perplexed as to what expression befits the occasion – ecstasy, bafflement or horror! Not just their body language, they became a laughing stock even at the oath-taking ceremony ! Our Telangana MLAs story is similar to those sour toddy consumers who are offered the best foreign brand liquor !

People voted them to power and gave a 'short-cut entry' into the Assembly, but the leaders scared them with their very first performance at the oath-taking ceremony! Not straight out of their beds – thank God for that – but fumbled even to read from a paper when asked to take oath. And on top of it, Laptops were given to such incompetents! What will a loincloth-clad person do when offered with a Laptop? Where will he tuck it? Wonder if they shove it inside their loin or sell it somewhere! But the T-MLAs took them with both hands just as a drunkard would crave for spicy pickle! MLAs were put to severe hardships and confusion gripped them big time once they entered the Assembly wondering where to sit and how, which way to take for wash-rooms, whether to use papers given as tissues, how to switch-off the ACs etc.!"

The MSOs of seemandhra never broadcast Telangana TV channels. Telangana Newspapers are not allowed in seemandhra. In the last A.P. Assembly session in Hyderabad Telangana TV channels and Telangana Newspapers were not given accreditation passes to cover the proceedings in the Assembly. When approached, the A.P. speaker, alleged to have opined that there is no need for Telangana press to cover Andhra Pradesh Assembly. If MSOs are not within their rights they could not have continued the ban for 3 months. Even the central minister for I&B could not make them lift the ban. The Press Council of India also could not interfere.

In such circumstances, there is no point in blaming KCR, for the abominable acts of 'apartheid' of Andhra press and the TV channels. He or Times Now TV should have tried to drill some sense into their minds instead of trying to bully the leaders of Telangana, to uphold the freedom of people. Even if KCR was wrong, there was no point in insulting his representative. It is like an attempt to 'kill the messenger' as the old saying goes. The poor man, an MP, was left high and dry even without getting a chance to complete even a sentence in the debate. A pun is in circulation in Hyderabad Public schools if some boy bullies other boys and will not allow them to speak in the school, the teachers would say that 'Don't behave like Arnab Goswami'. That is his reputation.

Anyway his treatment of Sri Vinod Kumar, MP has exceeded all the limits of journalistic decorum. There is a need to examine if there is any violation of privileges of an MP in this case. The behavior of Goswami at least in this case does not enhance the reputation of Times Now TV. There is a need to make the live debates more democratic and meaningful without bullying the participants. Whether you like it or not the participants should be allowed to say what they want to say. Delivering your sentence like denunciations and ordering them to do something peremptorily as if you are sitting in judgment without hearing the guest invitees does not behove for a national TV channel like Times Now.

12

TV CHANNELS BAN IN TELANGANA: PRESS IS NOT GOD

(The Hans India | 18 September, 2014)

Once again your frankly speaking in 'And not a dog barked!' makes us wonder, if you have understood the problem in the ongoing spat or simply trail the 'Andhra Press'. These two channels TV9 and ABN-AJ are not the Press and their behavior is not the freedom of Press you are so painstakingly trying to explain. Your being in Hyderabad and knowing the ground realities, yet choosing to champion this yellow press in the name of Indian Press makes a sad reading. Your discourse on freedom of press sounds misplaced here. For Telangana people are as democratic as any other people in the country. They know what freedom of press means. Their denouncing these two bigoted channels is not attacking freedom of Press. It is actually trying to save the Indian press from the ignominy of bigotry.

The freedom of Press and freedom of expression might be sacrosanct in democracy but Press is not God. As you have said, the press and government should complement each other. Whether pygmies or giants we need CMs also to run governments. All the press bosses cannot be said as giants. There will be pygmies and skunks among them also. The people do not need to put up with such pygmies and their abuse of freedom of press. CMs are temporary like the TV Channel heads; government is permanent like the press. The CM, just because you do not like his criticism of your press, will not become a pygmy. But whether KCR is a pygmy or a giant is not the point here.He is the representative of 3.5 crore Telangana people and he can question the press if they are erring against the people of his constituency. It cannot be seen as blasphemy.

If it is 'sheer arrogance on the part of KCR', what is it on the part of those two channels? TV9 says that all the Telangana legislators in the maiden assembly are uncouth ignoramus and do not deserve to be in an Assembly, meaning Telangana people do not deserve a state.ABN-AJ comments on insultingly on the physical features of KCR and calls him all kinds of obscene names in the name of press freedom and freedom of expression. You approve them nonchalantly as political satires. It is not a sporadic happening. It is a credo with them to constantly spike the self-respect of Telangana people and have become thorns in their flesh over the years.You are taking cudgels on behalf of these two yellow channels to defend their uncouth acts, in the name of freedom of press in India.

A CM who was elected by Telangana people cannot be an idle spectator, if they are insulted so blatantly by TV channels even if it is part of your powerful press. Added to this he was personally targeted by these paragons of your press. It should also be the concern of the PCI if the people of Telangana and its CM are being insulted by the Andhra colonial press as a regular practice.It cannot be like some human rights professionals who defend the human rights of extremists only, not the rights of the common people who are their victims. You cannot support the press who are transgressing into the rights of common people, because they are simply the press. Thanks to your appreciation of Shakespeare in KCR and for your respect growing many fathoms up. Then what about the 'pygmy' thing you have said earlier?

You talk of freedom of Press ! In Seemandhra Telangana newspapers are not allowed. Telangana news channels are permanently banned by their MSOs. Even they are not allowed to cover the proceedings of A.P. Assembly and you are not concerned about it. But if these two Andhra chauvinistic channels are taken to task by MSOs of Telangana you are making a big hue and cry about it. What are the anti-media unwarranted actions by the CM and the government? CM had said several times that the government has nothing to do with TMSOs boycott of the two channels. CM and his government will definitely have the right to comment on the anti-telangana tirades of the press. Like the press they also have freedom of expression. He has commented on these two anti-telangana channels for their vulgar and xenophobic satires. These horrific misdemeanors by these channels cannot be called critical scrutiny and constitutionally mandated norms of freedom of expression by any stretch of imagination. These sermons by you and your editor's guild sound very hollow here in this context.

KCR is not targeting Andhra press; his ire is directed at those who revel in insulting Telangana State and its people in the name of ethnicity and personal defamation. He and the people of Telangana will continue to do so, whatever be the diktats from the Press and its council, till the Andhra chauvinistic press gives up its anti-telangana campaign. Whatever press indulges in such sordid activity will be challenged. After all Press, freedom of expression and PCI all come after the self-esteem of people. Nobody has any right to attack the self-respect of people under any act or rules. Your expectation of all others joining the chorus of anti-telangana barking of your Andhra chauvinistic mutts is unfounded.

Your denigration of local press as 'And not a dog barked', also does not enhance the prestige of press. Frankly speaking, the only solution to this cantankerous problem would be to permanently ban these incorrigibly recalcitrant TV channels from Telangana, as they have banned Telangana press and channels from Seemandhra. There cannot be two solutions to one dispute.

13

TRS GOVERNMENT UNDER SIEGE OF 'POWER'

(Missiontelangana.com | 13 November, 2014)

A.P. is alleged to be not releasing power to the tune of about 2000 MW to TS as per its share in A.P.R.A. It is felt that the A.P. and the Central governments in collusion are manipulating the power problem to force the TRS government in TS into a political debacle. As most of the power plants are in A.P., TS is not in a position to meet its power requirement. In effect, the TS government is under siege and is impeded on the short term power requirement in the State. The working of TS government in other fronts other than this power problem is not of much immediate concern currently. It has another 4 1/2 years of its mandate. In fact, it has formulated several schemes as per its manifesto and started grounding them. But this badgering issue of power is most critical for its political credibility. The TS government's procrastination on it is causing a great deal of anxiety, as it should be, in the minds of the people in TS.

Whatever efforts ostensibly are being made for power do not appear to come to the state's rescue in less than 2 to 3 years. Government's action plan for power for the next 2 years, and or the problems in it are not being made public. But they need to go through this rabi sason, next kharif and thereafter in agriculture and meet the needs of the industry as well. It appears even if the weather is good the state may still be hard pressed for power, in coming years, if it does not get its share of power in real terms as proposed in APRA. It does appear that A.P. and Central governments will not be in a hurry to solve that problem in time to come to the state's rescue, based on the present political developments. Therefore the TS govt should have some short term plans to meet the shortfall of power and a political stratagem to realize their share of power withheld by A.P., as per A.P.R.A. simultaneously.

All the opposition political parties in TS are reveling in the troubled situation and the discomfiture of TRS government. They are not concerned with the stability of the state or the problems of the farmers or industries. The people in the state are also getting nervous and starting to put the government under great pressure. Their disquiet is understandable. The problem is also getting on to the nerves of the people in TNRI forums and intelligentsia in Telangana. The political affiliations, sympathies and animosities in them are coming to the fore. Some of them are embarking on an acrimonious campaign against TRS without regard to the sensitive state the Telangana State is in.

It is time for forbearance and cool thinking, not to get carried away by our political affinities and start denigrating the TS government. Either the government should be allowed to work out its solution keeping faith in it or, if we can brainstorm a solution to its problems, we should do it, without getting nervous and quarreling ourselves, based on our political preferences. It is pointless to make the TS government tense with our knee jerk reactions in the midstream. It will only aggravate the situation.

If it comes to brass-tacks, taking cudgels on behalf of political parties or denigrating TRS is not the thing we need to do most now. The consolidation of Telangana state into a full-fledged autonomous state is the most important factor for us at this stage of the nascent state. Changing our political allegiances now even if TRS falters, is not going to help us solve the problem, except playing into the hands of enemies of Telangana state who want to make it a failed state. Just because of this short term power problem, losing total faith in TRS and the present TS government is not the right thing. It has a mandate for all the 5 years of its term. It has not yet completed 6 months of it. It needs to be given its legitimate latitude.

As a matter of fact it will not end with this power issue. A.P. will be harassing TS in that weird 10 year probation period of common capital and other fetters, on some pretext or the other. There is lot more in store to come. Central government will be on its side by default, at least for the next 5 years. That way TS government cannot have a free run to implement its agenda, as expected by its people. Some of the TNRIs and other intelligentsia in Telangana are getting riled up against TRS in a hurry with real and imaginary lapses, so early in its governance, unnecessarily. Instead, there is a need for them to support the TS government in its fight with the central government in implementing the APRA in letter and spirit and addressing the legitimate concerns of Telangana as its tacit duty, since it is the author and the authority to implement it.

Here, we have to learn some lessons from Andhras. Andhra congress leaders did everything in their capacity to stop TS for 4 years and tried to stop the division. In the end when division was inevitable, they managed to get several concessions to Andhra and put many restrictions to TS in APRA. Yet, Andhra people never voted for Andhra congress in the general elections. Whereas we have voted for some. And are taking umbrage on behalf of those political parties who were lukewarm to TS and allowed or worked for imposition of the restrictions against it in the Act. Also, now asking to surrender to Center, just because TRS is in doldrums in this present power crisis.

It does not mean to say that everything is hunky dory with TRS. Like any political party TRS also has its foibles. They need to be criticized and prodded to act properly. But, as we are in the very first term of our maiden TS government with that peculiar probation for 10 years; with A.P. government breathing on our necks; a common governor monitoring over us; the center playing truant with its own APRA, we cannot afford to participate in a free for all politics like in other regular full-fledged states. It can be counterproductive and can jeopardize the consolidation of our new state.

Moreover, TRS cannot afford to be anti-people in its very maiden government. If it does so, it will get its lesson. As the things stand, we do not have much scope except to sail with TRS, at least in these 5 years of its government to help it to deal with the anti-TS capers of A.P. and Central governments. Once the state graduates to a full-fledged state and or finds its moorings firmly, we can practice our pluralistic politics to our fullest. Everybody can indulge in their idiosyncratic politics with a gay abandon, as we normally do in India. Till that time we have to be very circumspect and work with the TRS government through its thick and thin. Even if such a stand is termed as servility to TRS by some, it does not matter. After all, discretion is the better part of accomplishment.

'కొండనాలుకకు మందు వేయబోయి ఉన్న నాలుక ను పోగొట్టుకోవడం ఉచితము కాదు.'

14

CENTER OFTEN DANGLES 'GOVERNORGIRI' TO BROWBEAT TS

(Missiontelangana.com | 1 December, 2014)

The central government is acting like a stepmother towards TS in the implementation of A.P.R.A. There are too many meetings taking place, without central government's resolve to adjudicate the matters impartially and as a tacit constitutional duty. The bias by the center is quite apparent towards its ally the TDP govt. in A.P. It has never taken an objective view on several transgressions of A.P.govt and failed to decide the issues based on merit. It looks like the BJP government wants to keep things simmering like that for obvious political reasons.

There are several issues which are being delayed inordinately. One such example is PM keeping the division of AIS officers pending, though it is a simple matter with well laid out policy and practices adopted in the earlier division of states. It also does not include any regional overtones. The matter is languishing superfluously in the PMO under the very nose of the PM.

The dodging and complicating the issue of division of state employees; the inaction on the division of assets; The indifference to the power imbroglio between the two states; the predation of A.P.government on TS funds in the joint bank accounts of different departments; inaction on the institutions not covered in the reorganization act; not resolving the disputes on the institutions covered in the act etc. are important issues causing a great deal of inconvenience in the functioning of TS government.

Periodically, many meetings with the home secretary of the center and governor of the state are taking place, without resolving the issues. Whenever the TS government is raising these issues, the center is glossing over them deliberately and is raking up the issue of operationalization of the Section-8 of the APRA. The section deals with the special responsibility of the Governor to protect the residents of the common capital. As if it is the most pressing matter in the scheme of the things. As such a situation is developing, where it looks like that, the Center likes the TS government to compromise on many vital issues in favor of A.P. for getting its cooperation. TS with so many unreasonable restrictions against it, thanks to Congress and BJP in A.P.R.A. is in no mood to relent.

One such laidback meeting convened by Union home secretary Anil Goswami with the chief secretaries of both AP and Telangana state, to resolve disputes between the two states, on 28th November is reported to have failed to broker the peace, as usual. The Telangana CS, Rajiv Sharma, raised objection over the correspondence of the AP government with the home ministry without even informing the TRS regime and wanted that a copy of its complaints to the Centre be marked to the Telangana government.

He also objected to the manner in which the AP government was 'diverting' to itself funds lying in the accounts of the united state and requested the Centre to ensure that Telangana's share is protected. Sharma also pointed out that the C R Kamalanathan Committee should be given more freedom so that it need not visit New Delhi for every small clarification on the employees' distribution. Referring to the water row with AP, the Telangana CS said the then TDP government had issued several orders on water release from Srisailam complicating the issue and sought the Centre's intervention to ensure equitable distribution of the river water between the two states at the earliest.

On the other hand, the A.P. CS, apart from demanding operationalizing section 8 of the AP reorganization act and coercing TS government to agree for a common schedule for the intermediate examinations had nothing tangible to complain against TS. Goswami as usual said he would take a decision after discussing the issue of the intermediate exam with the law department. This minor issue, which is urgent, since it deals with the timely conduct of exams, could have been solved instantaneously consulting with the law department.

As for Section 8 of the AP Reorganization Act, it gives special responsibility to the governor for the security of life, liberty and property of all those who reside in the common capital of Hyderabad. Raising the issue, Andhra Pradesh chief secretary IYR Krishna Rao is reported to have said that several issues related to the joint capital region require its implementation. Responding to this, Telangana chief secretary Rajiv Sharma said the TRS government has already made known its objections to the Centre on this issue in writing and that a discussion on section 8 at this juncture was 'unwarranted. 'Goswami assured them that he would seek the opinion of the law ministry on the contentious issue and asked both the state governments to abide by the decision that would be taken by the Centre in consultation with the law ministry.

When TS had submitted its objections in writing earlier the law department could have examined them and come to a decision on the matter. Though the heads of the departments were present in the meeting why the issues were not discussed in depth and amicable decisions were not taken on the issues raised by TS is not known. If the law department's opinion was necessary it was not invited to the meeting to expedite the resolution of the contentious issues, at least minor issues like intermediate exams. It all suggests a lack of interest.

By the complaint of the CS of Telangana State it is quite apparent that AP was making complaints to Center without even bringing to the notice to TS, leave alone deliberating with it on them beforehand. The obvious indifference of the Centre to take these matters seriously also is quite apparent here. The whole purpose of the meeting appears to be to remind TS urgently of section 8 of the Act and dangle it over its head to make it fall in line. Earlier also in Power distribution and Krishna water board deliberations the same kind of dissolute attitude was shown by the Center towards TS.

Instead of providing a categorical concern to the issues raised by the TS, which are more urgent and are becoming bottlenecks in the administration of the state, the home secretary treated them as routine and promised to talk to the concerned departments. On the contrary, he has homed on to the section 8 of the act, as if it is more germane to the context. And promised to refer it to the Law department and asked the two states emphatically to be ready to abide by the Center's decision. It appears ominous.

For implementing the section in any form will again ignite passions and it will lead to a more deteriorating situation in the relationship of both the states. And moreover there is no apparent reason to invoke it at this time except granting the itching wish of A.P. to have a quarrel with TS to divert attention from its internal problems. And create a law and order situation where operationalization of the section or imposition of President's rule is probable.

Though the Center and A.P. with their nexus have succeeded in pushing TS government on to its back foot, it will not be possible for them to succeed in their designs of coercing it to capitulation. If the recent refreshingly meaningful conduct of the TS Assembly session and its pragmatic budget is any indication, the TS government is stuck to its task of governance of the state resolutely and promising to deliver the goods.

In contrast the A.P. CM is running away from the problems of his state and roaming around the countries in private planes canvassing for assistance to his 'world class' capital; while the Centre is taking care of TS on his behalf. He is behaving like the alter-ego of Modi with hyper publicity of his meetings with premiers and many company heads, reminiscent of his publicity glitz in his earlier stint allegedly spending Rs.350 crores of the state exchequer. Old habits die hard.

There is a need to bring out this undemocratic antipathy of the central government to TS. It should be made to act responsibly to perform its duty constitutionally in the impartial implementation of A.P.R.A. It should be expeditious and constructive to make both the states function effectively and without superfluous conflicts.

15

IS TELANGANA A RICH STATE !

(Missiontelangna.com | 11 March, 2015)

The claim that Telangana is a rich state should be taken in a different perspective — may be in regards to its potential. It means that it has rich resources and its riches were siphoned off by the Andhra colonial government in the last 58 years making it poor. Most of it cannot be reclaimed now. The much touted budget surplus now in TS is a temporary and a passing phenomenon. Based on that it cannot be construed TS as a rich state.

Surplus or deficit in the budget of a state, relates to its revenue earning and expenditure thereof. If in a year a state government spends less than its revenue it can result in some surplus. Next year if it spends more than the revenue it will be in deficit. Therefore the so-called budget surplus of TS on the beginning of bifurcation of the state should be taken as a short lived entity — may be for this year only. In view of the liberal spending of the TS government and the changing dynamics of revenue earning in the coming year or so, the scenario can change significantly. The migration of many Andhra establishments, division of assets, sharing of liabilities etc. can impact the revenue of TS. With the penchant of all state governments in India to spend more than their revenue, the surplus of TS budget can be a thing of the past within no time.

But the present surplus in the TS budget tells us a telltale story of the United state. It is a spillover of the erstwhile A.P. government's expenditure pattern. In the aftermath of 1969 Telangana agitation, Kumar Lalith and Bhargava committees found that Telangana surpluses were spent in Andhra region. After 1972 also the practice continued unabated and part of the revenue of Telangana was continuously spent in Andhra region. It indicates the habitual lopping off Telangana revenue for Andhra resulting in less expenditure than its revenue in Telangana. The same is now reflected as surplus. The so-called deficit in Andhra is the result of this unscrupulous practice. Not because of any unscientific bifurcation or injustice as crowed by Andhra politicians in their propaganda. The observation of the 14th finance commission corroborates this fact only.

As for Hyderabad revenue, it has a lion's share in erstwhile Hyderabad state, in A.P. and will have in TS also, like any metropolitan city in India. It will be the same story for Madras in Tamilnadu; for Bangalore in Karnataka; for Calcutta in West Bengal; so on and so forth. If A.P. is not getting the benefit of it, it is not the fault of TS. The residual A.P. has no claim whatsoever on it. For, Andhra state when it got separated from Madras state in 1953 and Gujarat when it got separated from Bombay, it was the same situation. Infact Andhras and Gujaratis were living in their parent states much more than the 58 years of Andhras' colonization in Hyderabad.

Therefore Andhras motivated propaganda of Hyderabad revenue for making them deficit, is a totally irrelevant issue and has no merit whatsoever. Any way some of the Hyderabad revenue will be transferred to A.P. as and when their revenue earning institutions and the government establishments translocate to A.P. If they want that part of the revenue they need to go to their state for good. If they want to be here and cry for the revenue it does not make sense. It is like they shall reap as they sow.

The central funds are devolved and shared among the states according to certain settled formulas. Of course the backward states get some additional funds and incentives as part of the formulas as central assistance. It can also provide funds to states for some special development projects out of turn. KCR's often repeated statement that Telangana is rich is creating some avoidable problems here. It is making Andhras indulge in irrational propaganda against bifurcation and trying to extort more funds from the Center. They are making the issue very contentious. It also is giving a handle to the center to give more funds to A.P., as TDP is the ally of BJP, as the difference in allotments to the two states in the Central budget indicates.

It is also not good for the TS government to give much importance to this temporary surplus and go on a spending spree on non-plan expenditure, which can have a deleterious effect on its economy in the coming days. Therefore thinking TS state is rich from the point of view of its present revenue is a misnomer. Maybe it could have become a rich state if it was not merged with Andhra and its resources and revenue was not siphoned off during the last 58 years. It has definitely pushed it backwards. The demerger will stop that diversion, and the state has the potential to be among the rich states like Maharashtra, Haryana and Gujarat in coming years. Yet, the government needs to be careful and use its resources prudently without getting carried away by the short-lived budget surplus.

For, the richness of TS is not like Brunei or Singapore, whose PCI is more than $ 50,000. Presently the PCI of the richest state in India does not exceed even $2500.

16

ANDHRA'S BUDGET DEFICIT IS THE LEGACY OF THEIR OWN MAKING

(Missiontelangana.com | 28 April, 2015)

Before the demerger of state, Andhras were saying that if A.P. was divided, Telangana will not survive as a state, alleging that Telangana is dependent on Andhra for its economy. But it is proved wrong. Actually Residual A.P. is on the receiving end. It is staring at a massive deficit budget. TS has emerged as a state with a balanced revenue and expenditure and is presently comfortable in spending for the state's administration and development. Whereas, the residual A.P. is reeling under deficit budget and resorting to overdraft from RBI. And looking for special assistance from the center, proffering the deficit card. The Finance commission has provided to adjust its deficit over a period of 5 years. The center also rustled up some 15000 cr, special assistance. The assistance to TS is tweaked to help Andhra. Yet A.P. is not happy. It is demanding for special financial status. There is also said to be a curious move for special autonomy to the state in some quarters.

It is, of course, between the Center and A.P. to settle for whatever financial assistance A.P. is eligible to get. But A.P. raising the bogey of bifurcation of the state as the cause of their deficit and trying to give an impression that the TS is benefited at the cost of Andhra is not true. It is a complete travesty of truth. As a matter of fact Andhra region was in deficit since 1953 and continued to be so after merger with Telangana from 1956 to 2014. Its deficit is the legacy of its partisan spending of Telangana revenue surplus in Andhra region. Andhra administration has done it continuously in all the 58 years of the merged state.

It is alleged by Andhras that they have created a large revenue base for Hyderabad and the lack of Hyderabad revenue is creating the deficit to them. Hyderabad city was providing lion's share of revenue to the state both in Nizam's dominion, Hyderabad state and united A.P. It is no surprise, as it is the same case with all the metropolitan city capitals like Madras, Bombay, Calcutta and Bangalore. Moreover, the peculiarity of united A.P. is that the per capita revenue in Telangana was much more than that of Andhra. The Dhar commission 1945-48; State reorganization Commission(SRC) 1955-56; Kumar Lalith commission 1956 to 68; Rosaiah's statement in the Assembly for 2003-2007; budgets of both the states for 2014-15; 14th Financial commission projections for 2015-2020 — all their estimations/findings will vouchsafe the fact. The per capita revenue excess of Telangana was ranging from 38.94 to 106.21% over Andhra.

The case of Andhra and Telangana was different from other states' reorganization. It was a merger of two states. Andhra was suffering from deficit finance from 1953 to 1956. Andhra, wanted to get merged primarily with Telangana for its revenue surplus and first class city capital of Hyderabad. In all the 58 years the Telangana region was revenue surplus and Hyderabad, was contributing more revenue to the state like before. Andhras were in the merged state only for 58 years. Whereas Andhras were in Madras state for more than 150 years with more than 30% population in Madras city. Likewise Gujaratis were in Bomaby for a few centuries. The new Andhra and Gujarat states could not get their old capitals of Madras and Bombay respectively. There was no contention for the revenue of the capital there. In such a scenario Andhras claiming that they are the reason for the large revenue of Hyderabad in just 58 years is an absurdity. Hyderabad is 400 years old and was 4th largest city in India in 1950's. It is now the 6th largest.

Let us now examine for veracity, the available statistics in the matter. The following table (source: Goutham Pingle, New Indian Express) shows the excess of per capita revenue of Telangana over Andhra since 1945, including the projections for 2015-16 to 2019-20 by FC. It ranges from 38.94 to 106.21%. Even if we take the figures of 14th Finance Commission projections for the period from 2015-16 to 2019-20 based on the statistics and financial history of the united state in the past it comes to 38.94%.

ANNUAL REVENUE CONTRIBUTION FROM TELANGANA AND ANDHRA

Period	Authority	Telangana (Rs/capita)	Andhra (Rs/capita)	% Telangana revenues over Andhra
1945-48	Dar Commission	12.80	9.04	41.59
1955-56	SRC	15.04	10.53	42.83
1956-68	Kumar Lalit	29.36	21.63	35.74
2003-07	Rosaiah	1978.72	959.56	106.21
2014-15	Both Budgets	13,777.30	9,598.40	43.54
2015-20	14th Finance Commission	22,167.48	15,954.49	38.94

The Two Telugu States after demerger

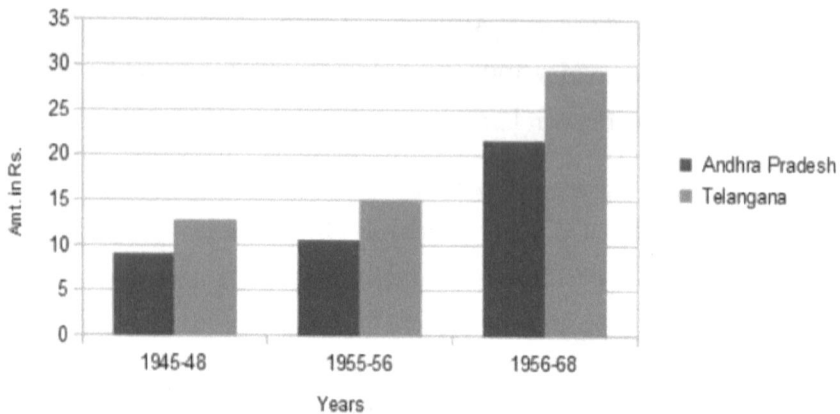

Per capita Revenue of AP & TS regions before 1969 :

(14th Finance Commission Estimates)

State: Andhra Pradesh

Assessed Own Revenue Receipts and Revenue Expenditure

(Rs. crore)

			2015-16	2016-17	2017-18	2018-19	2019-20	2015-20
A	GSDP		599295	678665	768546	870330	985595	3902431
B	Own Revenue Receipts		58624	68332	77784	88544	100793	394076
	1	Own Tax Revenue	47810	56058	63853	72732	82847	323300
	2	Own Non-Tax Revenue	10814	12274	13931	15811	17946	70776
C	Revenue Expenditure *of which*		90271	102155	115601	130816	148033	586874
	1	Interest Payment	9690	11083	12661	14447	16470	64352
	2	Pension	11066	12172	13389	14728	16201	67557
D	Pre-Devolution Revenue Deficit (+) / Surplus (-)		31646	33823	37817	42272	47240	

State: Telangana

Assessed Own Revenue Receipts and Revenue Expenditure

(Rs. crore)

			2015-16	2016-17	2017-18	2018-19	2019-20	2015-20
A	GSDP		500274	575667	662423	762253	877127	3377744
B	Own Revenue Receipts		57426	66340	76641	88546	102304	391256
	1	Own Tax Revenue	49981	57890	67051	77661	89950	342533
	2	Own Non-Tax Revenue	7444	8449	9590	10885	12354	48723
C	Revenue Expenditure *of which*		56607	64156	72711	82408	93402	369284
	1	Interest Payment	7057	8220	9558	11098	12869	48802
	2	Pension	8686	9555	10510	11561	12717	53030
D	Pre-Devolution Revenue Deficit (+) / Surplus (-)		-818	-2184	-3930	-6138	-8902	

Now if we analyze the Financial Commission figures given above, we will understand the following. The pre- devolution revenue of the 5 year period of A.P. is 78815 cr and TS is 78251 cr on an average per year. Though the population as per 2011 census is 4.94 cr for Andhra and 3.53 cr for TS, the revenue is almost equal. But there is a big variance in the expenditure. The average expenditure for Andhra is 117375 cr and for TS it is 73856 cr only. It indicates 48.92% more expenditure in Andhra. The average deficit for Andhra is 38360 cr. per year whereas TS earns surplus for all the 5 years with an average surplus of 4394 cr.

In per capita terms the expenditure in Andhra is 118800 as against the revenue of 79772 per person. In TS it is 104613 expenditure as against a revenue of 110837 per person. The average deficit of 38,360 cr per year is entirely on account of Andhra, as TS has a 4394 cr. surplus. Therefore it is a double whammy for Telangana both from the point of gross and per capita revenue collection and expenditure for all the 58 years. It clearly indicates that the entire deficit is due to excessive expenditure in Andhra.

In such circumstances holding bifurcation as the reason for their deficit or as a great injustice to them is an unsubstantiated claim. It has no merit whatsoever. The bifurcation did not do any injustice to Andhra. It has only paved the way for the full enjoyment of its revenue by the deliberately impoverished Telangana in all the years of coexistence with Andhra. It is only a hard earned justice to Telangana after a 58 year struggle, albeit a pyrrhic one with a compensation to its humongous loss of revenue.

If the exploitation of Telangana is stopped, after a huge loss of revenue and resources in all walks of life by demerger, how can it become an injustice to Andhra? Telangana was against the merger in the beginning itself. It was protesting time again on the use of surplus revenue from Telangana. In 1970 in the aftermath of 1969 agitation it was estimated that from 1956 to 1968 at least 65 cr surplus revenue of Telangana is spent in Andhra region. And it was agreed to spend that amount in Telangana in the subsequent years to make good the loss and also not to spend surplus Telangana revenue any more in Andhra. They have never implemented the agreements, like many such agreements, and continued the spending of Telangana revenue in Andhra without any qualms. Thus they were used to depend on the spending of Telangana revenue in Andhra for all the 58 years creating a permanent deficit budget in Andhra region.

Now because of the bifurcation of accounts of residual A.P. and TS by the 14th Finance Commission the truth of the matter is brought out so succinctly. The difference of availability of funds to the two states also explains the situation very clearly. In such a scenario, it is absurd for Andhras to blame TS and whine for their deficit. They have got in to this unenviable situation because of their avarice of eating into the revenue of Telangana continuously for all the 58 years of the united state, despite opposition to it. Their opposing formation of TS tooth and nail is also for the same reason.

Thus, their deficit budget is the legacy of their past and their profligate use of Telangana revenue. The responsibility is theirs entirely. Ironically, it translates to the saying 'ulta chor, kotwal ko dante', if they are trying to blame TS for their greed and impropriety.

17

A.P. GOVT. 'IN EXILE' IN TS - A SOLUTION OR A PROBLEM !

(The Hans India | 15 July, 2015)

On June 2, 2014 Telangana the 29th state of Indian Union came into existence. The residual A.P.with its 13 districts is separated. But even after one year after that the A.P.govt is still working from Telangana State and does not show any eagerness to move to A.P. in near future. It is on the pretext that Hyderabad is designated as common capital for 10 years in A.P.R.Act. Practically it is a govt.in exile from Hyderabad. It is some 250 kms away from the nearest border of A.P. and its entire government machinery is working from Hyderabad.

There are about 15 new states created in the Indian union after independence. There was no common capital conception in all those earlier state formations. Chandigarh was the sole exception, as it was situated on the border of Punjab and Haryana. It was also made a 'UT' to make it function lawfully as common capital for the two states. But, it is not without its nagging political conflicts. Yet, being straddled on the border it is functioning as a joint capital. Itcannot be repeated here in these two new states, as the geographic setting is entirely different. Such dispensation here will not be pragmatic and it has no constitutional approval too. Two sovereign state governments cannot exercise equal governing power over it, as the adage goes 'two swords cannot fit into one scabbard'. Therefore common capital for 10 years is an irrational proposition.

There are about 15 new states created in the Indian union after independence. There was no common capital conception in all those earlier state formations. Chandigarh was the sole exception, as it was situated right on the border of Punjab and Haryana. It was also made a 'UT' to make it function lawfully as common capital for the two states. But, it is not without its nagging political conflicts. Yet, being straddled on the border it is functioning as joint capital. It cannot be repeated here in these two new states, as the geographic setting is entirely different. Such dispensation here will not be pragmatic and it has no constitutional approval too. Two sovereign state governments cannot exercise equal governing power over it, as the adage goes 'two swords cannot fit into one scabbard'. Therefore common capital for 10 years is an irrational proposition.

Yet, the A.P. government, its politicians and their people in Hyderabad are enamored of common capital. They want all the 10 years of the period of the common capital and even more --- if possible permanently. The government on the plea of lack of capital, the employees on the pretext of accommodation, facilities, HRA, children education etc. do not want to move out. The excess Andhra employees do not want to be allotted to A.P. and those allotted to A.P. want to be here till their retirement. The A.P. Government wants equal sovereign powers in the city. It wants to use the wobbly section 8 in the Act, which was incorporated just to give reassurance to the presumed apprehensions, in a day to day administration as a regular statute. They don't take the division of the scheduled institutions seriously as per the Act. Andhra people from almost all the sections in Hyderabad are said to have a vested interest in the city and do not want to leave it. Ofcourse; they can be here and enjoy the fruits of their enterprise legitimately like any other people from outside the state. But they do not like it. They want special privileges over others. There lies the problem.

With this backdrop, the A.P. government is running a government from Hydearabad. A common capital is provided in the Act to facilitate relocation and establishment of a new capital and for extending certain benefits under article 371-D. But, the government is not making much effort to relocate. The capital construction is also proceeding at a snail's pace. The A.P. secretariat employees are not making it any secret to stay put in Hyderabad till their retirement. It is like tail wagging the dog. The government also is not making any serious effort to create necessary facilities to translocate the secretariat. It gives an impression that may be the govt. tacitly supporting the recalcitrance of employee unions with an agenda of its own. If we go by some statements of A.P.CM and other government functionaries, government does not appear to leave Hyderabad for all the 10 years of its common capital tenure for obvious reasons. Some of the statements also smack of a hankering for 'UT'.

The never ending Kamalanathan and Sheela Bhide Committees proceedings and power, Water, Institutions serial litigations etc. all are suggesting a deliberate long drawn war of attrition even after division, between the two states foisted by A.P. Also Read - Vijayawada: CJI Ramana to inaugurate new court complex The breaking out of Cash-for-vote scandal is the high point of this war. It was not a simple buying of one MLA vote for the election of one MLC of TDP.Euphemistically saying, it appears to be a tip of the iceberg. The plot seems to be a much larger conspiracy to buy about 30 TRS MLAs to destabilize the maiden TS government. This scam brings out with a jolt the sinister designs of TDP and the A.P. government in Hyderabad

If we see at the range and scope of the scam, we may be forced to think that the 10 year common capital, the section 8 and other additions in the last minute melee of A.P.R.A.as restrictions to TS is an intentional political strategy to harass the new state.Now, A.P. Government conveniently ensconced in Hyderabad, is trying to use them one by one. But, these things will no way help A.P. state and its people struggling to find the moorings in the new state. The A.P. government remaining in Hyderabad for all the 10 years, might help TDP to promote itself in Telangana and may be useful to the vested interests of many Andhra elite who have established many business/ property empires at the cost of Telangana. But it will not help to take the residual A.P. state forward unhindered.

The civil society and people at large in A.P. are not comprehending the implicit implication in it.They are getting carried away by the negative propaganda by TDP now, as by all of their political parties before bifurcation. They are still in the hangover of the political indoctrination against bifurcation.By now it should have been understood that, the merger was an historical blunder. Telangana people were never happy with it.They opposed it in the beginning itself and were agitating against it incessantly. It is Andhra political leaders who have always manipulated and foiled their efforts. By hindsight, it can be averred thatAndhra politicians are responsible for whatever bifurcation dejections are there for A.P.now. They should now realize that it is irrefutable and no use proselytizing on it anymore. And they should now embark on building their state with statesmanship, which their political leaders had abdicated between 1953 and 1956 itself, for their overriding political ambitions.

All the new states which were formed after 1956 proved that with a great measure of success.Gujarat, Haryana and Chhattisgarh states are some shining examples of it.Both Andhra and Telangana States would have been the front runners by now, if the forced merger has not taken place. They need to understand the futility and uncalled for TDP's political gamesmanship in Hyderabad and on the maiden TS government.It is a known fact thatChandrababu Naidu and TDP has stopped for four years the TS formation and caused inestimable suffering for the people of both states. It is time for them to behave responsibly now,at least for the sake of their own A.P.state. Like thoseinappropriate vishalandhra and samaikyandhra slogans earlier now also their cry for sovereign power on Hyderabad sounds as the extension of their imperialistic design.

In 1969 the agitation was suppressed by the killing of 369 people in police firing. In 1972 the mulki rules upheld by the Supreme Court were abrogated by the Constitution amendment. All agreements, formulas, plans evolved periodically in the 58 years of the united state to effect a level playing field, were observed in breach rather than in practice. The center was managed every time to coerce Telangana into submission. But this time fortuitously, because of the sacrifice of the lives of 1200 youth,a state is given. Albeit with many millstones around its neck as parting kicks..Now they are playing onthem remorselessly, as is their wont.

The center as usual is continuing its standoff attitude, not helping TS proactively for its legitimate interests.They show unambiguous indications of not leaving Hyderabad and play threatening divisive politics to make Hyderabad a contentious issue, which can have very volatile consequences. In addition, even before the expiry of one year, CBN's government has unleashed a clandestine program to destabilize Telangana state by its alleged 200cr. cash-for-vote scheme, running his government from its territory. It is tantamount to treason.

Therefore the purported government-in-exile in Hyderabad for 10 years appears to be a virtual breeding ground for spawning unsavory glitches for both the states. Instead of finding solutions to fictional problems, it has all the potential for getting entangled in a Gordian knot by itself.

18

'AMARAVATI' CAPITAL ECOLOGICALLY CHALLENGED

(The Hans India | 13, August, 2015)

The A.P. new capital christened as Amaravati, to be built in the vicinity of Vijayawada on Krishna river front is in the news for several reasons. A lot of discussion is taking place on political, economic, technical and environmental issues of the new capital. Some PILs are also current on it in the courts of law. Of all, on the ecological and environmental front, the concern is more acute. A PIL is also pending before the National Green Tribunal.

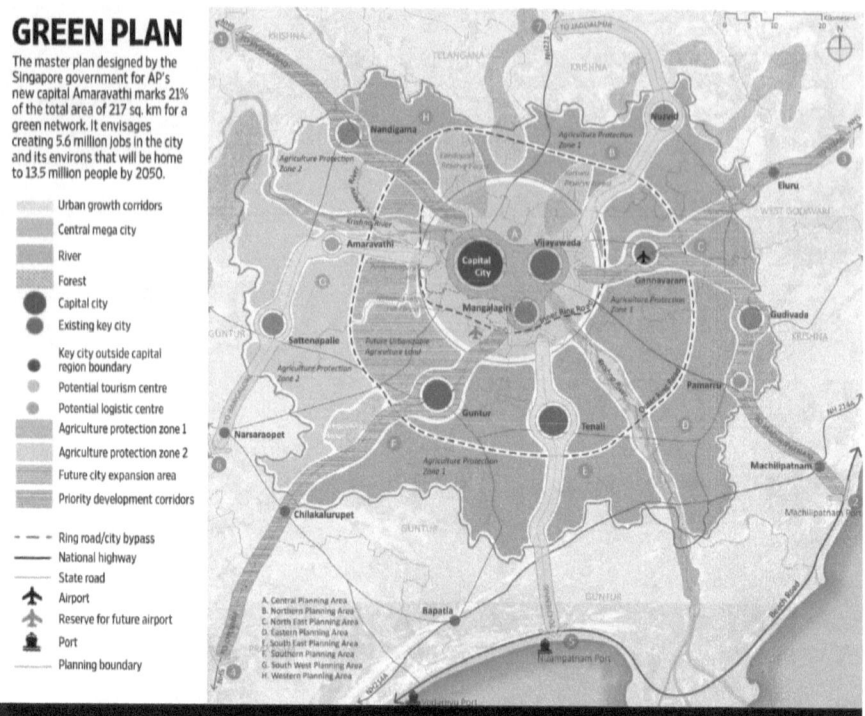

A P Capital Region

Green Tribunal

The tribunal has taken an undertaking from govt. of A.P. not to make any alterations in the lands purported to have been given by the farmers to government for the purpose of seed capital of Amaravati till the next hearing. The hearing is scheduled on 27th of August, 2015, where in the government is allowed to file its counter. The designated A.P.Capital Region, in the VGTM area is a prime agricultural zone in the state and also in the country. It has some natural endowments and some man made projects, which made the area one of the most productive areas from the point of agriculture.

The area has laid the foundation for the economic development of the area. Because of such lands the central coastal districts have become the most economically developed in the state. Now destroying such endowments, which were either natural to the area or made a century before, in the name of the capital, is felt as an inexcusable iniquitous act. The capital instead can be constructed in the denotified forest area available in the same zone without much ado. But, it is not happening so. We may now peruse some of the ecological and environmental issues connected to the enormous capital region development project.

Jareebu lands: The so-called 'jareebu lands', part of the 33000 acres core area for the capital, are natural endowments to the area. They are soils of deposited river alluvium with 'filter point' irrigation facility i.e. shallow wells with inexhaustible water supply, with well drained soils, facilitating growing a wide range of crops --- vegetables, fruits, flowers and other commercial crops. They say they grow 3-5 short duration crops in an agricultural year and also highly remunerative perennial horticultural crops there.

They are far more productive than the famous double crop wetlands in the nearby Krishna delta. It is a unique 'biome' with a fascinating cropping pattern of about 80 to 100 types of crops. It is said that these lands fetch Rs 60000 to 80000 lease per acre/annum. Probably; these are probably among the most fertile soils in the country. We may build 'Petronas' towers anywhere, but we cannot create such 'biomes', wherever we want. They are the natural endowment to the area and are heritage of the local people. Krishna canal ayacut: In the Capital Region of 7240 sq.kms, vast stretches of Krishna canal ayacut lands, the so called Krishna delta, which are double crop paddy growing areas are going to be affected by the capital region infrastructure. It is estimated that the extent of such lands could be about 2 lakh acres. The Krishna canal system is more than 150 years old built by SirArthur Cotton and was the springboard of the economic development of these areas.

It is also not easy to recreate such an ayacut elsewhere now. Obliteration of such historical delta ayacut is considered a monumental waste. Productive Agriculture lands: Besides, outside these jareebu and ayacut lands, all the cultivable area in the capital region is endowed with very fertile alluvial black soils, good rainfall, a high groundwater table, facilitating a very profitable agriculture under bore wells. Unlike in Telangana and Rayalaseema regions, which suffer with low rainfall, very low groundwater table with a very high cost and large scale failure of bore wells and are plagued by chronic droughts. By and large the entire Capital region of 7240 sq.kms is a prime agricultural zone in the entire country apart from the unique jareebu and canal ayacut lands endemic to this area forming part of it. Added to this, it is also reported that because of the deep alluvial and black cotton soils without hard strata and high water table the region is not suitable for high rise buildings.

This area is also situated in Zone 3 of earthquake prone areas in the country and is also prone to frequent floods and cyclones. It is also said that to obviate the high water table and flood threat and some lands being lower than river flood level, it needs to raise some area by 6 meters adding to the cost immensely. In addition to all this, a document prepared by United Nations Development Programme (UNDP) has identified that "Amaravati, the proposed capital of Andhra Pradesh, will face eight major environmental challenges that may affect the local atmosphere and lead to adverse climatic events in the region" ---- 'New AP capital to pose major threat to ecosystem' (TOI, 10 August, 2015). There cannot be any worse indictment than this. At Least UNDP cannot be blamed to have any bias whatsoever against the Project.

In such a scenario which categorically forebades, a grave ecological and environmental devastation, the need to go ahead with a mulish stubbornness towards such catastrophic capital adventure is beyond comprehension. Even if it is decided to have it in the vicinity only for the best reasons known to them, it can be built in that 43000 acres forest area or there about available in the area, shifting the constructions some 10-20 kms upwards with a limited area, avoiding many technical problems. Heavens will not fall because of it.

Even the capital scheme itself looks impossible.A.P.is one of the 29 states in India. It is not even a country, to model its capital on world class capitals of highly developed countries. Its DGP is around $80 B only. But It wants to imitate capitals like Singapore (DGP $360B), Tokyo (DGP $1617B) and Shanghai (DGP $594B) for its infrastructure. It is preposterous and foolhardy. Even India's capital New Delhi GDP is $294 B with a country's GDP of $7300 B, and cannot compete with these cities in infrastructure. The state's economy itself is in the doldrums presently. How can it pull off such dream capital even if it is that outlandish PPP model or FDI model?

It is beyond the capacity of A.P. to service these gargantuan investments. After all it is a city for the people and their distant future not for the vain glorious idiosyncrasies of some individuals for their short term gains. Just calling it a 'people's capital' and planning for the disaster, cannot make it a people's capital. Political leaders in such situations should behave like statesmen taking everybody into confidence.Follow the wiser counsel and take pragmatic decisions, not to jeopardize state's economy and lives of people.Let us hope that the Courts will drill some sense into their minds to stop this ecologically challenged gamble.

19

WITHER SCIENTIFIC STATE BIFURCATION !

(The Hans India | 9 May, 2015)

The govt. of A.P. calls Andhra Pradesh Reorganization Act-2014, as unscientific and irrational. They made the Governor, in his address to the joint session of A.P. Assembly and Council, say, the same. They harp on the allegation everywhere and badger the center for additional sops and impossible handouts in the name of it. This attitude without addressing the basics of reorganization is making life difficult for the people of both the states. There is no rationale behind this irrational refrain. Afterall it is a bifurcation of the earlier merged state, not a bifurcation in a mathematical study.

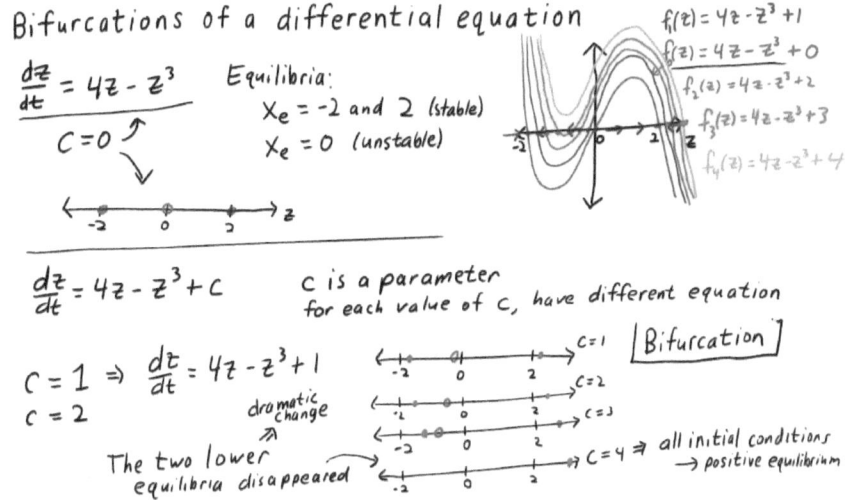

It is not for the first time a state is divided in independent India. Comprehensive reorganization norms are firmly in place. It was Andhra state which was the ancestor of this Act. What is good for the gander can be good for the goose. Actually several unusual provisions, partisan to Andhra, are shoved into the Act., because of the last minute politicking of two national parties.

1. A 10 year common capital.
2. An undemocratic 'Governorgiri' on TS.
3. A Polavaram Project, which cannot see the light in the regular laws of the land, including annexation of Bhadrachalam division as an inappropriate amendment to the Act.
4. A cumbersome special inter-state river water board.
5. Assistance to recommend a suitable place and necessary funds to construct a capital city.
6. Promises of several unsustainable sops like SCS etc.

On the floor of the Parliament such things were not considered necessary in earlier divisions. Some of them can be invalid in terms of Article 3. If they can be scientific, it is surprising how the regular provisions which were tacitly adapted and stood the test of time in earlier divisions can become unscientific here.

Not having the capital and inheriting a big financial budget deficit are two important complaints of the unscientific bifurcation theory of Andhras. Take the case of capital, Andhras did not have a capital in 1953. Many new states did not inherit capitals of their own either. The grant of financial assistance for building capital was also not a norm. There was some financial assistance for capitals for the states created in 2000. This was also not an outright grant. Whereas in the case of A.P., there was a committee of experts to recommend the capital. Presently, about Rs. 3000 cr is earmarked for capital assistance by the Center as grant. It is likely that they will garner some more in the coming years. But, A.P. govt. did not consider Sivramakrishnan's report apropos and stymied it even before the ink on it dried up. Then they went hankering after Singapore, Japan etc. for a world class capital at Vijayawada. And estimated Rs.one lakh cr.for capital construction and demanded all of it from the Center. They are now obsessed with that fantasy without regard to its feasibility. How scientific or rational that idea and efforts there on are left to its veracity into the future.

Now coming to the all important, 'deficit budget' issue. This deficit budget in new states is a common occurrence.And the Center as a tacit duty and was adjusting the deficit to neutralize it in the first one or two years. Here in case of residual A.P. the deficit is very high. It is not because of any unscientific bifurcation. It is because of continuous spending of surplus Telangana revenue in Andhra region.The 14th Finance Commission headed by Sri YV Reddy has clearly brought out this and has provided for adjustment of Rs.22,112 cr over 5 years from 2015-16 to 2019-20, neutralizing the deficit every year along with the devolution of funds from the Center. In addition, Rs.500 cr is provided towards non-plan revenue deficit also. By far it is the biggest adjustment of the deficit by the center for a new state. Yet, A.P.govt. is not happy. It wants the whole deficit at one go in the beginning itself and demands several other economic sops. It is clearly an irrational and unscientific demand.

There are the promises made by the PM Manmohan Singh in Parliament under duress such as special category status, special development package for backward areas, industrial incentives etc. A.P. demands these in addition to bridging the deficit budget gap for an allegedly level playing field with TS. Their earlier argument of holding light to Telangana economy proved to be wrong. Actually it was the other way round. When bifurcation took place, inevitably, it was caught plumb before FC and the state was left high and dry with a deficit budget. In view of that, the claim of unlevel-playing field with TS is a complete travesty of truth. Ironically it means to say that A.P. needs to be rewarded for its inappropriate appropriation of Telangana revenue in all the 58 years, in addition to bearing the huge deficit. There are many more states already in the queue for SCS. A.P. is not eligible for SCS as per the norms in vogue. It can be an unlevel-playing field for the neighboring states including TS if SCS and other industrial development incentives are given to A.P., which can start the migration of industries from these states. In such circumstances it cannot be called scientific to sanction SCS to A.P.

As for the package for backward areas, 8 districts in TS and 3 districts in A.P. were recognized as backward by the Rural Development Department of India. But now, unilaterally Rs.350 cr package is sanctioned to 7 districts in A.P.only. As per the Act such assistance should be given to both the resultant states wherever it is required. If A.P. is accorded SCS by any reason the facility should be automatically extended to TS to create the so called level-playing field. But, unfortunately it has become a one sided affair because of that surplus revenue which is the result of availability of its full revenue for Telangana for the first time in 58 years of united state.

Because of it, A.P. is trying to call itself an underdog unabashedly and demanding more sops. The Center is trying to acquiesce on the propaganda and trying to help A.P. at the cost of TS. There are several such incongruities in the implementation of the A.P.R.A. For example, the institutions in x schedule are to be divided between the two states within a year. Till that time the state in which they are located will have the primacy to own and run those institutions. A.P. is deliberately avoiding the division of these institutions and creating unseemly controversies in running these institutions. The employees division, shifting the secretariat and Andhra employees from Hyderabad to A.P.are some of the other issues.

The 10 year common capital itself is a big unscientific stratagem in the A.P.R.A. Such provision was never there in earlier divisions. Only in the case of Andhra, Madras was considered as common capital for 2-3 years by the Wanchoo committee and was shelved quickly as it was felt impracticable. Even if it is needed now it could have been enough to have a 2 year period of common accommodation. Now we all know how this 10 year period of common capital is causing the problems for both the states because of recalcitrance of A.P. The government is indulging in building a capital in the air and encouraging the secretariat and the employees to stay put in Hyderabad, affecting their own governance and administration. The power distribution, which was devised scientifically in the Act was rendered unscientific by the refusal of A.P. to honor it. The sharing of water is another bone of contention, which is creating more problems.In Fact when the new projects or the deliberately kept long pending projects in Telangana come on to the anvil the real difficulties of new interstate river boards will be unveiled.

TS is busy grappling with the running of the new state and appears to be making some good progress. Thanks to the availability of its own full revenue to itself. A.P. on the other hand is running in to rough weather creating unnecessary complications with TS with its obstinacy of not reconciling with the stark reality of the bifurcation. The complexities it has built up in the 4 years from December 2009 to June 2nd 2014 and the inappropriate subterfuge in the final hour of the passing of the Reorganization Bill are haunting both the states. Some of them are acting against A.P. like 'Bhasmasura hasta' as the saying goes.

Its profligate spending despite the heavy budget deficit is aggravating the situation. The incongruity of its SCS campaign with the slogans of unscientific, irrational and unlevel-playing field bifurcation on one hand and the bizarre obsession with world class capital and number one state on the other is causing bafflement. The A.P.govt instead of getting down to the brass-tacks of constructing the residual state, is indulging in building the castles in the air. Unable to make any headway in that fantasy,it is trying to find a scapegoat in TS surplus revenue inventing meaningless slogans. In their parlance 'scientific bifurcation' means getting everything they want.

20

A REPLY TO KANCHE ILAIAH

(Missiontelangna.com | 19 November, 2015)

Kanche Ilaiah the social activist has denunciated the new Telangana State and extolled residual Andhra Pradesh, in his chat with Hindu (Bifurcation proves bane for Telangana - 17, November 2015). He has cursed TS to dwindle in its economies because of drought and commended A.P. owing for its coastline, large agrarian base and Amaravati, its would be world class capital. He opined that coastal Andhra supplied food to Telangana all these years in united state. And says that, now TS has to import food from other states including A.P. and buy basic things such as salt. He thinks that bifurcation was due to the vested interests of few communities. He also says that Maoists were the game changer. And alleges that they thought Andhra upper caste industrialists were more dangerous than the feudal landlords of Telangana. He also avers that Hyderabad was developed by the business men from coastal parts of A.P. Here is the take on each one of his observations in the diatribe.

His prediction for Amaravati, the capital of Andhra to become world class, has no complaints. It is his whimsical wish like many others. It may become world class or not, it is anybody's guess. Presently there are no world class cities in India. It is not known whether our best cities like

Mumbai and Delhi can be called world class in the parlance of Amaravati baiters, who mean it to be Singapore, Tokyo, and Shanghai etc. Even our not so world class cities took hundreds of years to become what they are today. Even this, to be a world class city, cannot be created in a hurry in 5, 10 or 20 years. After hundreds of years even if it becomes world class, how it is going to help present residual A.P., it is difficult to comprehend now. Anyway, whatever happens there, it is of no concern to TS. Let Amaravati baiters like Ilaiah get a kick out of their yearnings. It is up to A.P. to have any class of capital it likes. Whether world or Indian class, TS has Hyderabad, whose revenue has been a bone of contention earlier.

'TS are land locked with a history of drought and AP has a long coastline and a huge agrarian base': Drought is not new to Telangana or A.P. In A.P., the whole of Rayalaseema and some parts of Andhra are also drought prone. Rivers Godavari and Krishna have more spans and more watershed area in TS. TS is eligible for more water than hitherto allotted.

The matter is before the Supreme Court. If the woefully neglected 46000 MI tanks are repaired; hundreds of tmc of water stole by Andhra without completing the irrigation projects pending since 1956, which are now being brought on to the anvil, is restored; redesigning and completing the deliberately ill-designed, neglected existing and ongoing irrigation projects is done, the drought in TS can be alleviated. And the state can challenge Andhra for agriculture production. Already district like Karimnagar has upstaged Krishna district in the production of rice. Telangana has a great agrarian base too, its population is less and its per capita revenue is more. The andhras' revenue deficit is the Telangana's revenue surplus spent on it in united state, which is now wholly available to Telangana. Presently Andhra is struggling to make both ends meet because of its less per capita revenue & the revenue deficit. Those are the ground realities.

Andhra is not supplying food to Telangana, despite drought. Perhaps Mr.Ilaiah was reminiscing on pre-independence or early independent rice-rationing days. Telangana is producing enough food for itself. Even if it is so, they would not supply it for free. Salt can be bought from anywhere else. Many states are getting salt from other states. That is not germane to development. There is absolutely no need for TS to import food from A.P. Referring to buying of basic things like salt in this context, sounds ridiculous, for the very primitive sense of it, in these modern times.

Long coast line to A.P. may have some advantages to it. Let the A.P. state enjoy those benefits. But, in India it is not TS alone —- there are more landlocked states than the coastal states. The line alone does not decree the economy of a state. Some landlocked states have more per capita income (PCI) than many coastal states in the country e.g., Haryana, Punjab & Sikkim. TS has more per capita income than A.P. even now.

Mr.Ilaiah's views on bifurcation are very intriguing. By saying bifurcation is because of the vested interest of few upper castes, is taking his dislike for caste system a little too far. Game changer here, is not his illusory premise. Many Dalit leaders argue that the bifurcation is because of Dalit support and it is felt good for backward and Dalit class representation in government. Actually the game changer is the renewed exploitation of Telangana by Andhra administration and participation of all sections of Telangana society in this episode of Telangana struggle.

Ilaiahs comparison of Andhra industrialists with now nonexistent Telangana feudalism makes a very interesting reading. Feudalism of Telangana is a thing of the past. The Andhra majority political-corporate hegemony has replaced the so-called feudalism. His love for Andhra industrialists who are the forerunners of the organized exploitation of Telangana by Andhra administration is very paradoxical. He does not know if Andhras developed Hyderabad or Hyderabad developed Andhra industrialists and corporate politicians. In posh colonies like Banjara Hills, Jubilee Hills etc. 80 to 90% are Andhra industrialists and political-corporates. A few lakhs of acres of land in and around Hyderabad is in the hands of these people. Most of the neo rich millionaires in erstwhile A.P. are from this class of people.

Mr.Ilaiah's views are completely inverted. It is because he considers his prejudices and biases without regard to ground realities, as facts of life. Everything cannot be looked at from the point of the caste system alone. There are several other parameters in the creation of a state and its survival. We must look at it with a holistic perception. The merger of Andhra and Telangana was an historical blunder. If both Andhra and Telangana remained separate states from 1956, they would have developed by now as front running states in the country. Though it is late, they can develop even now on their own in to two prosperous states. But, eulogizing Andhra and denigrating TS as Mr. Ilaiah tries to do perfunctorily has no valid basis. When Punjab and Haryana was divided in 1966, some had opined in the same vein. But, it is proved wrong. The backward and irrigation starved Haryana has now overtaken Punjab. It will be the same story in case of TS too.

Bifurcation of State is a fait accompli. It cannot be changed now. Umpteen numbers of new states were created in independent India. No new state had proved to be a bane for itself. TS has more resources and more positive credentials than many earlier new states to become a very successful state on its own. There is no need for any 'social activist' to worry about it with his imaginary premises.

Have we started buying salt and rice from Andhra after the demerger !

WHY HYDERABAD PEOPLE NEED TO VOTE FOR TRS IN GHMC ELECTIONS ?

(Missiontelangna.com | 29 January, 2016)

Telangana state is not like other 28 states in the country. It is a newly formed state still suffering from several baby blues. Though TRS has won a comfortable mandate to rule the state in the general elections 2014, still there are certain political hangovers that are nibbling at the full fledged political freedom of the new state. Now the ruling TRS winning in the ensuing GHMC elections is an important event to consolidate the formation of the new State. In that context, here are some of the reasons why people need to vote for TRS in GHMC elections.

- Telangana is a new state with several things pending for a full fledged state. The maiden TS govt. needs its sovereign control on its capital, for completion of the formation of the state. Hyderabad is designated as joint capital for 10 years with A.P. TS govt. needs its administration control on Hyderabad city to maneuver Andhra government presence in the city and to see it smoothly transit to its Andhra capital without causing any hiccups, given the antecedents of Telangana state struggle. Hyderabad is the capital of TS. The government needs control on it for its development commensurate with its mega development plans on the anvil to make it a world class city.

- In TS except TRS there are no other political parties with exclusive Telangana interests. All the other parties have their high commands from outside the state. Their local units are subservient to their high commands and cannot fully vouchsafe for TS interests.A. P. political leadership and its colonists want to have their proxy control on the city for their political advantage and vested interests. If they gain such control, they can trouble TS govt. and work for future political inroads into the state, which can be detrimental to the political and economic interests of TS.
- Andhra political outfits also entertain the ideas of 'UT' and other such redundant notions to deprive TS people to enjoy full rights in their capital like any other native people in other state capitals. TS people need to nip such unscrupulous ideas in the bud itself, by not allowing them political foothold in the city.
- Andhra politicians canvass an erroneous impression that Andhras are more in Hyderabad than the native telanganites because of the TRS not winning many seats in GHMC area in the general elections. It is now proved that it was because of lakhs of duplicate votes of Andhras in the city. Already 4.3 lakh voters are removed and another 7.9 lakh voters are identified. There is a need to correct this impression and establish the majority of native Telangana voters by winning GHMC elections to settle the issue once for all. And not to give scope to them to play any strife torn politics in Hyderabad.
- Winning Mayoral authority in Hyderabad for TRS is needed to make the cup of political sovereignty of Telangana people in their state full. It is essential to subjugate the political parties like T-Congress, T-TDP and T-BJP who harp on the cross border interests, rather than the interests of Telangana people. The people with origins from outside

state who made Hyderabad their home city need to understand the need for TS government to have its political control on the city for stability, peace and progress.
- Even people of andhra origin who made Hyderabad as their home city, should identify their interests with Telangana State as its citizens. They should not become pawns in the hands of political parties who want to foment trouble in the name of division of state. They should now vote for TRS for peace and prosperity in their own interest.Hyderabad is the heritage of Telangana people. Its status and future can not be negotiated in any way. it should be ensured that there is a resounding win for TRS, the only political party with unequivocal Telangana ethos.

22

NGRI REPORT ON MISSION KAKATIYA IN TELANGANA: A COMMENT

(The Hans India | 20 April, 2016)

This has reference to the news item 'Mission Kakatiya doomed, says NGRI report' –TOI, Apr 25, 2016. The news or the purported report of NGRI is not in consonance with ground reality. It is true that Mission Kakatiya is a programme of massive investment. If it does not create commensurate benefits it will not be cost effective. But, what is that comprehensive scientific approach that NGRI thinks appropriate and the state is missing is not explained here. The tanks that are being repaired have not dried up because of non availability of groundwater. In actual fact, they have not much to do with ground water directly. The tanks receive water from surface runoff of rainwater. The erratic rainfall because of change of climatic patterns has severely affected surface runoff of rainwater, which is the source for these tanks.

Added to this, the drastic lowering down of ground water table owing to very heavy overdraft of ground water by innumerable borewells in the state also affecting the free flow of surface water. The tanks are reservoirs of water on the ground, created by the bunds constructed across streams, and rivulets in the undulated terrain of the state. They are not dug into the ground and have nothing much to do with the underground hard rock geological formations. Over the years they have got silted up, reducing their water storage capacity. Now the accumulated silt is dug up and removed to restore its original storage. Obviously, the observation that "state having hard rock formations, …….. in hard rock areas, the occurrence of ground water and its movement are controlled by the thickness of the weathered layer and the presence of fractures and solutions cavities" has no relevance here.

These tanks are not either open wells or bore wells which were dug in the weathered zone or deep into the earth . They have nothing to do with groundwater regime. The present work done on the tanks is removing the silt accumulated over the years; repairing inflow channels, for increasing the water storage capacity; strengthening the weakened tank bunds and wiers to make them more durable ,thus restoring or increasing the reservoir capacity of the tanks. In addition to this, to augment the depleted inflows in to these tanks, it is planned to link the tanks to medium and major irrigation projects existing and the projects in the pipeline, wherever possible. Thus these tanks have nothing to do with the hard rock geological formations and the water movement underground. Actually, restoration of these numerous tanks to their original storage capacity will increase the replenishment of groundwater and help raise the ground water table, acting as a network of percolation tanks. As a matter of fact it is considered an excellent project to address the bane of bore wells in the state which has rendered its ground water resources very precarious, by lowering its ground water table to dangerously low level, making even drinking water scarce.

"Telangana is a comparatively small state with respect to geographical area and population, but it is not very favorable for water resources. The state government has to be extremely serious. The government's efforts are laudable, but there is a need for a scientific approach," NGRI chief scientist Shakeel Ahmed told TOI. It is not understood the connection of being a comparatively small state with geographical area and population and favorable water resources. There are many smaller states in the country with better water resources.

TS is a hilly region with low and moderate rainfall and a very undulated topography that is why it has so many thousands of tanks built historically to impound the water to make most of its limited water resources. These tanks have stood the test of time and have been the mainstay of irrigation and drinking water needs of the state's population. They have also helped to improve the water table in the hard rock geological formations, to draw groundwater for conjunctive use and irrigation.

The news report is very bald without providing the details of the scientific approach contemplated by NGRI in this matter. NGRI needs to make its purported scientific approach on this Project public. There is a need for the TS government to get in touch with NGRI and get to the brass tacks of the latter's observations for veracity and clarification.

23

TELANGANA VINDICATES ITS STATEHOOD

(Telangana Today | 23 May, 2017)

Telangana came into existence on June 2, 2014 as the 29th state of India. Several new state were created after independence, many of them on linguistic basis and some on tribal identities, geography and culture. The struggle for statehood of Telangana was different from that of the other new states. Telangana's struggle for its political freedom was long and poignant, took 58 years and the lives of over 1500 people. Even the end was a cliffhanger owing to the intense political drama and intrigue of vested interests to prevent it.

In fact, skepticism was systematically spread through a motivated campaign to show that Telangana can not survive as a separate state. It was made to believe that Andhra guides the political and economic development of Telangana. A misinformation campaign was unleashed in the media and an impression was created that separation of Telangana was not just bad politics but even unconstitutional. It was stressed that Telangana will trigger many new demands for bifurcation. All these have been proved wrong in the first three years after Telangana state formation.

> Truth is generally the best vindication against slander.
>
> (Abraham Lincoln)

Ahead of Andhra

From 1952 to 1956, Telangana, then known as Hyderabad state, was a separate state with surplus budget and a very high per capita revenue. During the reorganization of states in 1956, in spite of ceding some parts to Maharashtra and Karnataka, the residual state was sufficiently large and had a self-sustaining revenue.In 1955-56, according to the State Reorganization Commission (SRC), the per capita revenue of Telangana and Andhra was Rs.15.04 and Rs.10.53 respectively, in the ratio of 1.43 :1.00. In 2015-2020 as projected by 14th Finance Commission it is Rs.22,167 : Rs.15,054 (1.39 :1.00). Even earlier in 1948, according to the Dhar commission, it was Rs.12.80 : Rs.9.04 (1.42:1.00).

After the 1969 Telangana agitation,the surplus Telangana revenue spending in Andhra was probed by Justice Bhargava and Kumar Lalith Commissions and both confirmed it. Later it was agreed to transfer the estimated surplus spent in Andhra to Telangana region and from then on wards to spend Telangana revenue only in the Telangana region.But, it never happened and the revenue details were deliberately kept under wrap. It came out clearly only in the projections of the 14th Finance Commission for its estimations of 2015 to 2020 in 2014.

A Strong State

Telangana could have flourished even more if it were made a separate state in 1956, as recommended by SRC. In contrast, Andhra was struggling with its deficit budget since 1953, when it got separated from Madras state and was in dire need of a capital city. So they wanted a merger with Telangana. Even today, despite more share in the devolution of central taxes and the center making good the deficit in the budget, AP is still struggling to manage its finances. Telangana on the other hand, now has its full revenue for itself to go along with the high per capita revenue it inherited. Of the united State Budget of Rs.1.61 Lakh crore in 2013-14, Telangana regions was perhaps around Rs. 68,000 cr. But now the Budget of Telangana is increased from Rs.1,00,637 cr. in 2014-15 to 1.49 lakh cr. in 2017-18. The GSDP growth rate for 2016-17 is 10.17% as against the national average of 9%.

Taking advantage of this financial strength, Telangana has surged ahead. The majority of above 80 seats of the 119 in the Assembly makes Telangana Rashtra Samithi (TRS) in full command politically. These factors have provided confidence to the state government to take bold economic and political decisions.

Full Faith

Initially, there was an ambiguity over Hyderabad city and its adjoining areas, which did not favor TRS in 2014 elections. But, things changed subsequently in GHMC elections, with these areas backing the party. The identification of over 12 lakh bogus voters and preventing any fraudulent voting by Election Commission helped. Another factor is the change of heart among non-Telugu voters based on the improved governance after the State formation. This has brought both Hyderabad city and rural Telangana on to the same political page.

The financial position and political faith reposed by the people have encouraged the TRS to implement its manifesto with gusto. It has made budget allocations for all sections of the people and rural development schemes. The dramatic change in power situation, big emphasis on irrigation projects and industries,starting of housing scheme,pensions, promise of financial assistance to rural professions and farmers are big game changers. Though some of them are populist , they will all enable economic development.

Overcoming Impediments

The state is marching ahead well, but it is not without its problems. The Andhra Pradesh Reorganization Act.2014 was not fair to the State and it has imposed certain impediments. The division of assets, employees,institutions etc. The sharing of river waters and the execution of irrigation projects are the contentious areas.These issues have placed severe constraints on the functioning of the government . The opposition is not lending a helping hand to the state government in sorting out these things with a recalcitrant AP and the indifferent Center. Despite all these hiccups ,the TRS government has steered the nascent state very well and vindicated its competency for statehood in just three years.

Yet, there is a long way to go .The planning of various development schemes is very good, but, their successful implementation depends on the efficacy of officials and peoples' representatives working together with commitment and without pilferage.The state government needs to make it happen. It should use its finances in a prudent way and the outstanding issues with A P and the Central government resolved to the advantage of the State at the earliest.

24

KALESHWARAM PROJECT : SPRINGBOARD FOR STATE'S GROWTH

(Telangana Today | 17 January 2018)

The project cost will be more than compensated by the big benefits that include much-needed water security.

There continues to be apprehensions on the need and feasibility of the Kaleshwaram project in Telangana though it got clearances at a fast clip from many quarters in the Central government. These apprehensions are primarily political, technical and economic in nature.

Recently, the Central Water Commission (CWC) cleared it saying it is a unique project not only in India but also in the world. For, it combines lift, storage and gravity flow over a high gradient of the benefiting area. Such unequivocal approval by the CWC presupposes that the project is technically and economically feasible. It puts aside the apprehensions of the political opposition in the State.

Salient Features

1. **13 districts** to get water for irrigation, drinking and industrial use
2. **18.25 lakh** acres new ayacut, **18.82 lakh** acres stabilisation in old ayacut
3. To utilise **225 tmc** of Godavari water
4. **142 tmc** to be stored in **19 reservoirs**
5. **4,628 Mw** needed for the project
6. **30 tmc** of water for Hyderabad city
7. **16 tmc** of water for industrial use
8. **Rs 2,200 crore** economic benefits in several sectors
9. **17,220 crore** agricultural production
10. Benefit, cost ratio: **1.55**

The CWC approving it and the dedicated work happening on the project are important developments. The project's fast progress augurs well for low rainfall, drought-prone and water-starved Telangana.

Utilizing the Water

Telangana has a share of about 960 tmc of water in Godavari river yet the State at present is not even using 40% of it. This means the State is not using about 600 tmc of water, although it legitimately belongs to it. This water is going down the river though it was planned to use some of it by gravitational canals.

Telangana is not endowed with the type of landscape of coastal Andhra districts to get water to its cultivated lands by gravitational canal irrigation. Moreover, other States do not agree to submergence of land and resettlement of their people for providing irrigation in other States. A case in point is the aborted Inchampally multipurpose project and the Pranahitha-Chevella project, the precursor of Kaleshwaram project, which was designed with a barrage of 152 m in height. Maharashtra never agreed to it because it was causing submergence of a large area of its agricultural land.

The cultivated area in the catchment of the Godavari in Telangana is on a progressively increasing upward slope from the river. The slope can be as high as 400-500 m from the river at its higher levels. Practically, there is no other way, except building barrages on the river and lifting the water. Even then we cannot irrigate much land by gravitation. We have to take the water up by stages with intermittent lifts from the barrages to the highest possible point. The lifts need to have reservoirs linked to each other to store water and balance water flow. Water is fed to the ayacut from reservoirs via canals, tunnels creating new ayacut.

Challenging Project

In addition, the existing tanks and projects are filled using natural streams/canals to stabilize existing uncertain ayacut under those water bodies, creating as much irrigated command area as possible. The existing hundreds of tanks and medium projects in the command are a huge advantage. It has 17 lifts and 19 reservoirs, lifting the water from Medigadda in Karimnagar district to Mallannasagar in Medak district. The project envisages irrigation to new ayacut of 18.25 lakh acres and to stabilise another 18.82 lakh acres of old ayacut.

The project is complex and technologically challenging. Capital investment and maintenance cost every year post completion are also going to be very high thus making it economically challenging too. But, the benefits are also many. It is one-of-its-kind in the world designed to serve the peculiar ground conditions.

As things stand, Telangana has a large percentage of the catchment area of Godavari river, and it has its legitimate share of water awarded by the tribunal. The irrigation in the catchment area of the Godavari in the State is only about 30% and the remaining 70% rainfed area is largely drought-prone.

Sound Reasoning

Telangana's share of water in the Godavari has been going abegging down the stream for the last several decades. It happened in the united State by default or design. We cannot afford this anymore in the new State. We need to take into account the needs of our growing population and the large area under rainfed cultivation or under uncertain water sources. We also need to meet the growing drinking and industrial demand for water in future. Therefore, even if it is technologically or economically formidable, we do not have any other alternative except to use the water available and allotted to us in river Godavari. Dithering on it as in the past will not help.So, the State has taken a bold and determined decision to take up this project. Its detailed project report was scrutinized and whetted by the CWC. And it getting necessary clearances in a short time vouches for its feasibility.

Mere criticism based on apprehension cannot help arrive at a better solution. If there are sustainable technical and economic reasons, they should be presented in a rational way with competent technological and economic inputs. For example, renowned engineer Ch Hanumanth Rao had furnished a very detailed alternative plan for the Polavaram project. Eventually, the AP government did not agree to it. The Polavaram project is mired in several controversies.

Huge Benefits

The opposition's criticism on the redesigning of the project is also unfounded. At the previous site, the construction of barrage with a height of 152 m was out of question as Maharashtra never agreed to it. Shifting the barrage site was necessitated not just due to Maharashtra's opposition because a large extent (about 5,247 acres) of its land would submerge but also because of the CWC's revised report on the availability of water in Pranahita river at Thammidihatti.

The CWC had estimated water availability at Thammidihatti at 273 tmc but later revised it to only 163 tmc. And it would not allow more than 140 tmc to Telangana from there. Whereas at Medigadda, the water availability estimated by the CWC was 284.3 tmc, and it is easy for Telangana to use about 225 tmc of this water.

The protests by TJAC and other political parties are not very alarming when compared to the benefits. This does not mean taking away the hardship of people who have suffered because of the project. The people need to be compensated adequately and the government is doing it.Irrigation for 37 lakh acres, more than Rs 17,000 crore agriculture production and the huge rural employment potential thereof, make it a springboard for growth of other sectors of the economy as well. This can adequately compensate for the heavy expenditure on the project.

According to the feasibility report, the project will generate a benefit, cost ratio of 1.55. It is a bold bid by the Telangana government to provide the much-needed water security to the water-starved State.

25

FACTS AND FICTION ON DIVISION

(Telangana Today | 27 July, 2018)

It has been four years since the State of Andhra Pradesh was divided. Yet, the residual AP is still smarting under its impact and making untenable allegations. Its leaders, particularly the ruling TDP, and intellectuals call the division illegal, irrational, unscientific and unethical. This negative attitude is causing problems in settling down as well as in its working relation with Telangana. Let us examine these allegations and sift fact from fiction.

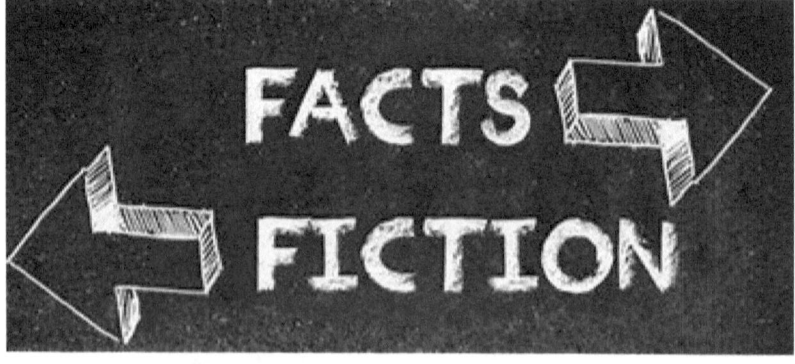

Illegal: They say when the State was reorganized on the basis of language in 1956, it should not have been divided again. It's the first time a

State was formed when the majority in Assembly did not agree to it. In Parliament, the Bill was passed with the doors closed.

Fact: Telangana was merged with Andhra in 1956 despite a majority in Telangana not being in favor. The SRC also recommended against it. It was a conditional merger with 14 agreements. Those agreements and the subsequent watered down formulas were never implemented. The cultural divide was never bridged. The majority of 175 v/s 119 MLAs in the Assembly widened the gap. Domination by majority and exploitation in every walk of life was felt in Telangana and so, the demerger was inevitable.

If the States are to be divided only with majority agreement, then there is no need for Article 3 in the Constitution. In fact, Andhra was separated from Madras despite the majority not being in agreement. This was even before the SRC in 1956 and as per Article 3. In earlier divisions, though in some States the majority did not agree, in deference to Centre's decision, they passed the resolution gracefully in the spirit of democracy. As per Article 3, it is enough to inform the Assembly. In Parliament, almost all the political parties agreed to the division but MPs from Andhra tried to mar the proceedings and stop the Bill.

Irrational: They say the division was irrational as they have no capital; they developed Hyderabad's infrastructure, centralized everything here, built Cyberabad and put Hyderabad on the world map.

Fact: Andhra getting separated from Madras in 1953 was a wrong move. They wanted Andhra with Madras as capital but could not get it. So, they were stranded without capital. Since Madras was on the border at least they could have bargained for a joint capital, like Chandigarh. It could have solved their capital and revenue problems. After suffering from a serious deficit for three years, they coveted Hyderabad, a metropolitan city with first-class infrastructure and revenue-surplus falling in Telangana. Despite the reluctance of the Centre, and opposition of SRC and Telangana people, they managed to get into Hyderabad using Telugu language.

Many Central organizations came up in Hyderabad because of its geographical location, cosmopolitanism and good weather. A few were also established in Visakhapatnam, but it was not developed. Regarding information technology, Bengaluru and Chennai were ahead of Hyderabad in IT. Hyderabad developed like any other city in the country. In fact, Hyderabad from the fourth largest city in the 1960s dropped to 6th in 2014.

As far as the capital city is concerned, In 1960, Maharashtra got separated from Gujarat and Bombay being in the Maharashtra region went to Maharashtra. Gujarat built a separate capital Gandhinagar for itself. Meghalaya was formed in 1972. Shillong was the capital of greater Assam. Shillong being in Meghalaya, went to Meghalaya. Assam built a new capital for itself in Dispur. In the same way, Madhya Pradesh lost its capital Nagpur to Maharashtra and selected Bhopal, a lesser town for its capital. If AP had continued with Kurnool as capital, it could have become like Bhopal or Bhubaneshwar.

They say they invested in Hyderabad. Yes, they did and all those investments are still there and with them only. They can keep them as long as they want or sell for profit. There are several such investors from other States too. Hyderabad, as said earlier, lagged behind other cities. So their claim is not sustainable.

Industries, particularly the IT industry, flourished in Hyderabad because of infrastructure. It was created from Hyderabad and Telangana revenues. Andhra revenue was never spent in Telangana in the united state. There was no restriction to develop other towns in Andhra. Some such effort was made and infrastructure like IT parks were also developed in Vizag. But other towns did not catch up. For instance, the Medha Towers in Vijayawada and IT Parks in other towns remained empty.

Unscientific: They say the division was not scientific and so AP has a revenue deficit. Many national and State institutions are in Hyderabad and in Telangana. We were sent away with just clothes on our bodies'.

Fact: The deficit budget was not caused because of the division. It is a legacy from their old Andhra State. The Andhra region had a deficit from 1956 to 2014 continuously every year. Telangana's per capita revenue was over 40% since the beginning. The Budget of the united state was balanced with surplus from Telangana. The deficit of AP in 2014-15 was Rs 11,000 crore, to be borne by Centre.

From 2015-16 to 2019-20, Rs 22,123 crore was sanctioned by the 14th Finance Commission to AP. It was for the first time any State was given such assistance. In addition, the central tax devolution and grants-in-aid are almost double to that of Telangana – Rs 2,44,591 crore for AP and Rs 1,37,941 crore for TS from FY16 to FY19 (Budget documents). With that AP has proposed a surplus Budget of Rs 5,235 crore for 2018-19. There is also a special package for seven backward districts with tax incentives for setting up industries and deficit revenue grant of Rs 30,000 cr. In addition, they have about Rs 1,00,000 crore revenue receipts of their own.

Haphazard division: The division was done just on the lines of any other 15 or so divisions earlier made. The same draft provisions for different sections of the division were followed.

Fact: The officer in charge for drafting of the Reorganisation Act was from Andhra and the Minister was Jairam Ramesh, an Andhra MP. No Telanganite had any hand or access to it. The specific recommendations or gifts given are:

1. Joint capital facility for 10 years. This, in fact, has delayed the new capital construction.

2. Section 8 for the safeguard of Andhras. Such provision is considered unconstitutional and was not there in any other division
3. A committee for selecting the site of the capital city and financial assistance for building infrastructure. Though the committee did its job, it was rejected by the State, which selected a different site
4. Polavaram multipurpose project whose cost has now escalated to Rs 60,000 crore. Paradoxically, it will serve only the over-irrigated Krishna and Godavari delta areas
5. AP gets 20 national institutions/projects whereas for Telangana, it's just 6.

One can now compare and see what is legal, rational, scientific and ethical in the State's division.

26

KALESHWARAM DESERVES NATIONAL STATUS

(Telangana Today | 8 August, 2018)

The Kaleshwaram project is in the news again. This time the opposition is questioning its economic viability and technical feasibility. On earlier occasions, it opposed civil liberties, land acquisition, R&R, environment and re-engineering. There were protests, meetings and PILs.

The TJAC prepared a report on it and placed it in public domain. But the Telangana government went ahead with the project as the courts cleared legal wrangles. The Central Water Commission (CWC) too is said to have cleared it fully.

Kaleshwaram is a complex capital-intensive project. Its operational and maintenance costs are very high when compared with traditional gravity canal projects. But it is a compulsion owing to the dire need for water and the topography of the benefiting area. The water needs to be lifted 525 m and carried through pipes, tunnels and open canals at a length of 1,843 km over a steep slope of land from the source of water. It is a unique project not only in the country but perhaps in the world too.

Much Desired

Telangana has been allotted 954 tmc of the 1,400 tmc water in Godavari basin. But the use is less than 200 tmc in TS and over 500 tmc in Andhra Pradesh. Much more water goes into the sea. In the united state, because of the limitation of technology to lift water over such a long undulated terrain and due to vested political interest of the lower riparian region, Telangana could not use its due share. Consequently, the semi-arid and low-to-medium rainfall area depends on lakhs of borewells depleting groundwater to a critical level. Now the conditions have altered. Political freedom and the availability of technology prompted Telangana to make use of its hitherto denied share of water.

Kaleshwaram was started in 2007 as Pranahita-Chevella — part of 'Jalayaganam' — by the Congress. A barrage was to be built at Tummidi Hatti, Adilabad district, with 152 m FRL to use 160 tmc water for irrigating 16 lakh acres from there to Chevella in Ranga Reddy district. But Maharashtra did not agree to 152 m barrage height. The CWC did not clear the project and alerted the new Telangana government about the non-availability of requisite amount of water for the project at that site. The Maharashtra government, meanwhile, agreed for 148 m after deliberations at the behest of the TS government.

As the State government found more water at Medigadda downstream than Tummidi Hatti, it re-engineered the project. The cost is estimated to be Rs 80,500 crore.

TJS' Rhetoric

The newly-formed Telangana Jana Samithi (TJS) harps on the cursory TJAC project report. Its spokesmen say that going by the BC (Benefit-Cost) ratio, the design of the project is not satisfactory. Capital expenditure, maintenance and operational costs are very high to make the project economically viable. However, it does not present any alternatives saying it is not its job.

A State does not do any project with its own assumptions. The Central government, through the CWC, scrutinizes the project and gives its clearances on many aspects. The Telangana government has explained adequately the need for re-engineering the project. Now, in all reasonableness, one can assume that the CWC exercised its due diligence while according clearances. The opposition can discuss it in the Assembly or in Parliament for whatever changes it wants to make on it.

As for its high cost and burden to the State, the concern of the opposition is not out of place. Perhaps, it is the costliest water project in the country. For a capital investment like this, the State needs to borrow and service the debt. It is within the bounds on its debt portfolio so far. Its debt-GDP ratio as at the end of 2018-19 is pegged at 21.36. But it can increase as these projects go forward. The State with its balanced Budget and revenue growth promises well for the future. But for a unique project like this, which is economically and technically challenging, the Centre needs to give its helping hand.

With Polavaram

Compare this with the Polavaram project, which is now slated to cost Rs 60,000 crore and is given a national status in the AP Reorganisation Act for obvious political reasons. Its operational cost will be less because of its traditional gravity canal design, but it's R&R itself costs more than 50% of it. It submerges 270 villages, about one lakh acres agriculture land and one lakh acre forest land against a modest R&R cost of the Kaleshwaram project. At least 80% of the benefiting area is already irrigated under lift irrigation projects. There the benefiting area is plain, rainfall is high and the area is groundwater-rich.

It has not even got many clearances. There are court cases on it from other States and some environmental organizations. The cost benefit analysis on its irrigation proves it is not economically viable, leave alone the humongous R&R problem. The only saving grace is its power production. But Andhra Pradesh is said to be power-surplus and does not need power at present. Moreover, the way the cost is escalating, eventually, the project may cost the same as Kaleshwaram.

TS does not have a grudge against the Polavaram project. Kaleshwaram deserves much more. If the Centre takes care of the capital investment or at least subsidizes some of the cost, this can reduce the debt burden of TS and the State can complete it with comparative ease. As for the operational cost, it is within the capacity of the State. It needs to devise more economical and imaginative methods to use the water, generate substantial revenue from its utilities and fine-tune other schemes.

Therefore, it would be wise for the opposition to demand national status to Kaleshwaram instead of nitpicking on it. For, it is a fait accompli by now. Yet, it can still engage the CWC to suggest better economic and technological inputs if it feels so.

27

DISCUSS TECHNICALITIES WITH EXPERTS

(Telangana Today | 29 August, 2018)

There was a round-table conference on the Kaleshwaram project yet again on August 26. The cost-benefit factor of last time was passé. This time, the goal post changed. It is technical feasibility now. Their concern with technical feasibility is understandable and relevant too. It certainly needs to be discussed and firmed up for such an extraordinary and technologically complex project. But it should be discussed strictly from a technological perspective only.

Political overtones and participation of politicians in it will smother its objectivity. The real discussion on technical feasibility should be left to the people who know the subject. This time there was some more information on reverse pumping, shifting of the main barrage from Tummidi Hatti to Medigadda and availability of the quantum of water at Medigadda.

Move Beyond DPR

Their insistence to confine the discussion to the detailed project report (DPR) alone as the agenda of the meeting appeared strange. The project has traveled past the DPR and has obtained the clearances from the competent authority, the Central Water Commission (CWC). The DPR is a government proposal submitted to the CWC to get the approval for the project. It is provisional and is a pre-feasibility report. It is not the final scheduled scheme. The DPR is subject to changes. The CWC has the mandate and is supposed to have the necessary expertise to scrutinize the DPR and demand changes, if needed. Or, it can also reject the DPR as a whole if it feels it is not feasible.

In this instant case, one can expect that the CWC exercised its due diligence as it is a special project. Now the CWC has become a proxy to the project. Therefore, it becomes incumbent to read the DPR along with the CWC clearances to understand the technical feasibility. It will also be meaningful if the CWC is made to answer some of the questions raised by TJAC.

As the cliche goes — it is always better to hear straight from the horse's mouth. Instead, forcing to confine it only to the untested DPR is not correct. It makes the whole round-table discussion redundant. There is no reason to believe that the CWC can be less circumspect towards the project and gives clearance in a routine way. The CWC has its own machinery to know the relevant information on projects and does not depend only on DPRs.

Playing Politics

Since the Central government is not of the same party and not even its ally, there is no reason to believe that the CWC politically favored Telangana. Since the DPR was scrutinized and clearances were given by the CWC, the ball lies in the court of CWC to explain its feasibility. Wapcos Limited, which was said to be the main consultant for the project, can be a better source to clear the doubts on the technical aspects.

Participation of the CWC, Wapcos and other technical specialists could have turned the round-table discussion meaningful. Or an expert on such lift irrigation projects could have been called to give his opinion. But it did not appear so. It looked like a show in a political campaign.

The meeting was predominantly political with all the opposition parties in the State, including the nascent TJS. The discourse was organized by TJAC. Though there were a few members of Telangana Engineer's forum, it was more of a political meeting than a technical conference with TJAC technical personnel taking time to present their case and calling the shots.

The Engineer's forum members were not allowed to speak fully on the technical aspects and were given less than 20% of the time. They were not even allowed to complete their answers when they tried to explain the reasons for re-engineering and that the DPR was not final and could be revised. But, they were shouted down by TJAC and political party representatives with their numerical dominance. It was like killing the messenger.

Losing Track

In such an atmosphere and political setting, the real intent of the conference got lost. It looked like a political shadow-boxing was taking place. We need to have a better discussion forum to know the intricate technical problem of the project. Certainly, not these political meetings.

Earlier in the united State, the very same politics made us forego our rights for water. We were stopped from using most water that legitimately belonged to us for decades. We need a definitive new approach in the new State.

The Congress has the necessary wherewithal to engage experts on such projects. They can hire an expert and ask them to present the real technical problems in the scheme. The State BJP can make the participation of Wapcos and CWC possible through their central government. Questions have been raised on the CWC clearance and the State BJP through its high command can get the necessary answers from the CWC.

Exhibit Altruism

It is absolutely important to know the technical feasibility of such a huge project. But in doing so, there is a need for political parties to exhibit some altruism instead of playing routine polemics and political one-upmanship.

It is also necessary for the State government to make the details of technical feasibility public with all the CWC clearances to remove the doubts of the people. Since it is past the tentative DPR stage and the CWC clearances are under its belt, there should not be any problem in doing so. Alternatively, the government itself can organize a technical round-table conference with all the stakeholders. This is important to convince the people and or to make corrections, if needed.

Faultless working of the project is more important than the gamesmanship of political parties and the government. This round-table on the project cannot be the last. There can be and should be more. Let us hope that in these meetings they discuss the technical feasibility with the relevant technical discussion, and with the experts on the subject.

28

BENEFITS DWARF COSTS OF KALESHWARAM

(Telangana Today | 24 September, 2018)

Major irrigation projects like Kaleshwaram need some gestation period for completion as well as for the accrual of full benefits. The benefits vis-a-vis costs cannot be compared in a few years after the initiation of the project. A longer economic period needs to be worked out for a logical cost-benefit analysis.

On such irrigation projects, governments will not be able to recover the cost from the direct beneficiaries through utility charges alone. They can, however, get increased revenue from intangible benefits of the associated areas because of the projects.

In view of economic benefits to the entire society, the government subsidizes the cost. Therefore, here the cost-benefit analysis for the borrowed capital repayment and the meeting of the operation and maintenance costs is mostly linked to the revenue budget of the government.

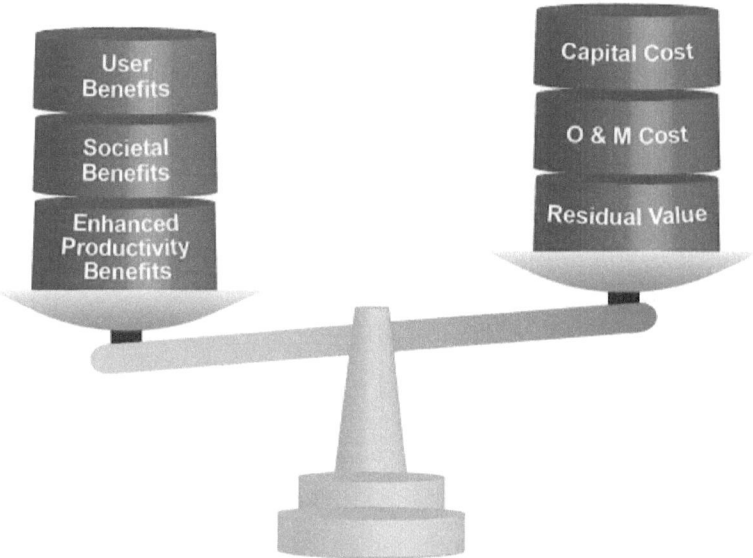

So, the identification of costs and benefits becomes very important. Identification of the costs can be fairly easy. But the benefits can be tangible and intangible and come over a period of time. The tangible benefits are irrigation, drinking water and water for industrial use, which can be quantified. The intangible benefits are many, like groundwater storage, public health, fisheries, dairy, tourism and environmental change, which are difficult to quantify. But they form a very important part of the economic analysis of such projects.

Funding Matters

In the case of the current major irrigation projects in Telangana and Andhra Pradesh, the Central government foots the bill for Polavaram. However, for Kaleshwaram, the cost is being borne by the Telangana government. It needs to meet the cost on its own or borrow from financial institutions.

The State cannot bear such a high capital investment from its revenue Budget. So it is mostly borrowing, and the financing institutions will be making their cost-benefit analysis on the State revenue Budget, its loan outstandings and the ability to service the debt.

The Central Water Commission, which clears these projects, looks at many aspects — mandatory and non-mandatory. The availability of water, inter-State water use, cost estimates and technical feasibility can be mandatory to it. The cost-benefit analysis can be a non-mandatory general economic analysis.

Economic Period

Thus, demanding to work out the whole span of cost-benefit analysis on the Kaleshwaram project assuming irrigation only as the benefit is not rational. Even if a general economic analysis is made, it should be done on an economic period of time, taking into account the gestation period of the project and accruing of full benefits. It is not as simple as working out the value of incremental benefits in the benefiting command area and comparing it with the total cost of the project.

The cost-benefit analysis is a tool for assessing the financial and economic profitability of investments. It is carried out from various perspectives — one from the point of view of individuals/groups of individual beneficiaries and the other for the implementing/financing agencies.

The main objective of the financial analysis is to assess whether incremental project benefits are sufficient for fully recovering incremental costs, which ensure the project's long-term financial sustainability. For the individual beneficiaries, the major objective of financial analysis is gross margins of major project-induced activities to know if they are contributing to the intended improvement. Economic analysis, on the other hand, looks at project profitability from the point of view of the economy or society as a whole.

Limited Target

If the projects' aim at the benefit of individuals or groups of individuals, it will be different. For example, a minor irrigation project, which may include a district or a few districts, can be proposed by some primary level financing institutions under the aegis of a State government. Here a project needs to be prepared working out the economics on a representative development unit. It is like a household with say five acres of land, a well and a pumpset and some working expenses. There the cost-benefit analysis includes financial analysis, BC ratio, fixation of repayment period and the installment amount on the economic period of time of the project.

Here the primary institutions have to borrow from bigger financial institutions like NABARD, ADB and the World Bank with the government infrastructure support and guarantee. The beneficiaries need to pay back their loans and the financing banks, in turn, have to pay to their higher financing agencies with the recovery from the individual beneficiaries There they need to work out the full span of financial analysis at the beneficiary level and the financing bank level.

However, in the case of projects such as dams and anicuts (irrigation projects), it is different. Here, the government executes the project with its revenues or centrally-assisted or externally-aided finances or a combination of them. So, here the perspective of cost-benefit analysis changes.

For government revenue or central grants, there will not be any mandatory cost-benefit analysis. There will be cost-benefit analysis in the case of an externally-aided component, which will be a borrowing to the government. There will be a cost-benefit analysis based on the revenue and fiscal budgets of the government to assess their ability to service the debt. So, the cost-benefit analysis is not a straightjacket calculation, its application can vary with the type of investment, investing agency and the clientele.

The tangible and intangible economic benefits of the Kaleshwaram project are numerous. They make the project economically viable. Its benefits far outweigh that of the Polavaram project, which is mostly stabilizing the already irrigated command. Its dire necessity for Telangana makes the State's bold attempt at it clearly worthwhile. All that it needs is Central assistance like in Polavaram to render equal justice to the two new States.

29

UNDOING THE SPIRIT OF TELANGANA

(Telangana Today | 6 October, 2018)

Telangana got its political freedom in a fractious struggle with the Centre and its other counterparts. It was expected that the political parties in the State would be more altruistic in the firming up of the new State. Yet, the politics that developed in its maiden term in Telangana was not very savory. Now as the result of the State government dissolving its Assembly and opting for an early election, the testy politics in Telangana has come to a boil and turned interesting.

In the last election, all the major parties in Telangana claimed credit for State formation. But, people gave a mandate to the Telangana Rashtra Samithi (TRS) with just enough majority. It made the disgruntled opposition parties take a very hostile stance against the ruling TRS. The initial overtures of the TRS for cooperation were spurned. The Congress felt a proprietary right to the new State as the party gave the State and called the TRS an upstart.

The TJAC said it was instrumental in getting T-State but the TRS stole the credit. The BJP claimed that without their support in Parliament, Telangana would not have been a reality. The TDP said its December 7 letter gave Telangana its State. In the conceit of their self-importance, they have forgotten the very purpose of the State and started to oppose the Telangana government ad nauseam without any regard to their own responsibility in strengthening the new State.

On and Off Opposition

The TJAC went hammer and tongs against the TRS government from the beginning. It joined hands with Congress and Communists on and off to oppose every move of the government. It differed with the government's development model and was crying hoarse for an alternative plan. But in the last four years, it could not muster up any such plan. Meanwhile, it has lost many of its associate societies and has formed a political party – TJS – outside of it as its adjunct.

The Congress along with TJAC was opposing indiscriminately everything the Telangana government was doing. The BJP was doing the same from the sidelines. The TDP was busy undermining the TRS in its efforts of consolidation of the State. It even went to the extent of destabilizing the government as the infamous 'vote for the cash' case revealed.

It is like the story of the proverbial fly forgetting its name flustering the floor on a festival day. These opposition parties in their disappointment of not getting into the political power structure, have forgotten the very essence of the new State – its sovereign entity in terms of the AP Reorganisation Act.

While the maiden Telangana government was grappling with it, these opposition parties did not lend any support to it. There are several issues lingering. Division of employees and institutions, river waters, power dues, high court, etc and establishing a few new institutions awarded in the Act.

They berated the State government for spending money on big projects instead of helping it get deserving aid from the Centre. There can be good and bad in the acts of government. But there is a need for criticism based on merit. But here, it is everything bad for them without exception. That does not make any democratic sense.

Unnatural Alliance

On top of it, it is now the Congress, TDP, TJS and the CPI's grand alliance for the next elections. It is not unusual for such alliances in the country nowadays. But, here it is very unnatural, considering the background of the new State and the roles played by these parties in its formation.

The Congress played an unconscionable callous game with the Telangana declaration for more than four years at the behest of the TDP and its own Andhra unit. The T-Congress was reduced to a helpless onlooker, lacking the gumption to force the issue. The TJAC though worked for Telangana along with the TRS, inexplicably balked at the last moment. It declared itself neutral and almost handed over a hung Assembly for the new State. And after the elections, it behaved like the main opposition to the TRS from outside the Assembly.

The treacherous role of the TDP and its chief in Telangana formation is common knowledge. He stopped it for four years and caused the death of about 1,200 Telangana people. Now, he is creating all kinds of troubles in the implementation of APRA related to Telangana. He tried to unsettle the Telangana government in this Assembly and is trying to sneak into it this time via this alliance to create more trouble.

His antagonism to Telangana and his negatively manipulating politics can be the sword of Damocles hanging on the head of Telangana if he gains some strength in its Assembly. The TDP is a party with Andhra ethos in every facet of it. Its place is in Andhra and it has lost its raison d'etre in Telangana.

TJS Hopelessly Hypocritical

The most absurd feature of the alliance is the TJS (Telangana Jana Samithi) with its probable 3-5 seat partnership trying to impose Telangana martyr-centric common minimum programme on the alliance. It is hopelessly hypocritical.

The T-Congress and the TJS can make an alliance with any party with the soul and spirit of Telangana or they can contest on their own. They can win political power if they have a better agenda than the TRS and if Telangana people vote for it. At present, for Telangana, it is more important to get all the provisions of APRA implemented and get rid of the Andhra colonial hangover. But not by a partnership with them. It will not work.

The very antithesis to the Telangana State, the Telugu Desam in the ruling dispensation can be an anticlimactic letdown. It will be a mockery of the martyrdom of hundreds of youth. The people of Telangana should not allow it to happen.

30

TELANGANA REASSERTS ITS IDENTITY

(Telangana Today | 17 December, 2019)

The first elections for the Telangana Assembly were held on December 7, 2018. The ruling Telangana Rashtra Samithi (TRS) swept the elections, winning 88 seats of the 119.It was an overwhelming victory.

It was expected that TRS will win the elections owing to its good governance and multiple welfare schemes.But, the margin, many believed would be small and not as huge as it has turned out, primarily some vocal sections of the population differed with the government on certain issues and were expected to vote against it.But it actually did not happen.

On the contrary it was a reverse swing in favor of the TRS. The obvious reason was the unholy alliance of Prajakutami, the brainchild of Chandrababu Naidu, the bete noire of Telangana. Prajakutami was an alliance of the Congress, TDP,TJS, and the CPI. Its principal members - the Congress and TDP are arch enemies. Infact. The Telugu Desam party (TDP) took birth as a feudatory rival to Congress. So, it was expected that the twain would never meet. But Naidu's unscrupulous politics made it possible. He is under intense pressure after severing his relations with BJP. His graph has gone down in Andhra Pradesh and he needed some partner to make good that loss.

The advanced elections in Telangana provided the opportunity for the TDP to cobble up such an alliance with the Congress and test it as a sample for a possible front in A P and at the national level.

Changing Dynamics

Every election is different. The mood and combination of issues are dynamic. They never remain static. They change according to the exigencies of the time. Mostly the votes that swing according to the political exigency of the time decides the fortunes of the political parties. There can be many vote banks, depending on cadre, caste, and money among others. There will also be voters who will swing. All these behave differently in different situations.

If there is a serious political exigency, a mere 5-7% swing can make all the difference. In Fact, it is this phenomenon that is saving the electoral system in India. The same thing happened in Telangana this time albeit with an overwhelming intensity. The exigency here is the State and its avowed political freedom. The people of Telangana saw the ganging up of parties to dilute the State's political freedom and reacted to it.

Role of opposition

Let us now see how these opposition parties played their roles in the very first term of the State. All of them forgot the very purpose of the State. They did not evince any interest in the State Reorganization Act, the implementation of which will enable the consolidation of the State and its much-needed sovereignty.

The Congress took it simply for granted and in addition it wanted special treatment for itself, because it had granted the State. The TDP dictated by Andhra Pradesh's interests was creating all kinds of impediments of the AP Reorganization Act. Its local outfit was simply following its high command's dictats from Andhra rather than espousing Telangana's interests.

The TJAC/TJS is an interesting study. They were crying hoarse about Telangana and implementation of 'udyama akankshalu'. But they just forgot the big picture of the State. its consolidation and the APRA. They were making inconsequential protests, on their own and in association with other parties, on certain archaic and imaginary issues against big projects. Finally, they morphed in to a political party and joined hands with the 'kutami'. The CPI continued playing its customary anti-government role.

The BJP which was not in the grouping, also did not do anything better. Its high command was not well disposed to Telangana because of its alliance with TDP. Even after its separation, it did not change its attitude much. The local BJP, except joining other opposition parties in berating the TRS, has not done anything special to use its party central government to help solve Telangna's problems.

In effect, all the opposition parties failed to appreciate the special status of Telangana in its first term. In fact, they were talking lightly of this

Telangana angle in their post-election discussions. That was their major mistake, which antagonized the people of Telangana to them.

Righteous Anger

There was some anti-incumbency in certain quarters of the Telangana society before Prajakutami came in to existence. If the Congress, TJS and the CPI had formed a front, they could have got that vote and made some difference. But their alliance with the TDP and the Prajakutami being run under the direction of Chandrababu Naidu changed the situation. It triggered the righteous anger.

The section that was ambivalent or antagonistic to TRS also changed its direction and voted for the party and that made this overwhelming victory possible. This is the essence of Telangana ethos at this particular point in time.

It was a remarkable exhibition of political sense by the people of Telangana. In 2014, they voted for the TRS party defying the BJP wave all over the country to celebrate their Telangana ethos in their new state. Now in 2018, while neighboring states preferred a mixed front, they rejected the front to protect their political freedom from the proxy governments of Andhra and Kendra domination. It is a lesson to Chandrababu Naidu for his unproductive and negative politics in Telangana. All parties should learn the right lessons from this verdict.

31

AVOID HOSTILITIES BETWEEN TWO TELUGU STATES

(Telangana Today | 4 January, 2019)

The bifurcation of erstwhile Andhra Pradesh State is not like the division of States existing at the time of independence. It's a demerger of States created after independence which was necessitated because of the continuous incompatibility between the two merged regions. Since the Andhra region continuously opposed the demerger, it was naturally uncomfortable for the Andhrites. They say the division was unfair to them and find fault with its process and provisions. The maiden government of Andhra Pradesh has created a big political agenda on it. In contrast, Telangana was delighted and just went about developing the new State while enjoying its new-found political freedom.

Different Demerger

Unlike other original State divisions, this demerger was dealt with differently. In addition to adopting the time-tested draft provisions in the State bifurcation, certain extra monetary and infrastructural garnishments were added to it. Most of them such as a joint capital for a 10-year period, a mega national irrigation project, a special deficit grant, a special grant for the construction of government building infrastructure in the new capital, sanctioning of several national institutions and the promise of many mega infrastructure projects went to the residual AP. Telangana got only a few token benefits as if to indicate that granting a separate State in itself was a big boon to it.

Despite many embellishments in the AP Reorganisation Act (APRA) to mollify AP, its maiden State government did not take to the division kindly. Leaving aside many ameliorating provisions, the ruling TDP indulged in a great deal of politicking and sought more concessions like special category status. Initially, the NDA government was supportive of its ally without understanding its implications. The State government without regard to the State's economy dreamed of creating a world-class capital in a hurry with the help of foreign direct investment (FDI) and made a big brouhaha about it. The BJP-led government in the Centre unwittingly encouraged the state to indulge in such extravaganza.

After wasting a few years and scarce resources of the State on it, they faced its impracticability. It has also boomeranged on the Centre. The AP government started demanding heavy financial assistance from the Centre in place of the failed FDI. Certain misgivings cropped up between them in the utility of central funds. The relations between the two deteriorated to the extent that the TDP came out of the NDA and started making BJP a scapegoat for its failures.

Defining Progress

Telangana got a slight revenue surplus economy as its full revenue was made available to it for the first time because of demerger. AP inherited a deficit budget. This and the attitudes of two maiden governments have defined the progress of two States. The Telangana government went about its task of consolidating the State with its own resources. It devised a mixed development model of welfare and infrastructure without unduly worrying much about the APRA and the Central assistance. It went about increasing its revenue to its balanced revenue budget. Using its resources as per the FRBM rules, it launched ambitious capital investment projects and reached out to all sections of the people with welfare schemes. Its efficacy was exhibited in the resounding win of the TRS in the December, 2018 Assembly elections.

Bubble Bursts

On the other hand, the maiden AP government of the TDP started its governance with a vainglorious agenda of world-class. It hyped and played on the emotion of public resentment to State division. But the impracticable hyperbole has failed. Its world-class capital plan came unstuck. The construction of the mega irrigation project of Polavaram has run into rough weather. The mismatch between revenue receipts and expenditure continued. Many promises could not be implemented. Its FRBM and fiscal management have come into severe strain. The TDP, to divert the public attention from its failures, resorted to negative politics of blaming the Centre, its opposition and Telangana.

Sticking to Basics

In fact, there was no need for such a pompous approach for residual AP, which had a big revenue deficit. Like many other States, which were divided, had AP stuck to the basics of State-building it could have made big strides in the last five years. If it had used the special provisions granted to it under the APRA and the devolution of Central taxes and grants-in-aid — which were twice that of Telangana — judiciously, the progress could have been very substantial. But the AP government wasted its precious resources on unnecessary things and got stagnated in the process. It is a case of much ado about nothing. On top of it, the TDP needlessly continued to meddle in Telangana and tried to put brakes on its progress and blamed Telangana for its own failures. It also played negative politics with its NDA ally BJP and jeopardized its potential partnership, which could have helped in the development of the State.

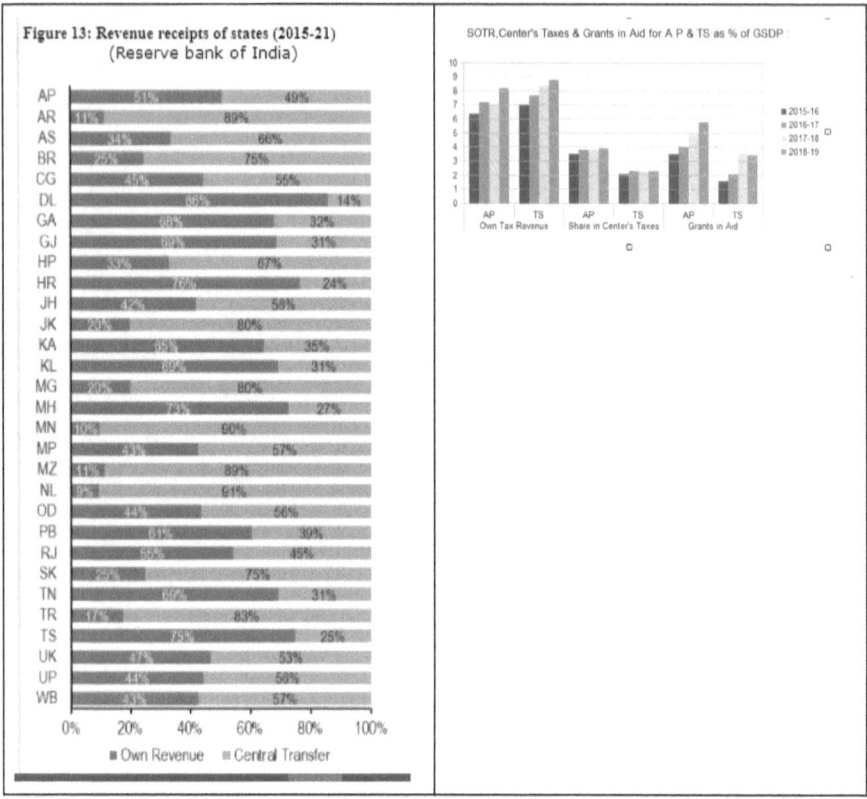

In all these, the Andhra media played a deleterious role. The combination of the TDP and its captive media is creating all the sludge that is messing up the progress of AP and trying to put spokes in the momentum of Telangana's progress. This needless hostility towards Telangana is also not helping AP in any way. The people of Telangana have weathered their propaganda and taught them a good lesson in the recent elections.

32

MARE'S NEST IN ANDHRA PRADESH

(Telangana Today | 4 February, 2019)

The maiden government in residual Andhra pradesh is in the saddle for over four and half years now. Its functioning during these years is a mixture of hyperbole and despair.

After coming to power in 2014, the TDP decried that the Centre had handed over an unfair state division with a big revenue deficit budget and a state without a capital. Yet, immediately it went to an overkill of embarking on building a world class capital city.

Though it won with a wafer-thin majority, it did not try for consensus in the state on the choice and scale of the capital. Ignored the report of Central committee for capital appointed by the previous UPA government. The NDA government acquiesced over it for obvious political bias, without realising its implications. This aberrant misdemeanor by both central and state governments, in case of capital has put the state in deep trouble.

The state government without regard to the state's finances and to the very need for such an impracticable project went about canvassing for FDI from several countries spending its scarce resources. After a couple of years of fruitless effort, the state government turned to the Centre to support the vainglorious scheme. The center realized its impossibility and tried to finance the capital infrastructure on a prudent scale.

This caused the relations between the two to get sour. Disagreement cropped up between the two on many of the other provisions of the A P Reorganization Act. Finally the alliance was broken, the TDP exited the NDA. Now the TDP and NDA have become bitter political enemies.

Enabling Provisions

The TDP government in the beginning, kept reiterating that injustice had been done to A P in the State's division and won power. But it was not proved right. A P was compensated for the deficit revenue not only in the first year but also during all five years of 14th Finance Commission period amounting to about Rs,30,000 cr. it was also sanctioned by 10 national institution. In addition it was also proposed to examine the feasibility of eight national level infrastructure projects. Polavaram, a mega multi-purpose project. was included in the Act. as a political gift.

Financial assistance for government building infrastructure, tax incentives to promote industrialization, economic growth and expansion of physical and social infrastructure in backward areas were provided. If we go by the earlier state divisions, these are the most enabling provisions to the region. Perhaps all the more than 10 new states together did not get so many institutions/projects from the center.

Added to that, the state was better placed in the devolution of the central taxes and grants-in-aid because of its larger area and more population than Telangana. The center also provided Rs. 2500 cr for building capital infrastructure. The UPA government was generous to A P for obvious electoral reasons. But the TDP government was not happy.

Half-hearted Approach

The state government could have worked positively on these provisions, utilizing the central funds prudently and could have demanded more,wherever needed.Instead, it went on censuring the center ad nauseum on the division.It also announced a plethora of welfare schemes in its manifesto but was half-hearted in implementing them.

The capital project has become a paradox with a few temporary structures and many exotic international designs,big publicity,fanfare and many controversies.The construction of Polavaram was affected due to misuse of funds and lack of coordination between the Centre and State.

The government undertook several 'deekshas' and created many political hassels with huge expenditure castigating the APRA and the Centre. The campaign escalated and the people started believing that the Centre is causing the trouble.All political parties in the state finally zeroed in on to the special category status as the panacea for all the problems.They have now started competing in demanding SCS.Attention was diverted from the availability of funds, their use or misuse and floundering of the schemes.Even the civil society, without going into these issues, has come up with a huge demand for funds from the Centre along with the SCS. The confusion and obfuscation proved to be complete.

Wrong Picture

A P received Rs.2,81,000 cr as against Rs.1,64,791 cr of Telangana as devolution of central taxes and grant-in-aid from 2014-15 to 2018-19, in addition to funds for capital,Polavaram and other projects. there was no deliberate discrimination as alleged.The pompous expectations were not justified and the Centre was not in a position to grant them.

After the State government was provided with adequate revenue deficit compensation and provisions for tax incentives for industries and financial support for physical and social infrastructure projects, there was no need for such a hue and cry for the SCS.

Infact,A P presented Rs.5,235 cr revenue surplus budget for 2018-19. The government was also claiming a very high economic growth rate in the state for all these years.This itself shows that its funds position was not as bad as it was portraying.Or it was indulging in unnecessary political hyperbole.

If the government worked on the funds provided by the center diligently,started industries and other physical infrastructure and claimed relevant incentives, it would have helped the state better.. Instead, the focus was on just demanding the SCS and spending huge funds on the agitation, which is simply imprudent.The government could not devise a prudent reconstruction plan for the state and frittered away its resources.

The state government is also taking loans and issuing government bonds to mop up the money for its welfare schemes. The Centre and APRA are not the reasons for the bad state of affairs. The Centre has certainly failed in disciplining the state government in the implementation of APRA.

But the major responsibility lies with the maiden state government in the residual state for failing to implement a judicious reconstruction plan with the available resources. In Fact, it has created a mare's nest in the state with its vainglorious and egotistic governance ; it is time to correct it.

33

ELECTIONS A REFERENDUM ON TDP GOVERNMENT

(Telangana Today | 10 April, 2019)

This is very much true that the Andhra Pradesh government failed to deliver on its promises because of its unpragmatic politics by self-centered politicians. Elections in Andhra Pradesh are being held on April 11. But there is a difference between the general elections in the country and the elections in AP.

These elections in the residual AP are the second after the division of erstwhile Andhra Pradesh. The first elections in 2014 were held on the agenda of division of the State, the provisions or lack of them in the Reorganisation Act, and the manifestos of different parties.

The TDP won the election with a wafer-thin majority of 1.6% votes. The BJP sided with the TDP, promising to help it in the reconstruction of the State. Much water has flown under the Krishna barrage in the last five years on the functioning of the TDP government. A great deal of political changes has also taken place. So what should be the agenda at the end of five years? Naturally, it should be the review of the reconstruction of the State by the TDP, its success or failure.

Issues of Contention

The main issues of contention were balancing the economy, construction of capital, Polavaram project, division of institutions, establishing national institutions, feasibility study and clearance of state infrastructural projects, and industrial development. In addition to these were popular schemes like loan waiver, Dwacra and providing employment to youth. So at the end of five years, it should be the review of this agenda and evaluating the performance of the TDP government. In effect, it is a referendum on the functioning of the TDP government.

But it is not happening. The TDP is not talking much about them. It is simply targeting the BJP, YSRCP and even the TRS to make them responsible for its non-performance. This strategy is simply because it was not able to do much on those promises because of its unpragmatic and unsustainable politics. Basically, the state was not ready to undertake such presumptuous projects like world-class infrastructure, as it was just one of the many States in India with a heavy revenue deficit Budget.

Projects a Non-starter

The Centre's insouciant support to it for the best part of the five-year term, without ground level feasibility in the name of its political alliance, has compounded the issue. The State government was not able to garner much of what it publicized and hoped for FDI. The Centre was not in a position to help in the grandiose plan. So the alliance broke and the political war of attrition started.

If we scan the agenda of 2014, we will know how its schemes were either non-starters or poor performers. The financial management of the State government is an area of serious concern. The AP government received almost double the central taxes and grants compared with Telangana in the five-year term. It also received Rs 30,000 crore as deficit grant, the highest by any State divided.

Yet, it has not matched its revenue and expenditure and still has the deficit Budget in its Vote on Account for 2019-20. It has also taken loans in excess of debt-GDP ratio going into excess of 29% as against 25%. In addition, the government is also said to have taken huge loans outside FRBM with government bonds or through SPVs to run the show. So, despite the assistance from the Centre as part of the Reorganisation Act, AP still could not balance its Budget because of its financial mismanagement.

Mega Failure

The capital city project came a cropper. It was a nonstarter. Not even a single permanent government building is completed. On the contrary, about a lakh acres of prime agricultural land was made to go to seed. With all the 90-plus conditions imposed by the NGT, even if the government manages to get the funds, it is next to impossible to execute the project.

Actually, there is no project in place. The design of the city has not been finalized even after five years. It is simply a case of the end of a pipe dream. The scheme is going to be a drag on the State in future also.

The TDP through its unscrupulous politics has messed up the Polavaram project. It was a sumptuous gift given by the Congress to AP. It was like a blank check to the State. But the greedy politics of the TDP chief has put the project in jeopardy. He took its execution into his own hands for obvious reasons and messed up the whole project.

Its estimates were hiked, its R&R was made controversial. The TDP government's spending on it became questionable and it could not respond to the queries of the Central government, which was fully funding it. So in a way, it was stalled in its tracks because of the inefficiency or political machinations of the State government.

There were 10 national institutions like IIT, IIM and AIIMS sanctioned as part of the APRA. The Centre had no reservations about them. The State government was not very enthusiastic in providing necessary land and utilities for them, as they were not very lucrative in its view. The progress is very tardy. Both the Centre and the State are not revealing the progress.Airports, sea ports and other infrastructure projects like railway zone and steel plant have turned controversial and are even facing delays because of the State government's vested interest in them

Several populist schemes like establishment of industries, loan waiver, Dwacra loans, employment schemes and unemployment dole-outs too have not lived up to the expectations. But there is an attempt to show a make-believe success of some schemes. The TDP government has failed in all areas. The State has stagnated because of its failure. The general election in the State is a referendum on its performance.

34

CAPITAL DILEMMA OF ANDHRA PRADESH

(Telangana Today | 12 September, 2019)

There is a debate on the feasibility of the continuation of the Amaravati project in Andhra pradesh political circles.It is rather disappointing that A P has not come to a final agreement even after five years on it. There was no such confusion in the several new states established in india after independence.The foundation stone for Gandhinagar, Gujarat's capital city was laid in 1965 and the capital was fully functional by 1971.All other states which needed a new capital, settled the issue quietly.Chhattisgarh separated in 2000, too built a full-fledged modern integrated capital by 2015. It is the best example of a green field capital city.

The bifurcation of A P was somewhat different from other state formations.it was a demerger of an earlier merged states.It had its own peculiar factors - mainly Andhra peoples' victimhood emotions over hyderabad.AP had acquired a first class capital in Hyderabad in 1956 and was using it and its revenue readily with their political majority.But, with the demerger, they lost Hyderabad and re-inherited a big revenue deficit of erstwhile Andhra State.

Against Committee

In view of these, special provisions were made for the residual A P in the Reorganization Act.

These included a committee to recommend a place for the capital, financial assistance from the center to help build the capital quickly and a revenue deficit grant to balance the state Budget. Chandrababu Naidu, who won the election in 2014, publicized that he would build a 'world class' capital for A P. The high level central committee on capital gave a report after a six month study making some recommendations. But the state government never considered it and chose the riverfront Amaravati site for the capital.

The NDA government of which TDP was an ally, supported him against the recommendations of the committee because it was a committee appointed by UPA. That was the beginning of the bad luck for the capital city. The central government simply forgot about its own committee and gave a long rope to CXhandrababu to indulge in his pipedream of constructing a capital city, which would be one of the top 5 cities in the world. In Fact, Prime Minister Narendra Modi in his overexuberance promised to build a better capital than Delhi, believing that Chandrabau will get all the funds needed from foreign direct investments.

Environmental issues

Bolstered by the center's bonhomie, the TDP chief went around the world inviting FDI for about three years. But nothing happened. He thought that the companies which invested in Hyderabad, would make a beeline to Amaravati. But it took some time for him to understand that the companies came to cities in India because of their urban infrastructure and the available human resources.

He then desperately tried to get the missing FDI from the Centre and demanded about a lakh of crore rupees for the dream capital. But, as the relations between NDA and the TDP soured, the Centre washed off its hands with Rs, 2,500 crore financial assistance. Meanwhile, the environmental credentials of the riverfront capital were questioned.

The A P government acquired 33,000 acres of the most fertile riverfront land in a bizarre land pooling scheme for the capital. In another one lakh acres of Krishna delta and other prime agricultural land as part of the 7400 sq.km capital area region a very productive agriculture was disturbed. It was also destroying a fresh water aquifer, replenishable yearly to provide drinking water for a million people. The area is flood-prone because of a small river during the flood season. Many such environmental and technical issues came to the surface.

The issue went to the NGT and the Tribunal asked the government to constitute supervising and implementing committees to implement its conditions in the construction of the capital. It is next to impossible to construct the capital with all those conditions and committees. All these together have brought the world-class capital project to a grinding halt. Except for a temporary secretariat, a high court building and some quarters for government officials. no other government complex could be constructed. This year's copious rains and flood flows in Krishna river also exposed the vulnerability of the site to floods.

Financial Mess

Moreover, the financial situation of the state was also grim. In 2014, the state inherited a deficit Budget of more than Rs.7300 core. The Centre provided a revenue deficit grant of Rs.4500 crore per annum from 2015-16 to 2019 to balance the Budget. But the deficit went on increasing - over Rs.16000 crore in 2017-18 as per the audited accounts. In such a scenario, embarking on constructing a 'world-class' capital with over Rs.1 lakh crore budget is a foolhardy attempt. The needless fixation on it has led to a waste of precious resources and five years time of the state and left the government in the lurch.

Now whether to continue the capital there or construct elsewhere is the moot political point. As the realities on the ground indicate, it is impracticable to build a national class, leave alone a world-class capital there. If continued with it, it can be a drag on the state. So prudence lies in shifting the site to a more conducive place like the uplands in the same vicinity or to Donakonda, where plenty of government land is available without causing much burden to the treasury, or near to Visakhapatnam, which can give a seafront capital with some good urban infrastructure in place.

If A P wants to have a good functional capital keeping aside its pent-up division emotions and vainglorious politics, there can not be a better example than Naya Raipur of Chhattisgarh.

35

KALESHWARAM PROJECT BENEFITS BEYOND AGRICULTURE

(Telangana Today | 4 July, 2019)

There is again a lot of debate on the Kaleshwaram Lift Irrigation (KLI) project, mainly on its costs and benefits, apart from its complex technical aspects. Many pundits think that it can perhaps irrigate about 20 lakh acres, not the scheduled 38 lakh acres.

Spending Rs 80,000 crore on it, needing to run it with over 4,000 Mw power and other operation and maintenance (O&M) costs can be more than the increased agricultural production. They opine that the increased yield and its value will not be sufficient to make the project economically viable.According to the International Water Management Institute (IWMI), Colombo, the opinion is not right. For, irrigation projects will create many socio-economic and environmental benefits, which should be taken into account in the

the impacts in secondary and tertiary markets.

While the cost-benefit analysis can be used as a basic approach for impact assessment, it should be supplemented with additional analyses through full economic, social and environmental impact assessments. All the outcomes and impacts that change the net benefits to society should be included in the assessment. Thus, in a project like the KLI, we need to include the components of environmental, social costs and benefits. They can be properly identified, quantified and valued in monetary terms in the cost-benefit analysis, making it Impact Assessment and Integrated Water Resource Management (IWRM) analysis. It provides a holistic approach.

Development of agricultural water resources brings significant changes at various levels. These include changes in production patterns, land and property values, expansion in the use of inputs and overall economic activities through backward and forward linkages. The impacts of these changes vary from one level to another. Some are confined to only farm level, while others spread to the whole project command. Some others spread to a wider region, province/State or at the national level.

Uses of surface irrigation water

OFF-STREAM	IN-STREAM
○ Irrigated agriculture	○ Commercial/recreational fish production
○ Urban domestic	○ Hydro power generation
○ Commercial and industrial	○ Water transportation
○ Rural domestic, livestock and small-scale enterprise	○ Recreational uses of river flows like swimming, river rafting
	○ Religious use of river, bathing

SOCIO-ECONOMIC IMPACT OF IRRIGATION

PRIMARY IMPACT

Increased agricultural production
- ○ Increased crop productivity
- ○ Expansion in crop areas
- ○ Increase in crop intensity
- ○ Increase in crop diversification

Increased commercial fish production (inland fisheries)

More water for industrial, commercial and residential sectors

Increased farm forestry and vegetation in irrigated areas

Increased health benefits – improved sanitation due to better access to water

Direct positive impact
- ○ Increased benefits from flood control
- ○ More water for rural domestic and livestock purposes
- ○ Increased groundwater recharge, recreation from water bodies, sight-seeing, fishing
- ○ Reduction in opportunity costs of water uses

SECONDARY IMPACT

More jobs in agriculture due to increased cropping intensity, area and output from irrigation

Increased employment outside agriculture in related industries such as input industry (backward linkages) and output industries (forward linkages); poverty reduction through increased productivity

Increased food security

Lower food prices

Improved nutrition, calories intake and better health

Primary impacts are relatively easier to evaluate in monetary terms. The secondary impacts, which are important in irrigation decision-making, are relatively harder to assess in monetary terms. As the scale of the project expands, secondary impacts also get amplified, resulting in more complexities in the impact assessment exercise. Irrigation impacts may vary considerably by the source of water and the nature of the project like dam, lift irrigation and groundwater-based irrigation. Surface irrigation infrastructure provides water for a variety of uses with wider coverage area, with potential impacts and likelihood of associated externalities. Water uses from surface irrigation water can be classified into withdraws uses and in-stream uses. Based on these uses, the socio-economic impacts of irrigation can be ascertained.

After identifying all the relevant important impacts, the next step is to quantify them. The method generally used is with and without comparison approach. The impacts can be measured as the difference between with and without irrigation access. In quantifying irrigation impacts, the views taken should be of society as a whole. It is not restricted to agriculture within the boundary of the irrigation command or the region. It should also include other socio-economic benefits in other sectors.

Once the impacts of irrigation are quantified, the next step would be to value them as far as possible in monetary terms. Where monetary-based measures are impracticable, non-monetary indicators of economic value should be used. Irrigation involves several types of costs like economic, social and environmental. They can be direct and indirect. Capital costs comprise annual depreciation and annual interest charges. O&M costs include administration costs. There are also rehabilitation costs. They may be classified as financial costs. Proper estimation of financial costs is important for determining the economic costs of the project. And the other indirect effects (costs) are estimated and valued in monetary terms.

Once the benefits and costs are identified, quantified and valued, the next step is to develop a common measure of index, which allows direct comparison of costs and benefits. The most commonly used measures include net present value, economic rate of return and benefit-cost ratio. They are used to compare costs and benefits of irrigation and to determine returns on irrigation investments.

Thus, it is not right to compare costs with immediate direct benefits, ignoring the economic value of other multiple distributary socio-economic impacts. For such irrigation projects meant to impact the economy of the

State, the government should be in a position to meet its annual capital commitments and O&M costs from its revenue expenditure and not just from the utility charges paid by farmers and other users. Confining the cost-benefit of the KLI project to agriculture alone is imprudent.

36

DO NOT BELITTLE TELANGANA STATE FORMATION

(Telangana Today | 11 February, 2020)

Prime Minister Narendra Modi in his reply to the motion of thanks to the President's address in Parliament on February 6 commented on the passage of Telangana State Bill by the UPA government. Apparently, he was comparing it with the passing of the Bills for abrogating Article 370 and CAA, 2019, by his own government. He said the Telangana Bill was passed amidst unrest, closing the doors of Parliament and the TV transmission switched off. He alleged that even Andhra and Telangana people were not consulted on it. He also said the BJP in 2000 created three States peacefully and all three of them are progressing very well.

Martyrs Memorial

It is a very politically incorrect statement. It seems the PM is not familiar with the history of Telangana State struggle, which was going on since 1956. Telangana State was not carved out from the original existing State formed at the time of independence like about 15 such divided States after independence. It was merged with Andhra, which was separated from the then Madras State even before the State Reorganisation Commission was formed in 1956 against the wishes of Telangana people and against the recommendation of the SRC with several guarantees and agreements, just to make an unviable Andhra State viable.

Civil Struggle

All the guarantees and agreements were flouted without exception. There were several campaigns for separate State since 1956 which were suppressed mercilessly. Some 367 people were shot dead by police and more than 1,000 committed suicides for the statehood. Such was the situation inside the forcibly merged State. These were unheard happenings in a civil struggle for political independence inside a democratic country. When such was the case of Telangana State struggle, for the Prime Minister to deride the State Bill is very galling to the people of Telangana. The Bill was not like the whimsical legislations passed by his government in Parliament.

His party also supported Telangana Bill in Parliament at that time. If it was not in order, they could have opposed it. Once a State is created by the Central government, all States are equal for the government and the Prime Minister, irrespective of party. He cannot endorse one State formation and denigrate the other. About his reference to the progress in the new States, it is already an established fact, endorsed by the RBI and other central institutions that within five years, Telangana has emerged as one of the frontline States in the country with its prudential financial management and a mixture of welfare programmes and big infrastructural development.

Growth-Oriented

All its programmes have been appreciated by premier central institutions. Some of its programmes/projects are being copied by other States. This clearly indicates the need, viability and legitimacy of the new State. It has done better than all the three States created in 2000, in the first five years. If he is considering residual AP, which is suffering from its inherited financial problems and the misrule by the TDP, till recently his ally, it is a different matter. Neither Telangana nor the UPA government is not responsible for it.

It is not for the first time that the PM is making negative comments on Telangana formation. Earlier, he said that they have killed the mother and saved the child. United AP was not the mother of Telangana. Andhra was with Madras State for over 100 years before its merger with Telangana. So the observation was factually incorrect. His party also was very lukewarm in its support to Telangana State before 2014. Only Sushma Swaraj wholeheartedly supported separate Telangana. LK Advani actually wanted to postpone the passing of the Telangana State Bill at the crucial juncture. Others were on the fence and Modi remained silent on the formation of Telangana state.

Avoidable Attitude

After the 2019 victory, the BJP government's attitude towards States has become more patronizing and condescending. Its legislative activities in Parliament have become shrouded in secrecy, are ushered in peremptorily and passed with a ham-handed approach. Abrogation of Article 370 and CAA are examples. These legislations have created a social polarization in the name of national security and majority nationalism. To ride on this polarization and win elections, such controversies are being created so as to sway the minds of the voters.

The comparison of abrogation of Article 370 and CAA with the Telangana State Bill is odious. After an arduous struggle of 58 years, Telangana State was declared on December 9, 2009. The Bill was brought in February 2014. Whereas Article 370 and Citizenship (Amendment) Bills were brought in clandestinely overnight without consulting the stakeholders and passed using political muscle in Parliament. Telangana and AP have now reconciled with the division and are going in their own ways to consolidate their respective States and move forward to progress.

J&K, CAA

Even after six months of Abrogation of Article 370, Jammu & Kashmir is still not normal. The political leaders who were kept under house arrest from day one are now being booked under the Public Safety Act (PSA). Business and tourism in the State are down. It looks like the impasse is going to be indefinite. In the case of CAA, it is a total mess. Even though the Act has come into force from December 10, 2019, there are no rules framed to grant citizenship for the intended groups. There are no lists of illegal immigrants/intended groups available.

The NRC, which is supposed to ferret out illegal immigrants for CAA, is totally impracticable and is kept under wraps for obvious political reasons. These resultant public reactions speak volumes about the feasibility of the Bills introduced by the NDA government. The Prime Minister should not belittle Telangana statehood time and again. People of the State, who struggled for six decades and sacrificed hundreds of lives for it, resent it. It is undemocratic as well.

37

MAKING REGULATED FARMING WORK

(Telangana Today | 6 July, 2020)

There is a great deal of discussion on regulated agriculture in Telangana. The State government is planning to adopt regulated agriculture to increase the income of farmers by bringing in market-driven diversified crop patterns instead of growing crops by rote, in a gambling fashion. It is good to regulate the cropping pattern to profitably use the available agriculture resources, ensure increased yields and assured marketing. It also enables the government to plan better in providing inputs, and forward and backward linkages to farmers without much red tape. It can add synergy to our agriculture growth. It is a desirable idea, but it should be made to work.

Every government promises to solve the problems facing agriculture. Some efforts were also made by certain special programmes. The ICAR and the regional research stations did a great deal of work to address agronomic problems, conserve soil, increase the yield potential of crops, control pests and diseases and to regulate marketing, etc. Several things improved. But an effective production and marketing chain linkage could not be established as the government efforts and the choices of farmers did not coalesce. If earlier agriculture in India was a vagary of the monsoon, it has now become a vagary of the market.

Market Dynamics

Availability of better crop strains, provision of quality inputs, subsidies, recommendation of better crop patterns, provision of MSP — all have improved. But the coordination between government plans and farmers' choices has gone awry. For, the government was not in a position to regulate crop patterns and market demand. This led farmers to grow crops without factoring in demand-supply and other market dynamics as they had no means to ascertain them. In such an unorganized situation, the government was not in a position to fulfill its MSP programme.

Regulated agriculture is needed to break this impasse with a premeditated action plan between the government and farming community. A consensus between the two on the plan is a must for its success. The government cannot force its plan unilaterally and farmers should not indulge in their laissez-faire cultivation of crops. The government needs to fulfil its designated obligations/guarantees of inputs and services all along the production line till marketing. And it should be in a position to decide the MSP for all crops and ensure the availability of it. Or more than that by itself or in the market as per the exigency with suitable market interventions. In this consensus, the government, State Rythu Vedika and the agriculture department have to play a critical role.

Areas and Crop Patterns

In every State, there will be canal irrigated areas, irrigated areas under wells and rain-fed areas. Under canal irrigated areas, it can be wet and irrigated dry cultivation. All these variables need to be taken into consideration while deciding the areas and crop patterns. The most important problems at present are cultivating more rice under projects and more supposedly high remunerative commercial crops like cotton, chillies in irrigated dry and rain-fed areas. This often causes glut and loss to farmers and unsettles agriculture. Though they are covered under MSP, the government more often than not is not in a position to fulfill that obligation even for designated crops.

To overcome this, the cultivation of such crops needs to be properly regulated depending on the forecast of market prices and the import and export of those commodities. Containing the burgeoning rice cultivation in the increasing irrigated areas under new projects is another major problem. It needs to be strictly regulated. Under the old MI tanks, the low lying water-logging areas under medium and major irrigation projects, rice growing becomes a must. It cannot be altered.

In the rest of the ayacut, the areas can be identified depending on the soil and other agro-climatic conditions as irrigated dry (ID) crops with alternative, commercial and other remunerative cereal, pulse and oilseeds. In rain-fed areas too, suitable cropping patterns must be adopted depending on the monsoon and market forecast. Here and in ID crop areas, there is scope for promoting the combination of cereal, millet, pulse to improve the variability of food crops and sustain productivity of the soil.

Planning Ahead

The regulated farm policy needs to be worked out well in advance every year. It should be ready by May well before the onset of the monsoon. Farmers should know in which crop zone they are and be prepared to grow the crops in the ensuing season. It will also help the government and the agriculture department to prepare their input plans and other linkage estimates depending on the crop areas.

The government also can work out its budget and other forward and backward linkages depending on the predetermined plan. Linking these plans to government schemes like Rythu Bandhu, input subsidies, insurance, MSP is a good idea. It can act as a catalyst with farmers to switch to regulated farming with a firm commitment. But its efficacy has to be monitored and assessed every year to bring in necessary changes and improvement.

Regulated farming is a progressive idea. But it is complex and needs a great deal of coordination between the government, its departments and farmer associations. It also needs an efficient administration of the plan, reducing the ever-present red tape. The State-level apex farm association needs to play a vital role in this. It needs to develop an organisation, which will acquire the ability to get things done from the government as per the plan with some independent approach. The government needs to promote that ability in the association for creating and implementing a pragmatic regulated farming scheme over the long-run for sustainable and profitable agriculture in the State.

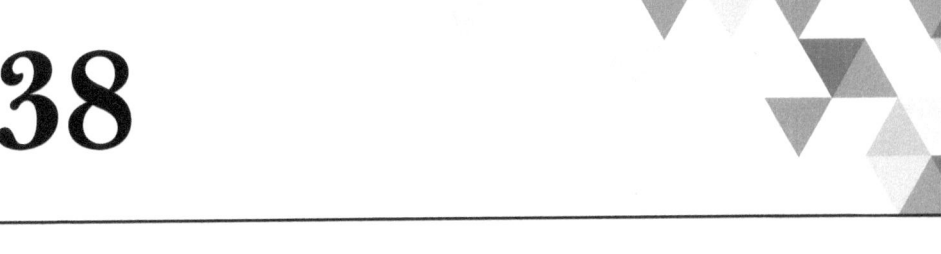

38

BJP'S DAYDREAMS WILL NOT COME TRUE

(Telangana Today | 15 September, 2020)

The social and election engineering of the north and BJP's religious ideology are unlikely to work in Telangana. The scraping win in Dubbak is making the BJP and other dissident elements in the State go into frenetic thinking of BJP barging into the State in a big way. Actually, in a 119-seat Assembly, this is only the second BJP MLA, and that too the seat was won with a slender margin of about 1,000 votes.

It is not that a political party cannot aspire to increase its tally in a State. It can do so. But the circumstances and credentials matter. Here it seems a clutch of minor local factors endemic to the constituency caused the upset. It does not look like it will have any larger implication, if we go by the ground realities in the State.

Bihar Case

The BJP winning more seats upstaging its partner JD(U) to form its proxy government in Bihar seems to have given them this improbable idea. The two States are too far between and have a different political situation and culture.

Telangana is not prone to the kind of peculiar social and political convulsions as in Bihar. Telangana is a progressive State. Its new-found political freedom, political stability and a forward-looking administration make the situation completely different. Telangana in its 6th year figures amongst the top 5-6 States in the country on most economic indicators. This is despite the State getting a low central devolution (2.4%) and no special financial help from the BJP-led Centre.

Bihar gets the second largest (9.1%) central devolution every year. In addition, Narendra Modi announced a big financial package of Rs 1,25,000 crore for it in 2015. Yet Bihar has stagnated at the bottom of all States and UTs on the economic front. Its per capita income has always remained the lowest in the country, despite the social engineering of Nitish Kumar for the last 15 years and election engineering of Modi during the last six years.

As for the performance of the BJP at the national level, it is very much wide open for all to see. The country's GDP growth had slumped from 8% to 3.9% by March 2019 even before Covid. Now it has contracted to -10.6%. So what is the need for Telangana to embrace the BJP?

Against Telangana

In the matter of Telangana's formation too, the BJP's role was at best lukewarm. Except Sushma Swaraj, the BJP senior leadership did not fully support the Telangana statehood demand after 2009. Advani wanted the Telangana Bill to be stayed in the crucial last session of Parliament in 2014, when Telangana State formation was in its throes.

Modi and his man Friday Amit Shah never liked Telangana's formation. During the inauguration of Amaravati, Modi disparagingly said that mother AP was killed and TS, the child, was saved. Both Modi and Shah, inside Parliament and outside of it, hectored the Telangana State Bill and the State formation more than once, belittling Telangana State.

Even after the formation of the State, the Modi government was not friendly with Telangana. Seven mandals of Bhadrachalam division of Khammam district were annexed to AP without even informing Telangana by an undemocratic ordinance, violating the AP Reorganisation Act. It was done just to make the tribals in the 270 villages to be drowned in the Polavaram project and make AP happy.

Even when Telangana wanted to be friendly with the Centre for the sake of the State, the BJP government cold-shouldered it. Though Niti Aayog recommended financial assistance for TS schemes to the tune of Rs.24000 cr. the BJP government did not give even part of it. The gap widened between the two governments, towards the end of Modi 1.0.

In Modi 2.0, the Centre started treating Telangana with more disdain for obvious political reasons. Leave alone any special assistance, even the regular statutory funds were released sparingly. In the release of GST gap funds and other Finance Commission grants, there was an inordinate delay even before the advent of the coronavirus. Once the virus entered, the Centre's economy went into a tizzy and its management of funds became unwieldy.

Political Discrimination

Telangana was left to fend for itself for funds amidst Covid. Not helping a wee bit in mega infrastructure projects is one thing and not responding with any financial assistance during unprecedented floods that caused an estimated damage of Rs 5,000 crore in Hyderabad city is another. There are statutory funds available for disaster management with the Centre. It is simply pointless political discrimination, compared to the flood relief given to the BJP-ruled States.

Telangana is not a BIMARU or an SCS State. It is one of the 6-8 States that contribute more to Central taxes and get very less back as devolution. As a new State, it needs help from the Centre, especially for fast development of infrastructure projects, which were badly neglected in the united state.

During the lockdown, a lot of Biharis lost their jobs and had to trek back to their native places weathering untold miseries. Neither Modi nor Nitish governments helped them. Yet, they voted for the NDA, even giving more seats to the BJP. They voted for the government, which did not help them in distress and started trekking back again for jobs outside Bihar.

Alternative Agenda

Without doing anything, not even providing the funds due to the State properly or encouraging real development, just depending on certain local political disgruntlement and religious undertones in its voters, to win elections will not yield results. Assembly elections are three years away and the political situation at that time is difficult to foresee now.

Dreaming to win the GHMC elections based on the Dubbak cliff-hanging result is not enough. No Telanganite would like to stop the momentum of the State's development and bring in a menace to disrupt the existing religious amity in the city.

The opposition in Telangana needs to find some positive alternative political narrative, instead of denigrating the TRS on personal aspects or playing religious politics. The BJP government at the Centre needs to treat Telangana with respect and recognise the needs of the growing new State and respond suitably to create some positive political mileage to make inroads into the State. The social and election engineering of the north and BJP's religious ideology are unlikely to work in Telangana.

39

REGIONAL PARTIES SUIT NEW STATES

(Telangana Today | 11 December, 2020)

Strong regional parties are more conducive for the consolidation and progress of the new States.

Normally, it is the local party organizations that participate and drive elections to local bodies. But in the recent GHMC election, the BJP's entire national leadership descended on Hyderabad in a furious raid to win.

The all-powerful Amit Shah, BJP president JP Nadda, UP Chief Minister Yogi Adityanath, Central Minister Prakash Javadekar, and many other bigwigs led the all-out raid. Even Prime Minister Narendra Modi made a backdoor appearance just before the election day through the Bharat Biotech route in a sudden overnight urge for reviewing the Covid vaccine preparation. And then, there was that wave to the people of Hyderabad! All this furious blitz, however, could not achieve the goal of winning a majority. Of course, it won many more seats than earlier.

Real and Forged

A lot has been said on the good and bad show of the BJP and the TRS. The TRS was in the GHMC seat for the last four years and has been in the Assembly for seven years. Naturally, there would be some anti-incumbency — some real and some forged. So, it was unrealistic to expect the TRS to win 100 seats.

The ground situation at the time of election matters most. The performance or the contribution to the city's upkeep and development by the parties is important. As the TRS was in power in the corporation, it was doing its duty. It was highlighting the importance of Hyderabad city for the State and envisaged several infrastructure development projects commensurate with it. It has implemented many of them and many more are in the pipeline. This is the reason why many foreign companies have set up shop here.

The BJP, as it had a small presence in the GHMC, did not do much. But, at the Centre, it had the ability to do much to help Hyderabad, yet it never did. It treated Telangana with condescension, especially in its attitude towards the State formation and in providing funds for its mega projects, despite recommendations of Central agencies.

The callous refusal to help the city in the recent unprecedented floods is the latest example. There was always a lukewarm approach to release even the statutory funds to the State. The local BJP also did not do anything to endear to the people of the city or the State. Forgetting all that, barging into the city with a big raid party at the last moment to win the Mayoralty is a farce. It has won a large number of seats with its propaganda machine, Hindutva nationalism, the presence of its many tinsel glitterati and by playing on the disgruntlement of certain sections of people. Though they were given more numbers, the people of Hyderabad have stopped them from grabbing the cake.

Weak Alone

Just because the BJP has won a majority at the national level, it thinks it has the suzerainty of all the States and tries to saffronize them in any election that comes in its way — whether local or State or national by-elections. The BJP has won power only in a few States on its own. In a number of States, either it has a coalition pre or post forged with local parties. Or it splits the winning opposite parties and hitches with them to cobble up a government to play a dominant role in it, brushing it with saffron. Saffronisation is its main motto. This kind of political avarice for a ruling national party looks unseemly.

The BJP thinks saffronisation is the sine qua non for development. First, it was the Gujarat model of development, where the per capita income (PCI) is around 11 in rank from 2001 to 2019. Their flagship States such as Uttar Pradesh, Bihar and MP too have more or less stagnated at the same low levels in the last 20 years.

The States are performing according to their inherent resources and strengths. Goa, Haryana, Karnataka, Tamil Nadu are performing better irrespective of the ruling party. The newest State Telangana is performing better than Gujarat since its formation in PCI and it is in the top 5-7 States in its macro development indicators.

We are all aware of the 'story' of the economic development of India since 2014 and the fall in many world indexes like Human Development, Democracy, Press Freedom, etc. So what do the saffronization and economic model of the BJP actually offer, if it is not improving the GDP or the indexes of living standards and democratic credentials of the nation?

Little Impact

In the GHMC, the TRS is the single largest party and has 31 ex-officio members, but it cannot win the Mayor post without a partnership with the MIM or some strategic understanding with it. The TRS allying with the BJP or the BJP with the MIM is unlikely. So the BJP's big dash appears to be a non-starter. If the MIM was not in the picture, the BJP could not have indulged in it.

The thinking that the BJP winning more seats will cause an upheaval in State politics seems to be a little far-fetched. If the BJP was a clear winner in the GHMC, it could have made some impact. Actually, the TRS was weak in the constituencies in and around the city even in 2014. The TDP's presence in the city in the 2016 GHMC election and the TDP-dominated 'mahakootami' in the 2018 general election had changed the situation, making it pro-TRS. Hyderabad is a cosmopolitan city with heterogeneous groups and some of them are non-Telanganites. So the voting in the GHMC is impulsive, and will change from election to election, depending on the political situation in the State and in the country.

The State elections are still three years away and the political situation can change a great deal by that time. Given the performance of the BJP in Modi 2.0, its political behavior, floundering of its reforms and controversies like farm Acts, the strength and spread of the BJP in 2023 is anybody's guess. Anyway, for the two new Telugu States, the BJP coming into their helm of affairs does not augur well. Strong regional parties of the present or new would be more conducive for the consolidation and progress of the new States.

40

NEW SECRETARIAT, NEW IDENTITY FOR TELANGANA

(Telangana Today | 23 March, 2021)

The new Secretariat complex will be like a memorial to the sacrifices that Telangana's people made for political freedom.

Telangana New Secretariat Design

The Telangana government's firm decision to construct a new government complex at one place with state-of-the-art facilities is good. In place of the old nondescript labyrinth of an office complex, a new complex is being constructed. In the 2021-22 Budget, the Telangana government also allotted Rs 610 crore towards its construction.

Like always, the naysayers and the opposition parties have started lambasting the government on it. They say the old complex, which was good for the 23-district united state is more than good for the new State, which is less than half of it. But the government averred that the present complex was randomly built at different times, lacked infrastructural facilities like adequate parking, fire safety and modern features for a State secretariat. The idea was mooted in 2016.

The government alternatively contemplated finding a suitable place for the new complex elsewhere like in Chest Hospital grounds, Erram Manzil and Gymkhana grounds to avoid demolition of the present structures. But for various reasons, the idea did not materialise. Because of its centrality in Hyderabad city, as the large part of the complex is old and required demolition, the government reverted to the idea of building a brand new integrated secretariat complex at the same site. A Cabinet decision to that effect was made on June 19, 2019. The foundation stone was laid on June 27. Meanwhile, five public interest litigations were filed on the government decision in the High court.

Old Structure

A ministerial sub-committee and high-powered technical committees were constituted to study the state of the old complex to make suitable recommendations. The technical committee, in its report, found that it was not possible to make any changes to the conditions prevailing in the existing buildings.

There were eight blocks located in the congested lanes where fire service vehicles cannot enter and it was not feasible to have fire safety measures. They observed that the secretariat complex had 10 blocks, with accommodation of 4.45 lakh sq feet, of different ages ranging from more than 100 years to 20 years — varying from dilapidated condition to working condition. Except for two blocks, other blocks were reported to be in dilapidated condition. The building blocks were disjointed and scattered over an area of 25.5 acres.

The repairs to the old buildings with very old plumbing, electricity, etc needed heavy expenditure. There were no adequate conference facilities, parking and a green area. The cost could be as good or even more than the new construction, if it was attempted to make the repairs and carry out renovation to create spaces and other suitable facilities, without demolition.

So it was felt that it was better to demolish the existing structures and build an integrated building complex with modern facilities. The ministerial sub-committee concurred with it. The government took the decision. The proposed integrated building complex with 7 floors is designed to have about 7 lakh sq feet floor area. The new complex is estimated to cost Rs 600 crore.

No Objection

The main grounds of the PILs were: no need for demolition; not a priority; unilateral decision by the government and huge expenditure. The HC bench refused to interfere in the State government's decision saying it does not find any irregularity in the Cabinet decision. The bench dismissed the PILs filed separately between 2016 and 2019.

Yet, the opposition to the new secretariat continued. The Pradesh Congress Committee president of Telangana went to the National Green

Tribunal (NGT) on the specious grounds of environmental damage. The NGT found no merit in it and dismissed his plea.

Every State has a Secretariat or government building complex depicting the history, culture and ethos of its people. Karnataka has the grandest of them all, built in 1956. Karnataka was not short of any buildings either in Bangaluru or Mysuru. Kerala, Himachal Pradesh and Tripura have beautiful Secretariat buildings. Even small States in the northeast region have beautiful government buildings depicting their architecture and culture. Ahmedabad and Naya Raipur Secretariats are modern examples.

Case for It

So what is wrong if Telangana wants to build a Secretariat depicting the architecture, culture and ethos of the State, in place of a drab and haphazard-looking agglomeration of old blocks? It is a new State and certainly needs to have its new identity. The Secretariat, the seat of the power of the State government, is one of the embellishments of that identity. Even the Supreme Court concurred with the decision of the HC.

Apart from the incongruity of the old structure, there is no need for a government to live in an unhappy place where the State's identity was ridden roughshod over for 58 long years. There is a need to have a complete break with that neo-colonial past and breathe a fresh air of political freedom in the new State.

The new design depicts the Deccan-Kakatiya architecture and culture expressing Telangana's quintessence, with all the Indian Green Building Council norms, meeting the stipulations of fire safety, disaster management and other mandatory regulations.

It will have concrete structures in 2.4 acres of the 27.5 acre campus and the rest will be dedicated to greenery, landscaping, footpaths, parking and other accouterments. If such a prestigious structure is coming up in place of an unorganized old structure at an affordable cost, there is no reason to oppose it.

When Andhra Pradesh is said to have spent about Rs 1,100 crore for a temporary Secretariat, what is the issue if Telangana builds a permanent integrated secretariat complex with half that amount? Telangana needs a new government building complex. It will also be like a memorial to all the sacrifices of the Telangana people made in their long and poignant struggle for political freedom.

41

SERICULTURE AS A MONEY-SPINNER IN TELUGU STATES

(Telangana Today | 24 May, 2021)

Telangana with its suitable climate, vast tracts of forest and a big tribal population is ideal for this cottage industry.

Sericulture is the growing of silkworms to produce silk. It has become an important cottage industry in many countries now. China and India are the two main producers, with over 70% of the world's annual production of silk. There are four types of natural silk – Mulberry, Eri, Muga and Tasar. India, the second largest producer of silk, has the unique distinction of being the only country producing all four kinds of silk.

Sericulture

Natural silk is an insect fibre. It comes from the silkworm cocoon, spun around itself to protect its pupal stage inside. A single filament from a cocoon can be as long as 1,600 metres. Like other animal fibres, silk does not conduct heat and acts as an excellent insulator to keep our bodies warm in the cold and cool in the hot weather. Of the four varieties of natural silks, Mulberry is produced from domesticated silkworms. Tasar, Eri and Muga are from the wild and are known as Vanya silks.

Mulberry Silk

The bulk of the commercial silk produced in the world comes from Mulberry. It comes from the silkworm, Bombyx mori L, which solely feeds on the leaves of Mulberry plants. These silkworms are completely domesticated and reared indoors.

Vanya or wild silks have their own fine attributes. These silks come from the North-Eastern and tribal zones of central, eastern India and sub-Himalayan regions. They are procured from the wild silkworms that feed on the leaves of different forest trees. Except for Eri, the cocoons are collected from the wild and the silk yarn is reeled. Eri silkworm feeds on castor leaves and is semi-domesticated. Each of the Vanya silks has its own unique beauty and individual charm. They are popularly used to create various designs for garments, lifestyle products and home furnishings. They form about 20% of the silk produced in India and have created their niche in the industry.

Mulberry silk is an agro-based cottage industry. To have a sericulture unit, first a Mulberry plantation needs to be established. Then the Mulberry leaves from the plantation are fed to the silkworms indoors in a rearing house in a certain controlled climate. The lifecycle of Mulberry silkworm of 45-55 days consists of the following stages — egg, larva, pupa and moth. At the end of the larval stage, the worm spins a protective cocoon consisting of a long single silk filament of 'fibroin' protein around itself. And is held together by 'sericin', another protein binding material. Inside the oval-like cocoon, the size of a cotton ball, the pupa forms and takes rest to become a silkworm moth. The moth cuts open the cocoon and comes out to live for 2-3 days to lay its eggs for continuation of its progeny. The lifecycle of the silkworm repeats again.

It is important to stop the cutting open of the cocoon by the moth. For, it cuts the single silk filament of 1,000-1,500 m length into pieces making it unfit for reeling. The cut pieces of the filament need to be spun, and the quality and the value of the silk is greatly reduced. So they stifle the pupa inside the cocoon, make the binding material dissolve in hot water and reel the silk filament into raw silk yarn inside the reeling units. Then the raw silk is processed to enhance its quality and made available for weaving.

Big Potential

Silk has lustre, drape and strength. There are three grades of silk. Each is a product of the three different stages of silk processing. The unwound filament makes the finest quality silk and is referred to as reeled silk. It is satiny smooth and pure white. Remaining silk from the reeling process becomes the raw material for carded or combed, spun silk yarn. The short fibres left behind after the carding or combing process are used to make noil yarn, a fine textured, rough silk.

The major Mulberry silk producing States are Karnataka, Andhra Pradesh, Telangana, West Bengal, Tamil Nadu and Jammu & Kashmir which together account for 92% of country's Mulberry raw silk production. Cocoon production is more in Karnataka, Andhra Pradesh and Telangana. The reeling activity is more in Karnataka. Weaving is spread wider in many States.

Of the total world raw silk production of about 1,75,000 tonne, India produces about 35,000 tonnes. Around 60 lakh persons are engaged in various sericulture activities in the country. It is estimated that about 57% of the gross value of silk fabrics flows back to the cocoon growers with a share of income to different groups. In 2019-20, India exported Rs 1,800 crore worth of silk products while imports stood at Rs 1,150 crore. Environmentally and marketwise, India has big potential for increasing its silk Industry.

Sericulture is labour-intensive, providing gainful occupation to lakhs of people in rural and semi-urban areas in India. Of these, a sizable number of workers belong to the economically weaker sections. There is considerable involvement of women in it. An investment of Rs 15,000-20,000 (excluding the cost of land and rearing space) is sufficient for undertaking Mulberry cultivation and silkworm rearing in one acre of semi-irrigated land. Mulberry takes only six months to grow and Mulberry plants are perennial. Five crops of silk production can be done in one year under tropical conditions. By adopting stipulated practices, a farmer can get a net annual income of Rs 50,000 to Rs 60,000 per acre.

Advantage Telangana

Telangana with a suitable climate akin to cocoon producing areas of Karnataka and Andhra Pradesh can undertake sericulture in a big way to help its marginal and small farmers in the upland areas to earn more. There is a need to increase the cocoon market and reeling units substantially commensurate with the weaving center infrastructure in existence in the State.

An acre of Mulberry garden and silkworm rearing can support a family of three without hiring labor. Features such as low gestation, high returns make sericulture ideal for weaker sections. It is an eco-friendly activity. There are vast tracts of forest and a big tribal population in the State for 'Vanya' sericulture. Tribals in the State are used to rearing/collecting Tasar silkworms.

Further promotion of it can offer more supplementary and gainful employment for them. So, sericulture can be a money-spinning micro enterprise for weaker sections in Telangana.

42

IF AP IS RIGHT, WHY DODGE THE TRIBUNAL !

(Telangana Today | 16 July, 2021)

KWDT2's mandate is to review water shares, make allocations, and there is no better way than the tribunal to adjudicate on it.

A virtual war is going on between Telangana and Andhra Pradesh on sharing Krishna waters. The issue is not new. It was always smoldering under the ashes and comes alive whenever AP ignites fresh trouble. It is a legacy of the erstwhile united AP administration — a case of majority political domination over a minority region. With 175 MLAs against 119, it was possible to browbeat Telangana in the united state and it has speciously happened in the case of Krishna water in favor of the Andhra region. Telangana was unable to get its legitimate share in the united state despite owning 68% catchment area of the Krishna river basin.

The Bachawat Tribunal, KWDT1, was appointed under the Interstate River Water Disputes Act, 1956, in 1969. The tribunal in its final verdict in 1976, awarded 800 tmc of water to erstwhile Andhra Pradesh, which included the Telangana region, at that time. Later, the AP government in the united state divided that water between regions in the State. They created a new region Rayalaseema, which was not a separate entity when Andhra and Hyderabad States were forcefully merged in 1956.

Arbitrary Division

The division of Krishna water by the AP government to its three regions was felt to have been made arbitrarily without regard to the catchment and cultivable areas, and the population, which were supposed to be the basic criterion for such division. (see Infographics)

As if the injustice in the distribution of dependable water as estimated by the tribunal was not enough, the AP government went into over-utilisation of the so-called surplus and floodwaters in the Andhra region with its Cabinet decisions and government orders. For that, the Srisailam reservoir has become a backyard water trough for Rayalaseema, making manipulations in the drawdown levels in the hydel project, in the name of drinking water to Chennai, a Telugu Ganga project, Srisailam Right Bank Canal (SRBC) and all kinds of 'srujala sravnthis' to take Krishna water to irrigate the old Tungabhadra ayacut and also all the way to Penna basin areas, which are outside the Krishna Basin.

Even before the dependable water share of Telangana was used, Andhra and Rayalaseema used their share and built reservoirs exceeding 200 tmc capacity to draw floodwaters from Srisailam via the ever-widening Pothireddypadu Regulator (PPR), through government orders. It did not matter much in the united State as long as it was an intra-State issue, because the minority Telangana region protests were stoutly ignored.

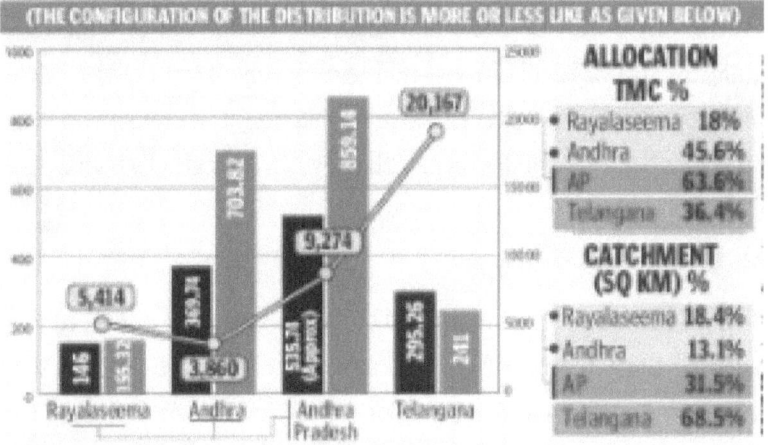

Manipulation Abounds

But even after the Telangana State came into existence, the manipulation has continued. The PPR which was originally designed for 11,000 cusecs, was increased to 44,000 cusecs before the merger, and now is being increased to 88,000 cusecs discharge capacity, to take water from the lowest level of the Srisailam project via its new controversial LI projects.

Another project is Pulichintala, constructed with 45 tmc capacity. The reservoir submerges 30,000 acres of Telangana lands but the ayacut is entirely in Andhra. Telangana has no share in its water for irrigation — the interesting thing is that the ayacut is Krishna delta and its adjoining areas. To stabilize a more than 150-year-old delta ayacut, water-starved Telangana lands were submerged. Even in the Nagarjuna Sagar project, so much manipulation took place. The ayacut, which was supposed to be 7.5 lakh acres for Andhra and Telangana each, ended up with more than 15 lakh acres to Andhra and 6-7 lakh acres to Telangana.

The Jurala project in Mahabubnagar — which is allotted 19.11 tmc — is built to utilise 6-7 tmc only for irrigation. It is an accumulation of such inequitable utilization of water in between KDWT I award and the government orders before the bifurcation of the State, which are ad hoc in nature and have a controversial legal status. They are the cause for the present political war. The present Rayalaseema lift irrigation scheme seems to have become the last straw that broke the camel's back.

KWDT, IRWD Act

The Brijesh Kumar Tribunal, KWDT2, came into existence to review the shares of the Krishna riparian States as a continuation to KWDT1 in 2010. It was about to give its final award in 2013 but it was stayed because of the bifurcation. The newly formed Telangana is the fourth riparian State in the Krishna river basin. The State wanted the central government to start the tribunal proceeding afresh as it was not a party to the earlier KWDT1 and KWDT2 adjudications.

Finally, the KWDT2 was extended and it was decided that the extended KWDT2 will restrict redistribution of water between Telangana and Andhra Pradesh States only.

There is also a specific provision in AP Reorganisation Act 2014 – Section 89 – Allocation of water resources. The term of the Krishna Water Disputes Tribunal (KWDT) shall be extended with the following terms of reference: to make project-wise specific allocation, if such allocation has not been made earlier, and to determine an operational protocol for projectwise release of water in the event of deficit flows.

The Interstate River Water Disputes Act, 1956, (IRWD Act) says whenever the riparian States are not able to reach amicable agreements on their own in sharing of inter-State river waters, Section 4 of the IRWD Act provides a dispute resolution process in the form of a tribunal. As per Section 5.2 of the Act, the tribunal shall not only adjudicate but also investigate the matters referred to it by the Central government and make suitable awards.

Tribunal Review

Telangana has requested the Central government to issue necessary terms of reference for the tribunal to review the water shares and make project-wise specific allocations. It has also withdrawn some cases pending before the Supreme Court, as advised by the Centre, to facilitate the issue of terms of reference. But the Centre is not issuing the terms of reference as laid down in the AP Reorganisation Act.

The issue is clearly a matter of inter-State dispute. The KWDT2 is in office and its mandate is to review the water share between AP and TS, make project-wise allocations and decide the operational protocol for the projects. Instead of referring the matter to the tribunal in all seriousness, the Central government indulges in never-ending and ineffective Krishna river board meetings, smacks of politics. It is a complex technical and legal issue. There is no better way than the tribunal to adjudicate on it and give a durable solution.

Why does the present Andhra Pradesh government, which is claiming to be right in all its Krishna river projects, not refer the whole issue to KWD2 as decided by SC and as is provided in the APR Act? Why this filibuster, political gamesmanship and dodging the issue in referring to the tribunal? It should understand now that Telangana is a separate State and has the right to demand its fair share of Krishna water and rectify the earlier unfair decisions as per the law of the land.

43

TELANGANA ON FIRM FINANCIAL FOOTING

(Telangana Today | 6 April, 2021)

The State has kept the Budget balanced maintaining the deficit regulations positive despite less Central transfers.

Telangana has emerged as one of the 10 States in the country with revenue surplus in the first six years of its formation through its prudential budget management. In the 7th year, as the coronavirus led to an unexpected fall in the revenue, it registered a small revenue deficit. Its fiscal deficit and outstanding liabilities are also within the stipulated limits. Its GSDP per capita for 2019-20 was at 6th rank, which used to be around 18 for united Andhra Pradesh before 2013-14.

A comparative financial statement of the residual AP and new Telangana (see infographics) portrays the budgetary management of Telangana from 2015-16 to 2019-20, being the full-fledged Budgets for the divided States, with their audited account numbers.

Comparative financial position (Telangana vs AP)

STATE'S OWN TAX REVENUE WAS 75%, HIGHEST ALONG WITH DELHI AND HARYANA WHILE ITS CENTRAL TRANSFERS WERE JUST 25%, AMONG THE LOWEST

	2015-16		2016-17		2017-18		2018-19		2019-20		Average	
	TS	AP	TS	AP	TS	AP	TS	AP	TS	AP	TS	AP
SOTR	54,309 (71,440)	44,042 (50,58)	58,190 (70,36)	49,378 (49,49)	64,345 (72,44)	53,627 (51,04)	74,691 (73,64)	62,413 (54,47)	74,957 (73,10)	60,926 (54,66)	72,16	52,17
Per capita SOTR	16,451	9,077	16,531	9,994	18,280	10,856	21,216	12,604	21,295	12,329	18,555	10,978
C.Taxes & Grants	21,745 (28,56)	43,606 (49,42)	24,629 (29,70)	49,630 (51,31)	24,479 (27,56)	51,436 (48,96)	25,733 (26,36)	42,168 (45,53)	27,586 (26,90)	50,358 (45,34)	27,76	48,07
Per capita CT & Grants	6,178	8,868	5,997	10,043	6,954	10,042	7,596	8,536	7,837	10,194	7,102	9,557
Total Revenue Receipts	76,134	86,648	82,819	98,984	88,828	1,05,063	1,01,420	1,15,81	1,02,544	1,11,034	90,348	1,03,662
Total Revenue Expenditure	75,896	95,960	81,432	1,14,478	85,365	1,21,214	97,083	1,28,569	1,08,096	1,37,475	89,574	1,19,877
Revenue Surplus(+)/Deficit(-)	(+)238	(-)7,302	(+)1,387	(-)17,194	(+)3,459	(-)16,152	(+)4,337	(-)13,637	(-)16,254	(-)26,441		
State GDP (lakh cr)	5,78	6,042	6,58	6,85	7,53	7,93	8,61	8,63	9,70	9,74		
Per capita State GDP (Rs)	1,60,640	1,09,002	1,93,45	1,20,676	1,80,404	1,29,660	2,04,486	1,50,173	2,26,216	1,69,519		
Loans outstanding (% to GDP)	16.2	24.5	19.5	37.2	20.2	28.9	20.3	30.6	21.3	31		

• SOTR (State's Own Tax Revenue) • CT (Central Taxes) • 2015-16 to 2019-20 CAG audited accounts data • Population figures amount and per capita data are of 2011 Census, the latest available (TS: 3.52 cr; AP: 4.54) • Revenue & Expenditure amounts are in Rs.cr.; per capita in Rs.; GDP in Rs.lakh cr. Note: Amt in Rs. (crore)

State of Finances

The performance of Telangana as delineated in 'The state of state finances: 2020-21' — a study by the RBI from 2015 to 2021, is summarized as under.

Revenue receipts of States comprise revenue from own sources and transfers from the Centre. During the 2015-21 period, on average 54% of revenue receipts of States came from their own sources, and 46% from Central transfers. The State's Own Tax Revenue (SOTR) of Telangana was 75%, the highest along with Delhi and Haryana. Its Central transfers were just 25%, among the lowest as against the national average of 46%.

Own tax-GDP ratio is a measure of a State's potential to generate taxes from its economy on its own. A higher ratio indicates a better ability to harvest taxes from the economic activities in the State. The average own tax-GSDP ratio of the States during the period stood at 6.3%. For most States, it ranged between 5% and 7.4%. For Telangana, it was 7.4%, the highest in the country.

Grants-in-aid are one of the four broad categories of revenue receipts. A higher shortfall is seen in grants-in-aid from the Centre to some States in the said period. Telangana had the third lowest Central transfers after Delhi and Haryana among the 28 States. It was also a recipient of much lower Central tax devolution than it collects for the Centre. It is a handicap to the State in spite of its better budget management.

Expenditure

Committed expenditure of a State typically includes expenditure on payment of salaries, pensions and interest payments. A larger proportion of the State Budget allocated for committed expenditure crowds out other developmental expenditures. Telangana's committed expenditure is 42% only, as against all India average of 50%.

Expenditure on economic sectors comprises spending towards agriculture, irrigation, urban and rural development, housing, energy, and construction of roads and bridges. Between 2015-16 and 2020-21, States on average spent 31% of their budget on these economic sectors. Chhattisgarh spent the highest (44%) followed by Madhya Pradesh (39%) and Telangana (38%).

The 14th Finance Commission reiterated the recommendation that the States should eliminate their revenue deficit by 2019-20. To do so, it also provided revenue deficit grants to some. However, despite receiving such revenue deficit grants, some States, including Andhra Pradesh, Kerala and West Bengal, continued to have a revenue deficit during the 2015-21 period. Telangana did not have a revenue deficit from 2015-16 to 2018-19. Only in 2019-20, it registered a .65% revenue deficit. The average fiscal deficit of the States was 2.8% from 2015 to 2021. Telangana maintained a fiscal deficit of 2.9% during the period.

Debt Servicing

Governments are required to service the debt by making periodic interest payments as well as repaying the principal amount on maturity of the debt. Higher debt servicing costs constrain spending on other priorities. Between 2015-16 and 2020-21, the States spent 23.4% of their revenue receipts on debt servicing. Punjab used the highest proportion of its revenue receipts (84%). Telangana spent 26%.

In 2017, the FRBM Review Committee recommended that a debt to GDP ratio should be targeted for the entire country, with a 20% limit for the States. In 2020-21, 26 States estimated their outstanding liabilities to be greater than 20% of the GSDP. Outstanding liabilities refer to the debt accumulated by the States from the borrowings in the past. Higher outstanding liabilities indicate a higher obligation for the States to repay loans in the coming years. Typically, these limits are set at 25% of the

GSDP in a year. At the end of 2020-21, outstanding liabilities of the State governments were estimated at 26.6%. For Telangana, this stood at 22%.

Spending

Agriculture and allied activities: It includes expenditure on subsidies, agricultural marketing, crop husbandry, horticulture, waiver of agricultural loans (in some States) and implementing schemes, including Prime Minister Faisal Bima Yojana and Rashtriya Krishi Vikas Yojana. The States on average spent 6.4% of their Budget on agriculture. Telangana spent 11.3%, highest after Punjab.

Energy: Expenditure under this includes subsidy to consumers, allocation for power projects and assistance to discoms under the UDAY scheme in certain States. The States on average spent 5.7% of their Budget on the energy sector. Telangana spent 7.3%. From facing extreme power shortage in 2014, Telangana has now become power surplus.

Social security: The States on average spent 4.1% of the Budget on social security. This consists of 0.1% of the Budget on capital outlay and 4% on revenue expenditure. Telangana spent the highest at 6.9%.

Irrigation and flood control: The States on average spent 4% of their Budget on irrigation and flood control. This consists of 3% on capital outlay, and 1% on revenue expenditure. Telangana again spent the highest at 8.4%.

Welfare of SC, ST, OBC: States on average spent 2.9% while Telangana spent 6.9 %, second highest among the States.

Housing: It was 1.3% on average for the States while Telangana spent 1.8% of the Budget.

There are a few sectors on which Telangana spent less than the average of States in view of the prioritization needs and the budgetary limitations.

But in most areas, its spending was above average and high-end. At the same time, the State kept the Budget balanced maintaining the deficit regulations positive. It is quite a creditable prudential financial management for a new State with less Central transfers and in need of finding its moorings to settle down.

44

PLUGGING CHRONIC ECONOMIC INEQUALITY

(Telangana Today | 8 October, 2021)

There is a wide variation in the key economic indicators of the Indian States. GDP, GDP per capita, GINI(ce) and percentage of poverty differ greatly, underlining the very uneven economic performance, in the country's 33 States and UTs. (See infographics). The configuration is as spiked as in the case of the countries of the world, indicating the great diversity and the contrast in the economic ecology of the States and UTs in India. The problem is that the inequality is becoming chronic — poor States continue to stay poor.

In India, the economy is improving and its GDP is also growing well. The GDP (nominal) which was Rs 10,596 crore in 1951-52 grew to Rs 19,745,670 crore in 2020-21. The GDP growth rate before the Covid pandemic was 6-7% and said to be the fastest in Asia.

The size of the economy, along with population, has changed enormously but it has also opened new challenges. India's GDP per capita also increased. But while the GDP of India ranked 6th in the world in 2021, its GDP per capita scored a low rank of 162 with $2200. The highest GDP per capita in the world is about $1,30,000. Although the increase in population and the techno-economic progress in the country increased the GDP, India did not do well in increasing its GDP per capita and the wealth distribution quotient.

Widening Divide

In India, along with the increase in population, economic inequality has also increased. There is a continuing upward march of the GINI coefficient and inter-State inequality. Coinciding with it, nearly 22% of the total population of India, about 300 million, have remained below the poverty line. (See infographics). Added to this, there is also a marked geographic disparity of income in the States. East and North are poorer than South and West.

According to a report by Johannesburg-based New World Wealth, in 2016, India was the second-most unequal country globally, with millionaires controlling 54% of its wealth.

Though the country is among the 10 richest countries in the world, the average Indian is relatively poor. Compare this with Japan, the most equal country in the world, where millionaires control only 22% of total wealth. As per Credit Suisse, in India, the richest 1% own 53% of the country's wealth and the richest 5% own 68.6%. While the top 10% have 76.3%, the poorer half jostles for a mere 4.1% of national wealth. What's more concerning is, things are getting better for the rich. The share of the top 1% now exceeds 50%. This is far ahead of the US, where the richest 1% own 37.3% of total wealth.

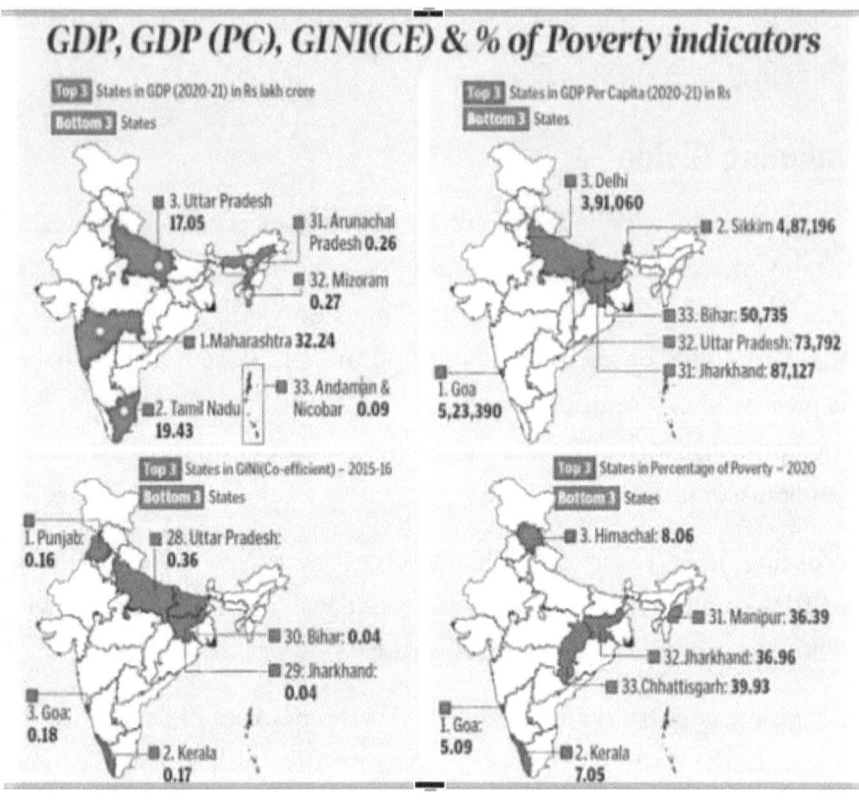

Oxfam International believes that this sharp rise in inequality is detrimental. Rising inequality will lead to slower poverty reduction, undermine sustainability of economic growth, compound inequalities between men and women, and drive inequalities in health, education and life chances. The World Economic Forum's Global Risks Report 2016 has found 'severe income disparity' to be one of the top global risks. A growing body of evidence has also demonstrated that economic inequality is associated with a range of health and social problems.

Government's Job

It is felt that the continued rise in economic inequality is not ineluctable. It is the result of policy choices. Governments can start to reduce inequality.

They need to implement reforms that redistribute money and power and level the playing field for the people.

Specifically, there are two main areas where changes to policy could boost economic equality — taxation and social spending. Progressive taxation is where corporations and the richest individuals will pay more to the state to redistribute resources across society.

Tax can play a progressive role, depending on the policy choices of the government. Social spending on public services such as education, health and social protection is very important. Evidence from over 150 countries – rich and poor, and spanning over 30 years, shows that overall, investment in public services and social protection can reduce inequality. The key indicators are commitment of government spending on education, health and social protection and the progressive levels of the spending on them.

India performs relatively poorly on both counts. Its total tax effort, currently at about 17% of GDP, is low and is about 50% of its potential. When it comes to social sector spending, India compares less well. Only 3% of GDP goes towards education and only 1.5% towards health. South Africa spends more than twice as much on education (6.1%) and more than three times as much on health (3.7%). While it's assessed as more unequal than India, South Africa ranks much higher than India in its commitment to reducing inequality.

Lacking Commitment

India, along with all the countries in the world, has committed to attaining the Sustainable Development Goals by 2030, and to ending extreme poverty by that year. But unless we make an effort to first contain and then reduce the rising levels of extreme inequality, the dream of ending extreme poverty for the 300 million Indians will remain a pipe dream.

In the post-reform period, the Indian economy got elevated to a high growth path triggered mainly by the expansion of economic activities across sectors. However, there are serious concerns about a number of imbalances in the growth scenario – intersectoral, interregional and inter-State. These have a serious impact on the goal of 'inclusive growth', which implies delivering social justice to all, particularly the disadvantaged groups.

One aspect of social justice is that all programmes that provide generalized access to essential services such as health, education, clean drinking water, sanitation should be implemented in a way that ensures that disadvantaged groups get full access to these services. This may need an innovative approach to public-private partnership.

There is also an imperative need to address the chronic geographical economic inequality, which is making some States stagnate at the bottom rungs. They need to be groomed properly and monitored closely to make them improve progressively in all the sectors.

45

DIVERGENT PATHS OF TELUGU STATES

(Telangana Today | 8 November, 2021)

Since the division, residual Andhra Pradesh and Telangana have presented seven Budgets. The Budgets are also audited by the CAG up to 2019-20. The final figures of the CAG report indicate the actuals of the income and expenditure and other economic parameters of the States. In a State Budget, the major financial indicators are revenue income, expenditure, revenue deficit/surplus and loan outstandings. The audited accounts of the two States say two different stories.

Telangana managed to balance its Budget with some revenue surplus for the first 4 years, ie, up to 2018-19. In 2019-20, it showed Rs 6,254 revenue deficit (0.65%) of GDP. In contrast, Andhra Pradesh reveals a mismatch between revenue income and expenditure. AP started with a deficit revenue income and this continued in all the subsequent years. In 2019-20, it reached up to Rs 26,441 crore. The deficit is likely to increase for both the States in 2020-21 and 2021-22 because of the shortfall in revenue collection owing to Covid-19. But AP's chronic and growing revenue deficit is a point to ponder over.

The Two Telugu States after demerger

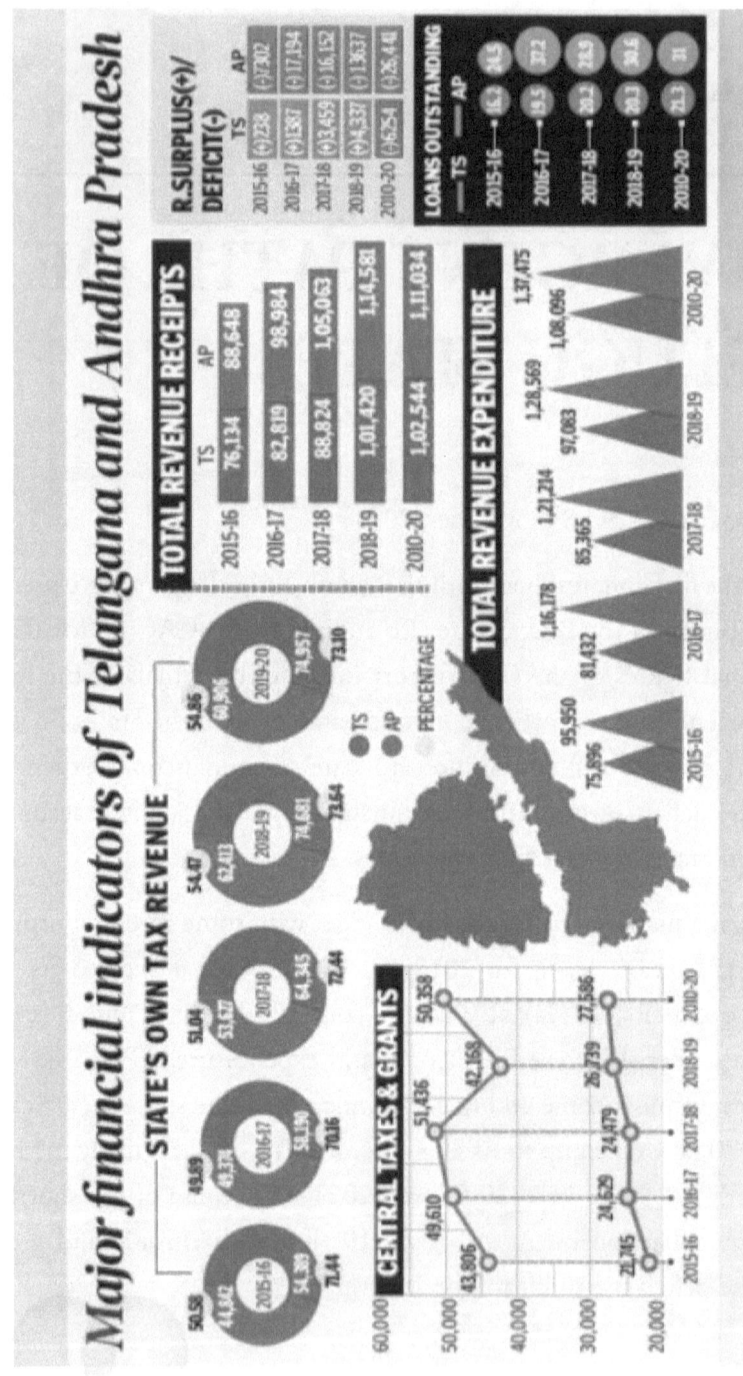

Driven by Need

Revenue deficit is the gap between revenue receipts and expenditure. This indicates the money the government needs to borrow to spend on non-capital components. It has several implications. It has to be met from the capital receipts, which a government either borrows or gets by selling its existing assets. This reduces assets. If the government uses capital receipts to meet its consumption expenditure, it leads to an inflationary situation in the economy. With more and more such borrowings, along with interest, the burden to repay the liability also increases and leads to a further deficit.

The needs of the two States were different. For Telangana, it was to regain its lost share of resources and rebuild the new State. For AP, it was to cope with the disadvantage of losing Telangana and reconstructing the State. The primary resource for both is State's own tax revenue (SOTR) and the Central tax devolution and grants. At the time of merger in 1956, Andhra State had a revenue deficit and Hyderabad (Telangana) had surplus. In the merged State, both Andhra and Telangana regions were contributing about 50% each to the SOTR. But the expenditure was 35-38% in Telangana and 65-62% in Andhra, making good the inherited deficit of the Andhra region. There was no effort to increase the revenue in the Andhra region to match its excessive expenditure in the merged State and that is being expressed even after the division now.

AP's Widening Gap

In 2014-15, the TS Budget was revenue surplus with Rs 369 crore and AP recorded a heavy deficit of about Rs 13,000 crore. This set the contours of economic planning in the two States. TS chose to follow prudential Budget making and implemented a balanced Budget after division. In AP, it was not so. The Centre had to bear the deficit in the first year. The 14th Finance Commission granted Rs 22,120 crore and the 15th

Finance Commission Rs 30,000 crore from 2015-21 to enable the State to balance its Budget. The State is using the grants but the gap keeps increasing.

In the case of Central devolution too, AP got more than TS, because of its more area and population. The borrowings of AP too exceeded the FRBM limit. Despite the restrained financial position, AP indulged in unrestrained spending. In the first term after division, the TDP government indulged in heavy unproductive spending in the name of world-class capital and administration, borrowing heavily.

The new YSRCP government too has embarked on an extravaganza of its large size welfare agenda continuing the heavy borrowing. The outstanding liabilities at the end of 2020-21 grew to 32.7% of GDP. AP spends 11.3% of its expenditure on the welfare of SC, ST and OBC, the highest in the country. While the average spending on economic sectors by States as a percentage of total expenditure was 31%, it was 29% for AP and 38% for TS.

Large SOTR

AP from the beginning should have tried to balance its Budget and consolidate the State finances. It needed to increase its SOTR gradually and rationalize expenditure with the sizable devolution funds and deficit grants from the Centre. The unwarranted hubris of the political leadership to play larger than life-size has pushed the State into an avoidable bad economic situation. AP's SOTR is 52%, its central devolution and grants constitute 48% of its revenue receipts. TS has 72% SOTR and 28% Central devolution and grants. The top-ranking States have an SOTR of around 70%. States need to have a large SOTR to raise more financial resources for their increased development.

The TS government represented by the TRS has stuck to prudential Budget management norms. Its pursuing a mixed bag of infrastructure development and welfare schemes. And it has achieved higher ranks in many macroeconomic indicators like GSDP, GSDP per capita, power production, irrigation potential and FDI, vindicating its claims of statehood. Though it has borrowed heavily for its infrastructural projects, it is spending them on capital-intensive projects creating assets and revenue. The welfare schemes are supported mostly by SOTR.

Own tax-GSDP ratio is a measure of a State's potential to generate taxes from its economy on its own. A higher ratio indicates a better ability to harvest taxes from the economic activities in the State. The average own tax-GDP ratio of the States during FY16 to FY21 stood at 6.3%. For most States, it ranged between 5% and 7.5%. AP has 6.4% and TS secured 7.5%, among the highest.

Considering the situation at the end of 2021-22, AP needs to drastically prune its Budget and increase its SOTR. TS also needs to downsize its ambitious big-ticket schemes and rationalize its Budget to curtail its growing deficit because of the pandemic.

46

BJP'S STRANGE TURF WAR IN TELANGANA

(Telangana Today | 17 January, 2022)

With almost no contribution, the party is trying to create an impression that it is the next big thing in Telangana.

The Bharatiya Janata Party (BJP) is indulging in a peculiar political turf war in Telangana. The party has just 3 MLAs in the 119-member Assembly. The Congress has 6 MLAs and MIM, 7. Yet the BJP is making all the noise as if it is the major opposition and is on the verge of toppling the TRS government. The Assembly elections are some two years away. The TRS has 103 seats in the Assembly and is batting very strongly on the placid wicket of the State. It is a rather curious noise, considering the circumstances.

Prior to the formation of the State, the BJP comparatively had more presence in Telangana than in Andhra. But, in the first Assembly elections in 2014, the BJP did not evince much interest in Telangana. It threw its weight around the TDP in AP and helped Chandrababu Naidu win. The jugalbandi with the TDP continued till Venkaiah Naidu was in the Central cabinet. Later, the TDP separated from the BJP. The present YSRCP government is wooing the Central BJP for obvious political reasons.

All Theatrics

In the 2019 Lok Sabha elections, the BJP winning 4 MP seats in Telangana whetted its appetite for increasing its strength in the State as part of extending its presence in the South. So it enhanced its political investment in the State. It attempted a big raid on the GHMC elections and won a large number of seats but could not win the mayoralty. The performance helped it win Dubbaka with a slender margin. And in the high stakes Huzurabad byelection with the connivance of its arch-rival Congress, it could wrest the seat from the TRS. The BJP now thinks it has breached the fortress and is encouraging the local cadre to indulge in all sorts of theatrics to create an impression that it is the next big thing in Telangana.

A national party like the BJP has every right to expand its domain in any State if it can win there. But its credentials, ability and promise to do better than the incumbent party in the State matters. Though the BJP promised Telangana State, it went back in 2000 while granting statehood for three other States where the demand for separation was not as intense as in Telangana. In the decider Statehood struggle, the BJP was on the fence, except for one or two individual leaders. In fact, in Parliament, LK Advani wanted to defer passing the Telangana State Bill.

Opportunistic Politics

Once the State was formed, Narendra Modi openly lambasted the State formation, in a trope calling it: 'killing the mother and saving the child'. He kept the friendly Telangana government at an arm's length and snuggled closer to residual AP for its more number of MPs. Seven mandals of Telangana were taken away through an ordinance to be submerged in the Polavaram project.

In AP, the BJP did not get traction because of the caste polarisation there. There was not much scope for the Hindutva factor. Moreover, though it was partial to AP's needs vis-a-vis Telangana, the BJP was not in a position to accede to many inordinate demands of AP. Thus continuing the political support to the AP government, the electoral focus was shifted to Telangana, as part of the saffronisation of southern India. The win of 4 MPs in the 2019 elections boosted the idea. Hyderabad and its comparatively large minority population helped it play the majority nationalism card.

Both the TRS in the State and the BJP at the Centre have won two general elections after the formation of Telangana. The performance of both the governments in their respective constituencies in the last seven-and-a-half years is there for all to see. Telangana has done exceedingly well among all the States. It is among the top 5 in all the major economic growth indicators. It has maintained a balanced Budget and executed many welfare and infrastructural projects in power, irrigation, drinking water, industries, IT, with its own resources. The same cannot be said of the Central government. The economy is in the doldrums and the country has fallen on many development indexes. The BJP-ruled States are lagging behind. The BJP's flagship States like UP, Bihar and MP still languish in the bottom rung of development.

More Bias

The BJP at the Centre has not helped the new Telangana State in finding its moorings. Much help flowed into AP in the name of deficit Budget. Two finance commissions provided about Rs 53,000 crore as a deficit grant. The Rs 60,000 crore Polavaram project is being constructed by the Centre and it has helped establish many national institutions there. Telangana, which was kept backward for 58 years, has spent heavily on several socio-economic schemes enhancing the per capita income of its people. The Centre did not extend any special assistance despite the recommendation of national institutions and the requests by the State government.

The BJP's political relationship with the Telangana government has not been not very sanguine from the beginning. In recent years, it started exhibiting more bias against the State. Krishna and Godavari issues are a major pointer. The BJP has delayed and blocked the legitimate interests of Telangana in the river water projects with political intent, causing a great loss to the State.

In the case of rice procurement under MSP, it has created a great deal of discomfiture to the State. While it was procuring more quantity of rice in kharif and also wheat in rabi seasons from many northern States, it has refused to procure more rice from Telangana. In addition, it has encouraged local BJP leaders to agitate and make political capital out of it.

Even for a small local issue of GO 317 zonalisation of employees transfers and recruitment, a big ruckus has been created. The BJP national president and former and present BJP Chief Ministers are sent to raid the State as a preparation for its political railroading into Telangana. It is a strange political turf war considering BJP's almost nil contribution to the consolidation and development of Telangana.

47

CENTER NEEDS TREAT TELANGANA WITH RESPECT

(Telangana Today | 22 February, 2022)

Prime Minister Narendra Modi again said in Parliament that Telangana State was not formed properly. It has been more than seven years since the State was formed. The AP Reorganisation Act (APRA), 2014, was passed in Parliament unanimously. His own party, the BJP, was a willing party to the passing of the Act on February 18, 2014. His Home Minister has also found fault with the formation of Telangana.

It is a misdemeanor by these constitutional functionaries to call this Act improper and unconstitutional. It can invite a privilege motion for contempt of the House.

Phobia Continues

It is not new for the Central government to look down upon the Telangana region and treat it as a political orphan. History records how Telangana got liberation from the feudal rule on September 17, 1948, while the rest of India got its independence on August 15, 1947. Since then, even in independent India, Telangana's tryst with its destiny is about discrimination, exploitation, oppression and angst.

The very liberation from Nizam's rule by the Indian army had started the discrimination. The Congress and the Indian union with their phobia of communism had brutally assaulted a section of Telangana people during the liberation from Nizam.

During the military and civilian government from 1948 to 1952, the iniquity against Telangana people in the name of containing communism was initiated. Outsiders were imported with the excuse of replacing the Urdu official language and weeding out communism. Though its own government was formed and functioned as Hyderabad state from 1952 to 1956, the administration was dominated by these outsiders, continuing the bias against Telangana people.

Then came the biggest of all misfortunes — the merger with Andhra State in 1956. Pandit Nehru, despite the SRC opposition, was influenced for the merger. It initiated a neo-colonisation and organized exploitation of Telangana and reduced its people to second class citizens in their own native land.

There was an agitation against the attitude of the civilian central government and against outsiders as early as 1952, which was brutally put down. The attitude continued with the Congress party, before and after the merger with Andhra State. Andhras used their closeness to the Congress because of their British India politics. Telangana people who were holed up in Hyderabad state under Nizam had no influence with the Congress in Delhi. Again in 1969, there was an uprising in Telangana which was ruthlessly put down by killing 369 people. In 1972, the mulki rules were abrogated by amending the Constitution by the Indira Gandhi government.

BJP's Slogan

It was the BJP which first raised the slogan of 'one vote, two States' way back in 1998 when the party passed a resolution in Kakinada extending support to the statehood cause. But when it came to the formation of new States in 2000, the BJP ditched Telangana and created three States — Chhattisgarh, Jharkhand and Uttaranchal, where the separation demand was of recent origin, ignoring the 50-year-old Telangana demand.

In 2004, the Congress led by Sonia Gandhi again stoked the fire for Telangana State. She kept the Telangana State dangling before the people of Telangana and won the elections in 2004 and 2009. But went back on it and it escalated into a bigger campaign. Under tremendous pressure, the Congress passed a declaration in Parliament for Telangana State. But kept it in abeyance for very long. Due to deteriorating political status in the hands of YSRCP in Andhra, just before the 2014 general elections, and after about 1,200 people died in the agitation, the Congress passed the Telangana State Act.

Telangana now is a full-fledged State along with the other 28 States. In just 5 years, Telangana emerged as one of the top States in economic progress. It has also proved the SRC right on its recommendation to keep it a separate State in 1956. This is despite no help from the Centre. In contrast, the residual AP is struggling to come to terms with its ill-balanced economy. This also clearly underlines the loss of Telangana revenue to the Andhra region in the united State to keep the united state's budget balanced.

Telangana is a sovereign, self governing and top performing state in India.

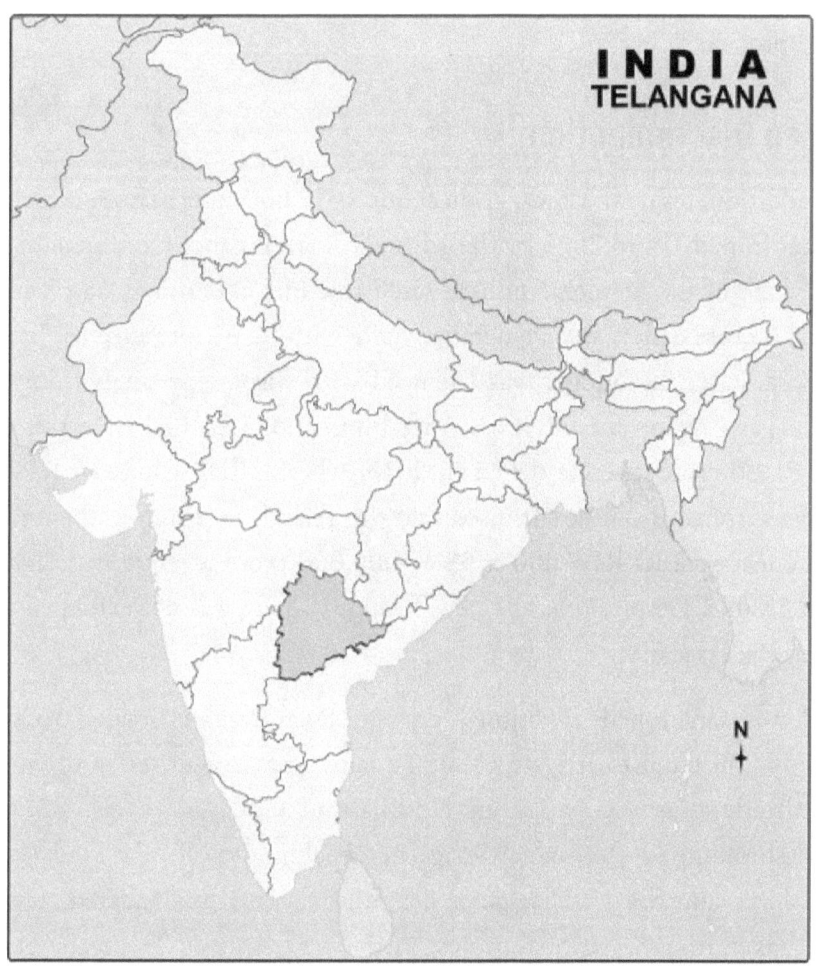

A look at APRA 13th schedule reveals the discrimination. Residual Andhra Pradesh was sanctioned 10 national-level institutions like IIT, NIT, IIM, IISER, Central University, Petroleum University, Agriculture University, IIIT, AIIMS, Tribal University and a National Institute of Disaster Management and one state port, apart from examining the feasibility of 8 infrastructural projects (10+2+8 =20). Whereas for Telangana, it was one Tribal University, one Horticulture University and examining the feasibility of 4 infrastructural projects. (2+4 = 6). There is also a big disparity in the sanction and execution of these institutions and projects.

Deep Discrimination

In addition, residual AP was given about Rs 52,000 crore as revenue deficit grant from 2014 to 2025 by the 14th and 15th Finance Commission. At the time of the merger, Andhra State came into the united state with a Rs 3.6 crore deficit and Hyderabad State with Rs 6 crore surplus. In the united state, the budget was balanced with surplus revenues from the Telangana region for 58 years. After bifurcation, residual AP registered Rs 7,300 crore revenue deficit in 2015, whereas Telangana saw Rs 238 crore surplus. It can be surmised that the Telangana region in the united state lost at least Rs 7,000 x 58 = 4,06,000 crore revenue in terms of 2015 value. Despite this, the new Telangana State was not extended any financial assistance.

AP was sanctioned a national project, Polavaram, estimated to cost Rs 60,000 crore to irrigate about 10 lakh acres ayacut, 80% of which is already under irrigation in Krishna and Godavari deltas. But the Kaleshwaram project, which irrigates 18 lakh acres of new ayacut and stabilizes another 18 lakh acres old failed ayacut was rejected. It was not taken up as a national project in the water-starved Telangana State. Projects like Mission Kakatiya, Mission Bhagiratha, were not funded in spite of the recommendation of Rs 24,000 crore grant by the Niti Aayog, which is only a part of their total estimate. In such a scenario where is the injustice to Andhra Pradesh as alleged by the Prime Minister in Parliament.

Instead of complimenting and felicitating the new emerging State, denigrating the State's formation time and again in Parliament by the Prime Minister in such uncharitable terms is undemocratic and unconstitutional. The Central government should know that Telangana is no more a political orphan. It is a sovereign State on its own and a rightful member of the Indian Union. And it is among the few States funding national economic development with their higher contribution of Central taxes to the national exchequer. Telangana demands its due place in the comity of States in India.

48

G.O. ON RIVER WATER IS ANTI-FEDERAL

(Telangana Today | 15 May, 2022)

The Ministry of Jal Shakti issued a gazette notification on July 15, which gives complete control of all projects in the basins of Godavari and Krishna in Telangana and Andhra Pradesh to the Krishna River Management Board (KRMB) and the Godavari River Management Board (GRMB). The notification usurping all the rights of the two States came into effect from October 14. The protocols for the takeover are being worked out but there is not much headway because of the ill-conceived plan.

The Telangana Development Forum found it to be unconstitutional and anti-federal. It made a memorandum on it to the President and the Centre demanding immediate withdrawal of the draconian order.

There is not much of a problem in the Godavari basin since adequate water is available in the river, though taking over the projects there is a disagreeable invasion. But a virtual war is going on between Telangana and Andhra Pradesh on sharing Krishna waters. It is a legacy of the erstwhile united AP. Telangana was unable to get its legitimate share, despite owning 68% of the catchment area of the Krishna basin.

Bachawat Tribunal

The Bachawat Tribunal, KWDT1, in 1976, awarded 800 tmc to erstwhile Andhra Pradesh, which included the Telangana region. Later, the AP government in the united state divided that water into its three regions. This was felt to have been done arbitrarily without regard to the catchment and cultivable area, and the population, which were supposed to be the basic criteria for such a division.

Region	Allocation	%	Max use	Average Use	Catchment sq km	%
Rayalseema	146	18	155.32	116.15	5,414	18.4
Andhra	369.74	45.6	703.82	511.98	3,860	13.1
Telengana	295.26	36.4	241	198.32	20,167	68.5
Source: Irrigation department (1977-78 to 2007-08)						

The AP government then went into over utilization of the surplus and floodwaters for the Andhra region with many non-statutory government orders. For that, the Srisailam reservoir has become a backyard water trough for Rayalaseema, making manipulations in the drawdown levels in the hydel project, in the name of drinking water to Chennai, Telugu Ganga project, Srisailam Right Bank Canal and all kinds of 'srujala sravnthis' to take Krishna water to irrigate the old Tungabhadra ayacut and also all the way to Penna basin areas, which are outside the Krishna basin.

sanciliary

Another project is Pulichintala, constructed with 45 tmc capacity. The reservoir submerges 30,000 acres of Telangana lands but the ayacut is entirely in Andhra. Even in the Nagarjuna Sagar project, the ayacut, which was supposed to be 7.5 lakh acres for Andhra and Telangana each, ended up with more than 15 lakh acres to Andhra and 6-7 lakh acres to Telangana. The Jurala project in Mahabubnagar — which was allotted 19.11 tmc — ended up utilising 6-7 tmc only for irrigation. It is an accumulation of such inequitable utilization of water in the Andhra region in between KDWT-1 award and before and after the bifurcation of the State with the GOs which have no statutory sanction that is considered illegal. The latest Rayalaseema LI scheme is the last straw.

Brijesh Kumar Tribunal

The Brijesh Kumar Tribunal, KWDT2, came into existence to review the shares of the Krishna riparian States as a continuation to KWDT-1, in 2010. It was about to give its final award in 2013, but it was stayed because of the bifurcation. Telangana wanted the Centre to start the Tribunal proceeding afresh as it was not a party to the earlier KWDT-1 and KWDT- 2 adjudications.

The KWDT2 was extended with the express purpose of review and redistribution of water between Telangana and Andhra Pradesh and also to make project-wise specific allocation as per the provision in the AP Reorganization Act, 2014. It is based on the Interstate River Water Disputes Act, 1956, (IRWD Act), which says whenever the riparian States are not able to reach amicable agreements on their own on sharing of inter-State river waters, Section 4 of the IRWD Act provides a dispute resolution process in the form of a Tribunal. As per Section 5.2, the Tribunal shall not only adjudicate but also investigate the matters referred to it by the Centre and make suitable awards.

Inter-State Dispute

Telangana had requested the Centre to issue necessary terms of reference for the Tribunal to review the water shares and make project-wise specific allocations. It has also withdrawn the cases pending before the Supreme Court, as advised by the Centre, to facilitate the issue of terms of reference. But the Centre did not do so as promised by it. Instead, it has issued the GO to take over all projects.

The KWDT-2 is still in office. Instead of referring the matter to the Tribunal in all seriousness, the Centre dodged the issue, indulging in ineffective Krishna river board meetings, wasting over seven years. It is a complex inter-State issue. There is no better way than the ongoing or new Tribunal to adjudicate for a long-lasting solution.

It is incomprehensible for the Centre to have stonewalled the issue for 7 years. And now it is indulging in an unconstitutional takeover of the projects in the two river basins. This is resulting in obstructing Telangana from completing the projects for the earlier unutilised share of its water and thwarting its bid for more allotment as a new State. It is clearly political discrimination.

The Centre should understand that now Telangana is a separate State and has the right to demand its fair share of river waters.

49

TELANGANA SCORES A BULL'S EYE

(Telangana Today | 27 April, 2022)

Telangana on June 2, 2014, became the 29th State of India. Many new States were created after independence — some on a linguistic basis and some on tribal identities, geography and culture. The statehood of Telangana was different from other new States. It was for political freedom. It was a demerger of the earlier coercively merged State, after a prolonged struggle for 58 years.

It was felt that it will be difficult for Telangana to sustain itself as a separate State. But all the hypothetical in-certitudes proved incorrect. On the contrary, Telangana not only vindicated its statehood but also established itself as the fastest-growing new State in the country.

Revenue Generation

The potential of the region was grossly underestimated by the critics in their actuated thinking. Hyderabad state, the forerunner of Telangana, was sufficiently large and had a self-sustaining revenue. In 1956, as estimated by the State Reorganization Commission (SRC), the per capita revenue of Telangana and Andhra regions was Rs 15.54 and Rs 10.53 respectively in a ratio of 1.43:1.00. The trend has continued in the same vein. It was 1.58:1.00 in 2015-16 and 1.59:1.00 in 2020-21 in the CAG audited accounts. This underlines the comparative revenue generation capability in the two regions.

But, the central tax devolution and grants configuration was different. AP being a larger area with a higher population is garnering more of them. It was in the ratio of 1.00:0.75 in 2015-16 and 1.00:0.64 in 2020-21 in favour of Andhra. In addition, AP got about Rs 52,000 crore deficit grant from the Centre from 2015 to 2026. As per the State Finance Minister, the taxes collected by the Centre from TS from 2014-15 to 2020-21 amount to Rs 3,65,797 crore, of which the State has got back

Rs 1,68,647 crore only as devolution. It is the reverse for AP. The Centre collects less tax but remits more devolution to the State.

Economic Resilience

Despite this handicap, TS balanced its budget from 2014-15 to 2018-19 with some surplus revenue. During the two Covid years of 2019-20 and 2020-21, it reported a revenue deficit like all the States but within the stipulated limits. Whereas AP registered deficit all the years from 2014-15 to 2020-21 despite higher Central devolution and grants, including deficit grant every year. TS has about 74% of its State's own tax revenue (SOTR) in its total revenue, which is among the highest in the States. AP has about 51% and the States' average is 54%. This shows its revenue potential and the inherent economic resilience.

Among about 15 new States created in India after independence, Bombay-Gujarat (1960) and Punjab-Haryana (1966) have some similarities with the Andhra-Telangana division. Both Gujarat and Haryana surged ahead after separation and are now on the frontline. It is the same case with Telangana. Separation gave it political freedom and full use of its resources for itself. Telangana followed Gujarat and Haryana, the two very successful States post-bifurcation. The compound annual growth rates of GSDP and per capita GSDP of Telangana are better than these States. That makes Telangana the fastest-growing new State. These two States which were kept bilingual post-1956 and were bifurcated subsequently, realised their potential after separation. If Telangana and Andhra were kept separate as recommended by the SRC in 1956 or divided in 1969 when the opportunity came, they would have developed like other premier States in the country.

But all new States formed did not get that kind of progress. In the three States formed in 2000, Uttaranchal did very well, Chhattisgarh is making steady progress but Jharkhand is yet to make that grade. Many northeast

States continue to be overly dependent on the Centre's dole-outs. So it depends on the States' inherent economic strengths and political leadership. Strategisation, bold conception and execution of projects, and the prudential management of the State Budget are important. For the good fortune of TS, all these things have come into play in the last 8 years to make the desired progress.

Praise for Progress

There is wide recognition and appreciation for the progress made by Telangana. NITI Aayog's publication ArthNITI in its 7th volume, 31 August 2021, wrote a special feature on Telangana. NITI Aayog also said, "Telangana has clocked a CAGR (compound annual growth rate) of more than 11 per cent, since 2015-16. The State's economy has grown at an average annual rate of more than nine per cent since its formation, significantly higher than the growth rate before its formation". NDTV made an exclusive documentary titled 'Telangana, a Phoenix rises'. These reports lend great credence to TS' progress.

Critics may say whatever, the statistics provided by CSO, CAG, RBI, and NITI Aayog reveal the facts. In the power sector, TS which was struggling with 7,600 Mw inadequate power in 2014, increased it to 17,300 Mw in 2020-21 and is reaching 25,000 Mw by 2023. Spending Rs 1,28,000 crore, irrigation was increased to 90 lakh acres with 190% gross cropped area. Through the ease of doing business, the State attracted Rs 2,32,000 crore in investments. In the IT sector, exports reached Rs 1.5 lakh crore in 2020-21. About 450 welfare schemes have been implemented, making it a well-balanced infrastructure and welfare spending. This has been done without extra help and in uneasy political relations with the Centre.

It is a stellar performance by the Telangana government. Yet, there is a long way to go. Though on the macroeconomic side it is doing very well, at the micro-level, there are several censorious issues like in other States.

There is a need to take good governance to the lower rungs enabling the progress made at the top to percolate to the ground level. The revenue deficit which has crept into the Budget during the Covid years needs to be corrected. The State-Centre relations need to be improved for better coordination and financial support. There is a need to consolidate the ongoing schemes before embarking on new mega capital investments for better budgetary management like in the past years.

50

TELANGANA 8TH ANNIVERSARY - THE PROGRESS

(Telangana Today | 3 June, 2022)

June 2, 2022, marks the eighth anniversary of Telangana State's formation. In these 8 years, the State's forward march was very eventful and inspiring. For a region which was denied its statehood for six decades, forced to be in the company of a majority region and was fighting with its back to the wall for its rightful share of its own region's resources, it is very commendable progress. A revelation of its denied potential and proving wrong the skeptics as well as an avowed vindication of its ardent protagonists.

At the peril of repetition, we need to recount Telangana's outstanding progress among the comity of States in the nation on its anniversary. It has risen to a position of above 5 in the larger States in terms of GSDP and per capita GSDP. The erstwhile united state was hovering at the 15-18th position before 2014. In most of the macroeconomic indicators too, it has secured its place among the top. Its Budget performance is acknowledged to be very prudential. Telangana has made a mark in every important socioeconomic indicator in these eight years. Official figures and estimates of the national institutions confirm it.

Little Acknowledgement

But the two national parties and other local parties in the State refuse to acknowledge it. The Congress does not talk about progress but indulges in perverse personal and family invectives. The BJP local leaders instead of trying to get help from their ruling Centre, promote anarchy and disgruntlement for their own political benefit. Other local parties like the TJS simply indulge in knee-jerk reactions of rejection of everything the Telangana government does.

The media is a peculiar mixture, dominated by 'two Telugu States' (a euphemism for Andhra) media, both print and digital. There are some local anti-Telangana and some pro-Telangana outfits. The latter is dubbed as pro-government, blithely by the antagonists. Even if they report the official Central and State data and the ground level situation as it is, it will be billed as pro-TS government. Yet, the Telangana media reporting dedicated news on the State's progress is doing a fine job. It has shown its merit and brought the real progress of the State to the fore.

The progress made by Telangana in the last eight years needs to be reviewed against the backdrop of its formation. Many States were carved in India after 1956. But only a few were created through bifurcation of old States, like Mumbai-Gujarat and Punjab-Haryana. Andhra-Telangana is not a bifurcation of the original old State. It is the demerger of two merged States. It was a conditional merger. There was disaffection between the two since the beginning. The States Reorganisation Commission (SRC) did not recommend it. The Centre forced it for political reasons. They did not gel like other linguistic States. There were vehement intermittent revolts against it with a great deal of loss of life.

Centre's Apathy

It was the misfortune of Telangana to have fallen for the wrong political calculations of the Centre, getting a very raw deal in its forcible merger with Andhra in 1956. The Centre had revised its decision in the case of Bombay-Gujarat and Punjab-Haryana and bifurcated them. They flourished better after separation. Subsequently, there were many such State divisions with several dimensions. In 2000, three States were created which were not in the purview of the SRC and their struggle for separate States was not as intense as in Telangana. Despite all these examples, everybody who was somebody professed that the demerger of Telangana was wrong and would trigger many such divisions. But nothing of that sort happened, except providing a profound new lease of life to the suppressed Telangana.

Nearly all the Andhra intelligentsia never appreciated the desire of Telangana people for demerger. They said it was unconstitutional, unscientific and irrational. They also solicited opinions from outside the State from eminent personalities like Kuldip Nayyar in support of their refusal to demerger. They wrote a book 'Refuting an agitation – 101 lies and dubious arguments of Telangana separatists'. Sanjaya Baru, former media adviser to Prime Minister Dr Manmohan Singh, released the book in New Delhi. Ashok Malik, renowned columnist, and Ajay Sahni, Executive Director of the Institute for Conflict Management, spoke on the occasion. They did not talk on why it is not justified like in the case of other earlier mentioned divisions later than 1956 and the need to make Telangana people go through such conflagration for as long as 58 years.

Discrimination Continues

As if the 58-year ordeal is not enough, the BJP Central government from 2014 started its own snatch of discrimination against Telangana. It called the division 'killing mother and saving the child' and said the Telangana Bill was not passed properly. Added to it, it cosied up to residual Andhra Pradesh and kept Telangana at an arm's length politically, in the first term after the merger. In the second term, it has become hostile outright. It has withheld central funds in a wilful manner, employed a deliberate political squeeze on the State – did not provide flood relief to Hyderabad and buy rice from the State, jeopardized Telangana irrigation projects with its draconian takeover of river water projects on Godavari and Krishna, did not sanction national institutes, medical colleges, Navodaya schools, so on and so forth.

It also made big political raids on the State to win the GHMC election and a few by-elections to corner the TRS to wrest the political initiative from it. It denigrated the State's development with unsubstantiated allegations, personal attacks on the Chief Minister and his government, and treated Telangana in a very condescending manner, exhibiting unseemly political phobia. It is a very surprising political attitude of a Central government towards a newly formed State. Leave alone helping it, trying to squeeze it politically to subjugate it is very undemocratic and does not behoove a national government.

In such circumstances, the progress made by Telangana is all the more commendable. The progress and achievements have vindicated in full the grievance, claim and aspiration of the progenitors and activists of the separate State. It is all because of the fine culmination of the State's inherent economic strengths and pragmatic political leadership. Strategization, bold conception and execution of projects, and the prudential management of the Budget proved to be key. For the good fortune of Telangana, all these things have come into play in the right measure at the right time to make the desired progress. Viva la Telangana!

51

NATIONAL PARTIES STOOP LOW IN STATE

(Telangana Today | 27 August, 2022)

The people of Telangana had elected the Telangana Rashtra Samithi (TRS) with 63 seats out of 119 for the new State's maiden government. The TRS government has implemented a mixed development plan of capital-intensive infrastructure with socioeconomic welfare schemes, commensurate with the objectives of the new State. For the capital investment, it undertook big projects like power, irrigation and infrastructure for their accelerated implementation, which were deliberately neglected in the united state. The State government invested heavily using its own resources and borrowings commensurate with its growing revenue and GDP. It has managed its Budget prudentially, without any additional help from the Central government. Because of its good show, the TRS won the mandate again in the 2018 Assembly elections with a massive majority of 88 seats.

In the second essay too, the TRS has continued its progressive development programme. Massive power projects, irrigation projects and city infrastructure, industrial, IT development etc, were made on a fast track. It is an outstanding performance and is duly recognised by the related national institutions. The State has improved its national economic development indices commensurate with its effort and achievements. In many macroeconomic indicators, it has climbed up to around the top 5 places in the national standings. In the united state, the position was around 15.

Some disputable political and administrative issues are there at the ground level but at the macro level, the State has acquitted itself very well. And all that was in consonance with the accelerated reconstruction plan of the new State. While the ruling TRS was engaged in the reconstruction of the new State in the right earnest, the opposition was indulging in peculiar pessimistic politics.

Congress

The Congress felt that since it has granted statehood, the power in the State was its right. But the people decided otherwise. The four-and-a-half years of heartrending dithering on the implementation of the declaration of the State formation and the loss of about 1,500 lives cost them their share in the power. But the party did not realize it. And now its role as the opposition is far from being constructive. It always opposed every move of the government in the reconstruction of the State with wild allegations. People understood it and gave it a suitable verdict in the 2018 elections too. Yet, it continued the same illogical opposition to the reconstruction of the State, giving an impression that their leaders do not have any idea of development except the obsession for the elusive power.

Bharatiya Janata Party

The BJP, the other national party, was on the fence in the formation of the Telangana State. After the BJP came to power in 2014, it did not treat Telangana with respect. It preferred Andhra Pradesh over Telangana for strange reasons. But the AP electorate did not favour it. It condescended with Telangana as long as the TRS supported its Bills in Parliament in its first term. In the second, BJP gradually became hostile to the TRS government. It has not helped the new State in any special way except with the statutory funds in both terms. It neither has the idea for the reconstruction of the State nor the intention to help it. It has denied sanction of funds on several counts despite recommendations of national institutions and in many other economic exigencies. Its winning a few MP seats in the 2019 general elections has ignited its political ambition in Telangana.

Of late, the BJP has started making many political incursions into the State, like creating by-elections and making big political raids into the State in the name of every election and occasion. It has also started to employ serious financial squeeze on the State to make it vulnerable to its political dominance. On the development front, the BJP's performance at the national level is on the decline since 2014. In the States, particularly in its long-ruled States, the progress is not comparable with Telangana. Even its best-advertised State Gujarat is lagging behind Telangana in economic progress, now. Thus though it is trying to gatecrash into Telangana electorally, it does not promise any better economic progress than the incumbent TRS, besides lacking the requisite regional Telangana ethos.

Local Parties

Coming to the local political parties, the newly-emerged Telangana Jana Samithi party, comprising some disgruntled elements from the Telangana Udyamam, is making some political noises in the State. It does not have any particular political or economic model, except opposing the TRS and its economic development plan at every step. It is regularly hobnobbing with other parties in trying to discredit the ruling TRS. It joined hands with Andhra TDP, the arch enemy of Telangana, in 2018 to form the so-called 'Maha Kootami' to dethrone the TRS government. It has opposed almost every project of the TRS government and tried to create obstacles, indicating its lack of constructive thinking on the reconstruction of the State. It also follows the national parties in trying to deprecate the TRS government in all and sundry matters.

The political climate in Telangana is caught between the fast reconstruction of the State on one side and the negative political skulduggery on the other. The national parties, except trying to capture power by any means, do not have any will or strategy of reconstruction of the State. Given the history of the State, they should have developed a meaningful regional party as a constructive opposition like in Tamil Nadu and Kerala, which is perhaps good for the State. But this too did not happen. The local outfits are disgruntled for their individual aspirations. In the milieu, it appears that the national parties are no good for the forward movement of the State.

Thus, there does not appear to be a credible alternative to the TRS for the time being to take the development momentum created by it forward beyond 2023-24. Neither the national parties nor the local political outfits in the State show the necessary wherewithal or the will to do it. They sound and act too pessimistic and too self-absorbed for the task.

52

DEFEAT OF BJP'S COVERT MOTIVES

(Telangana Today | 24 September, 2022)

It is a well-known fact that Hyderabad was the last princely State to join the Indian Union. While the whole of India got independence on 15th August 1947, Hyderabad State got its freedom from Nizam on 17 September 1948. There was some eventful history running up to the integration of Hyderabad State into the Indian union on that day.

In that history, the Communists, the Razakars and other freedom fighters, the Nizam, the Indian government and the Indian army played their different roles. The interpretation of their roles and the modus operandi of the celebration of the 'D' day became so controversial that it resulted in the non-celebration of the eventful day. Now taking advantage of the chronic ambiguity in the matter, the BJP and the Centre raked up a new political contention in Telangana.

Many Views

September 17 was in dispute for its celebration, its name and the credit for the integration of the State into the union by different political groups since 1948. There was no consensus on the nomenclature and the mode of celebration. Some said it is liberation, some annexation, some termed it integration and some even said it was treason.

The extremist Communists and Muslims supporting Razakars called it treason, for their own reasons. The others among them called it liberation. The majority of democrats called it integration. Because of the many debatable views, religious and political overtones and the bias of the ruling governments from time to time, the event was not celebrated officially since 1948 and that became a serious bone of contention amongst all political groups.

The BJP or its progenitors were not in any way involved in the freedom struggle of Hyderabad State, as they were not in the national independence struggle too. Nor was the party taking much interest in the celebration of the integration day all these years. All of a sudden this year, as part of its political slugfest with the ruling TRS party and as part of its grand plan of annexing Telangana in south India, the BJP national party evinced a great deal of interest in the event and wanted to celebrate it as liberation day, for creating a Hindu-Muslim divide in Hyderabad and Telangana as it is doing elsewhere as part of its Hindutva majority nationalism concept.

Building Plot

As a run-up to it, the BJP held its national executive meeting in Hyderabad. Almost the entire political pantheon of BJP descended on Hyderabad – 18 CMs, all MPs and the party 'hastis' were there. Their national leaders were nominated for each of the 119 constituencies for political brainwashing for the next Assembly elections in the State. In continuation, there were regular military-like political raids on Telangana by the BJP Cabinet Ministers, particularly by Home Minister Amit Shah, trying to ruffle the feathers of the TRS government, creating some incongruous political incidents. Amit Shah planned a mega event to celebrate 17th September as Liberation Day on behalf of the Centre in Hyderabad, without the consent of the State government. As is their wont to usurp local history to corner the opposition State governments.

To counter this predatory politics of the BJP, the TS government launched a three-day 'National integration Day' diamond jubilee celebration from September 16, to commemorate the 75-year-old integration of Hyderabad State with the Indian union. In Telangana as part of the united State of AP for 58 years and 8 years in its own State, the people have forgotten this controversy and are living amicably in a secular frame of mind.

The BJP which has nothing to do with Hyderabad state joining the union in 1948, trying to reignite the passions of 1948, is deplorable. The Telangana government has promoted the all-important Hindu-Muslim amity and forged ahead with a stable, progressive and peaceful State, and has made it a model to other States in the country. In that context, Chief Minister K Chandrashekhar Rao's idea of celebrating 17 September as National Integration Day instead of Liberation Day was commensurate with the democratic thinking and the Hindu-Muslim unity in the State for the last 75 years.

Celebrating Oneness

It was reported that the state-sponsored Telangana National Integration Day celebrations were held on a grand scale across the State. Ministers, MLAs, Collectors, SPs, Police Commissioners and other officials, students, youth and women took part in great numbers. The participation was beyond expectation. It included padayatras, dances to the drum beats and bike rallies. People from different walks of life joined it holding national flags. The rallies saw the participation of about 15,000 people in every constituency, totalling about 20 lakh people throughout the State. The slogans of 'Jai Telangana and Jai Bharat' echoed across the State. The CM hoisted the national flag in the Public Gardens and addressed a huge meeting at Fateh Maidan stadium.

The AIMIM held a bike rally in the Old City on the 16th of September. The rally was led by AIMIM chief Asaduddin Owaisi and attended by thousands of locals and party workers. Owaisi hoisted the national flag and addressed the meeting. He said his party is not run by the descendants of Qasim Rizvi, the leader of Razakars. Targeting the BJP for celebrating Liberation Day, he said the party should understand the multifaceted nature of the region's history and promote harmony instead of using it as an opportunity to create a feud.

In comparison to the celebrations by the State government, the meeting of the BJP and its rallies were reported to be a damp squib. It looked like much ado about nothing. It exposed the superfluousness and untenable political intentions of the BJP. It also exposed its double standards as it left out Junagadh in Gujarat, the princely state that was integrated into the Indian union in a similar fashion. While the people of Telangana have forgotten the animosities of 1948 and have imbibed a secular way of life, the BJP wants to revive the old animus, to polarize the communities.

But the bold and positive proposal by the CM of Telangana and the magnificent rallying of Telangana people for the national sentiment defeated the ulterior motives of the BJP roundly. And made 17th September 2022, the maiden National Integration Day for Telangana, an unqualified success.

53

BHARAT RASHTRA SAMITHI CAN BE A GAME-CHANGER FOR INDIA

(Telangana Today | 5 October, 2022)

The idea of floating Bharat Rashtra Samithi (BRS), an all-India political party, was hanging in the air for some time now. It was finally launched on October 5. The idea could be executed because the national parties such as Congress and BJP, who have been ruling the country, have lost their federal character. Several regional parties in States have emerged in the last several years, creating political confusion in the country. But the last eight years of BJP's rule in the country and the rapid weakening of Congress during this period have exposed a political vacuum. The BRS can fill this vacuum.

The Congress has been reduced to a shadow of its former self and has its governments only in a few States. The BJP came to power at the Centre in the name of NDA and has grown into a political leviathan. It has its own or participating governments in most States, which have become the extensions of the BJP-led Central government. The non-BJP State governments are at the receiving end and have been subjected to the dictates of the Central BJP government.

It has upset the federal nature of the relationship between the Central and State governments, which was the arrangement of the Constitution. In that context, the idea of BRS is the concept of a national party that can act as a federal national political party. In that the national party can think, plan and strategize to achieve inclusive national development. The State units can do it for the States and the plans are dovetailed into national plans, reviving the federal relationship between the Centre and States, as intended by the Constitution.

The debate of the party is not on economic development — of improving the nation's economy, improving the economic lot of States, or monitoring and evaluating the progress of backward States. The debate is on the past governments, past history and controversial historical incidents, which were asked to be closed by the Supreme Court. Majority nationalism and the non-implementable citizenship Acts, National Registers etc. The reforms are not on the issues agreed upon in Parliament by discussion or on the national need, but on their political goals, which, of course, have not reached their logical end. The grandiose schemes/projects are mostly either aborted in the beginning or struggling to go forward because of the lack of comprehension and holistic approach.

The Central administration is micro-managing the States, foisting the elections, trying to win the elections to spread its religious ideology, and is not focused on economic growth and overall development. The Planning Commission, which was semi-autonomous, was scrapped and made fully political in the name of reforms, with the so-called Niti Aayog which has not shown any improvement over the earlier. The terms of reference of Financial Commissions have not changed much. The funds are distributed in a routine manner without evaluating the progress made by the States receiving the larger funds in earlier years. The share of States gets reduced. The so-called poor States are staying poor and continue to get the Center's gratis. The good States give more and get less as usual as though they are penalized for their good performance.

Like always, some seven-eight States contribute high central taxes to the Centre, which are to be distributed to other States in the name of Central devolution and grants. This too, is not because of any proactive economic inducements by the Centre. It is because of the States' inherent economic strengths that they do better. It is only States like Telangana that are punching stronger than their weight despite receiving much less than what they are contributing to the Centre. But the flagship BJP States of UP and MP, among others, continue to garner the major share of Central devolution and grants. There has been no change in the economic weight of these States in the last eight years of the BJP rule.

The principal opposition, Congress, is in a weak position because of its internecine squabbles and lack of energetic and committed leadership at its helm. The ruling BJP is not doing good for the nation. In such circumstances, there is a big scope for a third national party, which can take their position to guide the nation forward with a progressive federal economic development plan, which is awfully lacking now. In that, the BRS, launched by KCR, seems to have the necessary credentials to fill that vacuum. KCR has fought for the creation of Telangana State and, in the last eight years as CM of Telangana, has moulded the State into a frontrunner with prudential management of its finances and implementing of a comprehensive development programme, making the State's net worth better than any other State. All this was done despite the non-cooperation and the deliberate financial squeeze by the Centre because of its political rivalry.

KCR has toured the nation, met several State and national leaders and discussed strategies for the nation's comprehensive rapid economic development with subject-matter specialists. His idea is not to just celebrate the 3.5-trillion economy (6) and continue to gloss over $2,500 PCI (160). It is to take India to a middle-level PCI like $10,000 in a short span, to make its economic development meaningful. If it catches the imagination of the people and political leaders across the country, it can be a game-changer for India, like the TRS was for Telangana.

54

AP'S CAPITAL DREAM KEEPS CRASHING

(Telangana Today | 17 October, 2022)

It is over eight years since the united Andhra Pradesh was divided, yet the residual AP is not able to establish its capital. About 15 new States were created after independence, in 1947, but there was no such long-drawn dispute over the capital in those States. In the case of AP, it has been made so complicated that it looks like they cannot come out of it even in the next few years.

It all started in 1953. The Andhra region, even before the States Reorganisation Commission took shape, separated from the erstwhile Madras state. It aspired to get Madras city as its capital but failed. It could have worked on a plan B of having Madras as a joint capital, like Chandigarh, as Madras was on the border of the two States. It could have settled the capital issue and the State's revenue problem. It was a big miscalculation on the part of Andhra, which is affecting it even today.

Persisting Problem

They chose Kurnool as capital and suffered heavily with a revenue deficit, from 1953 to 1956. Then, taking advantage of the SRC and manipulating the Centre, they gatecrashed into Hyderabad state. It solved its capital and deficit revenue problems with Hyderabad city as capital and the surplus revenue of Hyderabad state. But the merger started another inequity between Andhra and Telangana regions in the united State, which prolonged for 58 years till they were demerged in 2014.

The demerger brought out the two old problems of capital and the revenue deficit, which were kept submerged in the united state. The State is getting revenue deficit grants from the Centre and somehow managing the deficit. But the capital issue is not getting solved. It has become intractable because of irreconcilable sectarian politics in the State. Unfortunately, political parties of the State have taken an adversarial position on the all-important capital issue and pushed it into an unmanageable awkward situation.

Several Precedents

In fact, there were several precedents in the country on capital cities of new States. The division of Bombay-Gujarat resulted in a moderate Gandhinagar as the capital for Gujarat, not another Bombay-like city. Madhya Pradesh ceded Nagpur, the 2nd tier city capital, to Maharashtra and chose Bhopal as its capital. Assam gave up its capital Shillong to Meghalaya and built Dispur as its own capital near Guwahati. Chhattisgarh built an integrated capital in Naya Raipur.

Other new States too settled into their capital towns as per their circumstances and requirements. There was no such fractious controversy as in AP. Moreover, there is no need for it as AP has several large towns and also large government land areas at many places to make a new capital.

The Centre offered to help residual AP with the selection of capital location and also financial aid to construct government infrastructure. Accordingly, the Sivaramakrishnan Committee toured the State and recommended a few places for the capital to be built on government lands.

But the maiden government did not even consider the report. Instead, it decided to build the capital in and around Amaravati in Guntur district acquiring about 35,000 acres in 30 villages, in a bizarre land pooling system of complicated financial implications. The matter was steamrolled in the Assembly.

The Central committee report was not placed in the Assembly even for a cursory discussion. The opposition did not demand for it. It was a bad legislative action. Civil society also did not react. The report contained some very sensible recommendations, in keeping with the situation of the new State. But all were thrown to the wind and an outlandish world capital concept was created, which was way beyond the requirement of the State. The Centre's promised assistance was limited to the bare minimum of government capital-building infrastructure. There was no FDI, as was overly advertised. So the whole project has come unstuck because of its bad conception and impracticability.

The TDP government was trounced at the hustings in 2019. Though the YSRCP won the massive mandate, it was left with an escalating deficit budget and a rolling stone like the Amaravati project. The new government contemplated some changes in the project and brought in its own peculiar three-capital concept, which again brought several twists to the story via politics and judiciary. The objective of this government of making Visakhapatnam the administrative capital, Kurnool the judicial capital and leaving Amaravati as the legislative capital, is hanging in the air.

A P 3 Capitals

Unpractical Alternative

They could have followed any of the earlier instances of capital selection, like building a new capital near a city or town(s), as in the government lands in between Vijayawada and Guntur or near Tirupati. Or choose Vizag, the 10th largest city in the country by GDP with considerable urban infrastructure. Or a greenfield city in a place like Donakonda with plenty of government lands and situated in the middle of the State, to expand into a big city in future. It could have made the State afford the requisite capital infrastructure in the government lands, without much financial difficulty.

Instead, they chose the most fertile private land with a prohibitive financial implication, which the state could not afford. And it has some serious technical and environmental issues to contend with. The NGT has imposed several conditions, which will make the completion of the project very difficult.

The three-capital concept is also not a very practical alternative. Decentralization of development based on spreading capital infrastructure does not make much sense. Here, the Hyderabad example is also not appropriate because there was no centralized capital building in Hyderabad after 1956. Almost all the capital infrastructure was built before 1956. In a television discussion, it was said that if AP goes ahead with Amaravati it would require Rs 1 lakh crore and if it abandons Amaravati, the State may need to pay Rs 12,000 cr compensation. Even if the three-capital plan is upheld by the Supreme Court, it will be as daunting as building Amaravati because of the compensation conundrum.

It is a dicey situation to comprehend what will happen to AP's capital plan. It is not known when it will be solved and brought to its logical end. This is the result of the lack of egalitarian interest in the State's future and the egocentric political shenanigans by the caste and region-polarized political parties.

55

MUNUGODE BYPOLL IS A BLOT ON DEMOCRACY

(Telangana Today | 26 October, 2022)

All three – two national parties and the ruling TRS – have locked horns in a fierce battle for a prestigious win. The Congress wants to retain its seat, proving it is a censure for the betrayal of its candidate, and also that it is its stronghold. The BJP wants to wrest the seat to advertise its intending rise in the State. The TRS wants to take revenge on the BJP for the byelection debacles in Huzurabad and Dubbaka and cut short the brouhaha of its rise in the State.

Malafide Intentions

The very exigency of the byelection is questionable. The incumbent candidate resigned from the Congress and triggered a byelection for the express purpose of joining the BJP and becoming the candidate of the BJP in the election to give the party a chance of challenging the TRS. Rajgopal Reddy's resignation and joining the BJP may be right in letter but not in spirit. The malafide intentions are very clear.

Of course, the BJP has made such elections the new normal. If we see the happenings in the last eight years, in 10-12 States the BJP won elections by manipulating governments, with splits, links and several other dubious means. Winning elections or forming governments by hook or crook has become more important than ethics and democracy. The whole atmosphere is so vitiated, nobody knows who is in which party and which party is in power in the States at a given point. It is so ephemeral that it can change in just days, though the legislators" or State governments' tenure is supposed to be for five years. In comparison, similar shenanigans by the Congress earlier now look like small-time plays.

In the grand scheme of saffronisation of India, the BJP has been assiduously working on the spread of it in the States since 2014. In the case of Telangana (TS), which too came into existence in 2014, though the BJP supported the statehood during the campaign, it was on the fence in the end. In the deciding moments in Parliament, it almost backtracked but a section of the party prevented it. Narendra Modi and his Home Minister Amit Shah both have found fault with the method of formation of the new State and openly said it in Parliament and outside of it. They were partial to residual Andhra Pradesh for political reasons.

Centre's Harassments

In the first term, the Modi government was acting neutral with the TS government to get support for its Bills in Parliament. As its position became comfortable in the Rajya Sabha, it started keeping TS government at an arm's length. By the end of the first term, the divide increased. The BJP won 4 MP seats in the State in the 2019 elections. This stoked its ambition and it started targeting TS, politically and economically, for its saffronisation scheme. There were electoral raids on the State in the shape of interim elections. Its somewhat improved performance in these elections encouraged it to increase the intensity of its turf war. The local BJP leadership was encouraged to make an all-out effort to tarnish the image of the TRS with repeated unfounded allegations.

The BJP started applying financial squeeze on TS. Many projects slated for TS were diverted to other States. There were inordinate delays in releasing the regular funds and grants from the Centre. No central funds as recommended by the national institutions were sanctioned to the State. It refused to reimburse the rice procurement cost causing a very heavy financial burden to the State. It also caused trouble in granting permission for loans even within the agreed FRBM limits. Virtually, a financial siege was laid on TS by the Centre. Even for the projects earlier cleared and appreciated, problems are being created deliberately, affecting their progress or completion.

TS was singled out for high-octane political bullying. The BJP national executive meeting was conducted in Hyderabad and the whole of the BJP pantheon descended on the city in a big ostentatious show of strength. National BJP leaders were allotted to all the 119 constituencies for canvassing and local leaders were primed and allowed to make increased propaganda on the fictitious misrule and failure of economic development in the State. But all this did not work.

As if it was not enough, the BJP raked up Hyderabad State integration day on September 17, not celebrated for 60 years for several political reasons. The BJP taking advantage of the Hindu-Muslim element involved in it, tried to cause religious strife in the State. Regrettably, the Home Minister who is supposed to be the keeper of peace of the nation led the attempt. A Hyderabad liberation day was organized in Hyderabad presided over by the Home Minister, against the three-day State National Integration Day. Deservedly, the ulterior attempt failed miserably. The whole State celebrated National Integration Day with the spirit of nationality. Muslim political outfits and the Muslim population too joined the celebration exhibiting a great spirit of nationalism.

Undemocratic

Not making any headway, the BJP invented a new subterfuge in foisting the byelection in Munugode to keep the TRS and the TS government in a quandary. The idea is to win a byelection before the ensuing general elections and show the TRS in a poor light to make inroads into the State. It is a strange political thought. Politically bullying a State, squeezing it financially and trying to create religious strife are very undemocratic. And now foisting a false byelection to win over the State is a manifestly wrong political practice. In fact, the Munugode byelection is electoral fraud.

Here, the incumbent Congress legislator is made to resign and join the BJP to force the byelection. And he becomes the official candidate of the BJP in the seat vacated by himself. It is an open secret that he was given a Rs 18,000-21,000-crore contract for a project by the central government in a quid pro quo for enacting this fraud. It is reported that the candidate himself has vouched for it in public. There cannot be any more damning proof of perfidy than this.

It is unbecoming of the Centre to allow such electoral fraud. After all, India is a democracy and the largest democracy in the world, not a banana republic.

56

PREDATORY POLITICS OF BJP EXPOSED

(Telangana Today | 8 November, 2022)

The Moinabad farmhouse expose of political horse-trading is a revelation that should stun us all. It upstages such earlier happenings. Here the scheme was Rs 50-100 crore for each MLA, and it could be for 30 or even more MLAs. Had it been successful, it would have brought down the TRS government in Telangana.

In the expose, it is revealed that it has happened in eight States, with the involvement of thousands of crores of rupees. The details were brought out in a sensational expose by the TRS' counter maneuver. This extraordinary expose can have serious implications for politics in the country.

As usual and as is the wont in Indian politics, there was a cacophony of opinions on the episode. Some called it a farce or fiction, some others termed it a drama. It is argued that the politicians who exposed it themselves are not the paragons of virtue. So it is not such a sensational event as it was made out to be. But the fact is, the incident took place, and it went to the High Court which initiated certain proceedings against the actors involved in it. The case is on.

Turf War in Telangana

Horse-trading has only grown in the country. The loose anti-defection law and its partisan political interpretation by the authorities have not helped matters. The present Central government, which is enamored of so many reforms, has not brought in any worthwhile reform in it. On the contrary, amendments like removing the cap on donations to political parties and the audit on them, and the new electoral bonds have increased the money flow into the ruling political party coffers.

It is said that the BJP is the biggest beneficiary of anonymous political contributions from electoral bonds. It is also said the BJP is the richest political party in the country accounting for more than 70% of the assets of major political parties. This and the compulsive desire for the expansion of the BJP all over India have increased horse trading as never before.

In this background, the revelation in Moinabad does not come as a surprise. The BJP has been waging a tough turf war in Telangana in the last two years and was using all means to upstage the TRS in the State. The GHMC and a few by-elections were used to increase its vote share. It also used other political and economic means in the TRS government. It included economic siege on the State, withholding the regular funds and not extending any additional financial help from the Centre. It found fault with its schemes, which it had approved and appreciated earlier, and tried to stall them, causing a deliberate financial strain on the State.

The latest was foisting of Munugode by-election on the TRS to corner it and win the election by any means and show that the TRS is losing its ground in the State before the coming general elections. This by-election is an archetypal example of the predatory politics of the BJP. In this bizarre plot, K Rajgopal Reddy was inveigled into the BJP and made to resign from the Congress and as an MLA to force the by-election. Then he was made the BJP candidate in the by-election. The price for the whole artifice is a Rs 18,000-crore contract for mining in the Chandragupta coal mine in Jharkhand.

Mining Corruption

It is said that the Chandragupta opencast coal mine operated by Central Coalfields, a subsidiary of Coal India Limited, was awarded to Adani Enterprises Ltd, in a global tender bidding in December 2020, for about Rs 28,000 crore. But for reasons best known to the government, a second-time national tender was called for it in Feb 2021, cancelling the first. This time too the Adani firm participated. But Shashi Infra, belonging to Rajgopal Reddy, got the contract for Rs just 18,264 crore. It is reported that many bid conditions and other stipulations were altered to make the ineligible Shashi Infra eligible for the contract, violating the established norms. The experience of the company is in construction, roadworks, waterworks, etc. Its mining experience is said to be just 0.88%.

Rajgopal Reddy's gambit looked like a perfect quid pro quo act here. In the 2G spectrum case, wherein the BJP was the major electoral beneficiary, it was an alleged notional loss to the nation. Here it is a direct real loss of

Rs 8,000 crore. Rajgopal Reddy revealed the nexus between this contract and his becoming a BJP candidate openly during campaigning. It was also complained to the CEC. But as expected no action was taken.

Therefore, the predatory politics of the BJP, spending crores of illegal money toppling the legitimately elected State governments should not be taken lightly. This Moinabad poachgate is real and its exposure is very important to stop this rapacious politics of the BJP. The victory of the TRS in Munugode rejecting the electoral fraud endorses it emphatically. Telangana shows the way!

57

ANDHRAS' DESTABILIZING POLITICS

(Telangana Today | 7 December, 2022)

It's been eight years since separate Telangana was formed. But, the absurd politics of Andhras continues to create a nuisance for the State. With not much improvement in Andhra Pradesh, the earlier 'powerful' residents and important government functionaries continue to stay in Hyderabad, as the capital issue is not yet settled. They do not want to leave Hyderabad and do not identify with Telangana either. They call themselves people of 'two Telugu States,' a euphemism for Andhra. They have properties, voter and ration cards in both States. They milk both governments for their benefit. They vote for their caste parties in Andhra and Andhra parties in Telangana. A questionable duplicitous citizenship.

The progress of Telangana does not interest them. Some of them don the leadership mantle and indulge in a political rigmarole here. They canvass against the Telangana government and deride the progress made by the State. Some undertake political tours in Telangana boasting to bring down the present government and usher in a government, like in the united State, which was anathema to Telangana. Some go to Andhra and campaign against Telangana and its government, without much intelligible meaning in it. They talk condescendingly about the history and culture of Telangana. A peculiar mixture of chauvinism, misplaced victimhood and a vindictive mindset!

Unfounded Fear

There is nothing wrong if the people commemorate their Andhra roots in Telangana. After all, Andhra Pradesh is divided into two States, not into two countries like India and Pakistan. Many other States were divided in the country before. The people of those States are living amicably with each other. Punjab-Haryana and Maharashtra-Gujarat are two good examples. And the new States are progressing in cooperation with each other. That is the objective of the division of the States. Lakhs of people from other States are settled in Hyderabad and Telangana. They have integrated with Telangana society and are living harmoniously. Why our Andhra brethren do not like to live like that is a moot question.

Their grievance that they have to suffer due to Telangana is wrong. It is Andhra which is responsible for that. Firstly, the merger of Telangana with Andhra in 1956 was a historical blunder. It was a forced merger. It was a dire necessity for Andhra and was totally unnecessary for Telangana. That is why the merger was made with 14 pre-conditions in favor of Telangana but all the conditions were flouted in the united state with impunity.

Secondly, Andhra had a huge Budget deficit in 1956. Andhra always had more revenue expenditure than its income. Hyderabad state was revenue surplus. This continued from 1956 to 2014 in the merged State too. The deficit of Andhra was made good with the surplus from Telangana in all 58 years to balance the State's Budget. There was not much effort to increase the per capita revenue of Andhra in the united state. There is a basic difference in the revenue structure of both regions/States. The SOTR in the total revenue of the State in Andhra is around 50% only, while it is more than 70% for Telangana. The proportion of SOTR in the total revenue generally influences the financial situation of a State. (see infographics)

TS & AP Comparative financial position from 2015-16 to 2020-21

Amt.Rs.in Cr.

Details	2015-16 TS	2015-16 AP	2016-17 TS	2016-17 AP	2017-18 TS	2017-18 AP	2018-19 TS	2018-19 AP	2019-20 TS	2019-20 AP	2020-21 TS	2020-21 AP	Average TS	Average AP
SOTR	54389 (71.44)	44842 (50.58)	58190 (70.16)	49374 (49.89)	64345 (72.44)	53627 (51.04)	74681 (73.64)	62413 (54.47)	74957 (73.10)	60906 (54.86)	72751 (72.09)	60823 (51.93)	- 72.15	- 52.17
Per capita SOTR	15451	9077	16631	9994	18280	10856	21216	12634	21295	12329	20684	12312	18555	10978
C.taxes & Grants	21745 (28.56)	43806 (49.42)	24629 (29.74)	49610 (51.11)	24479 (27.56)	51436 (48.96)	26739 (26.36)	42168 (45.53)	27586 (26.90)	50358 (45.34)	28163 (27.91)	56313 (48.07)	27.85	48.07
Per capita CT & Grants	6178	8968	6997	10043	6954	10142	7596	8536	7837	10194	8000	11400	7112	9557
Total Revenue Receipts	76134	88648	82819	98984	88824	105063	101420	114581	102544	111034	100914	117136	90348	103662
Total Revenue Expenditure	75896	95950	81432	116178	85365	121214	97083	128569	108096	137475	123212	152677	89574	119877
Revenue Surplus(+) / Deficit(-)	(+)238	(-)7302	(+)1387	(-)17194	(+)3459	(-)16152	(+)4337	(-)13637	(-)6254	(-)26441	(-)22,298	(-)35541		
State GDP (Lakh Cr.)	5.78	6.042	6.58	6.85	7.53	7.93	8.61	8.63	9.70	9.74	9.85	9.52		
Per capita state GDP (Rs.)	140840	108002	159395	120676	180404	139680	204488	151173	228216	169519	257894	189930		
Loans Outstanding (% to GDP)	16.2	24.5	19.5	37.2	20.2	28.9	20.3	30.6	21.3	31	25.17	35.63		

1. SOTR (State Own Tax Revenue)
2. CT (Central Taxes)
3. 2015-16 to 2020-21 CAD audited accounts data is taken
4. The population figures to work out per capita data are of 2011 census, the latest available.(TS:3.52 Cr; AP:4.94 Cr:)
5. Revenue & Expenditure amounts are in Rs.Cr.; per capita in Rs; GDP in Rs.lakh Cr.

After the demerger, Andhra registered about Rs 11,000 crore revenue deficit in 2014 (which was in dispute & revised from from7302 cr.). Telangana gained that much and recorded a surplus Budget. In fact, it was the revenue of Telangana that the Andhra region was enjoying in the united state and it has now come back to Telangana. To offset it, the 14th and 15th Finance Commissions provided Rs 52,000 crore deficit grants from 2015 to 2026 to residual AP, in addition to meeting the entire revenue deficit in the first year of demerger. Such a huge deficit grant for a period of 10-12 years was never given to any other divided State in the country. Despite this, there is not much commensurate increase in the revenue income of Andhra. Its revenue deficit is increasing by the year.

Thirdly, there is also a general refrain from Andhras that AP has sustained a big loss because of the demerger. It is absolutely unfounded. In the united state, Telangana lost hundreds of lives, and a few lakhs of crores of its revenue. It also lost a great deal of river water, jobs, lands etc for which there is no estimation. In such a scenario, how is the demerger a loss to AP?

Biased Center

The Centre, as if Andhra is the sufferer, has sanctioned about 20 national/infrastructural institutions and other grants to it. A national project of Polavaram worth Rs 60,000 crore was sanctioned to AP despite Andhra drawing much more river water than it was eligible for. Even if a few institutions were mentioned in the reorganization, the Centre has not deemed to give them to Telangana so far.

As per the CAG audited accounts from 2014-15 to 2020-21, the amount given to AP as devolution and grants is Rs 2,93,691 crore and for Telangana, it is just Rs 1,53,341 crore. That shows the losses and gains of both the States in the division.

The BJP-led central government continues to give huge grants and other central funds to Andhra for its political reasons. In addition, it has imposed a financial siege on Telangana and is hampering its reconstruction with malafide political intentions. As if it is not enough, political outfits from Andhra are playing bizarre fractional politics here. The civil society of Andhra in Telangana should see the facts and promote responsible citizenship here since they have made it their home. Positive politics is welcome, but negative politics is subversiveness.

57

AP MUST SHELVE FALSE COMPLEX

(Telangana Today | 26 January, 2023)

The political and economic contours of both Telangana and Andhra Pradesh have now clearly emerged. Eight years is a long time for people to understand the ground realities and separate facts from fiction. It's time to draw a blueprint for sustainable development and progress depending on the strengths and resources of each State. The myths and false prestige of the past need to be shelved. Pragmatism and democratic cooperation must be ushered in for the benefit of both the States.

Fact Vs Fiction

However, it does not seem to be happening. Politicians, media and the educated elite from Andhra in Andhra Pradesh and in Hyderabad are repeating the same old fiction of developing Telangana at their cost. This facade worked before the demerger because of the unverifiable and fudged accounts in the united state. But post-demerger, the CAG audited accounts of the two States have made things quite clear.

The audited accounts are available from 2014-15 to 2020-21 which clearly show where the two States stand in their financial parameters.

After the demerger, the Centre continues to support residual AP's deficit Budget in place of Telangana.

Telangana is self-reliant and is forging ahead. Andhra was in a revenue deficit right from 1953 to 1956. The Budget in the united state for 58 years was in balance, regularly. Immediately after the demerger, residual AP registered a big revenue deficit of about Rs 11,000 crore in 2014-15, while Telangana reported Rs 238 crore surplus. That provides the true financial picture of the two regions. AP always had more revenue expenditure than its revenue income. It was the same while it was in Madras State, in separate Andhra and in united AP.

Hand Holding AP

The Finance Commission, both 14th and 15th, together has provided Rs 52,000 crore revenue deficit grant to AP from 2015-16 to 2025-26 averaging about Rs 5,000 crore every year. It is an exceptional and the highest deficit revenue dole-out to any divided State in the country. Yet, the revenue deficit of AP doesn't show any improvement. In fact, it is growing rapidly every year. It has grown from about Rs 11,000 crore in Rs 2014-15 to Rs 35,541 crore in 2020-21 — a hard and verifiable fact. And, every year, Andhra gets double the Central devolution than Telangana.

If we take the audited figures of the two States from 2015-16 to 2020-21, it reveals that AP has its average State Own Tax Revenue (SOTR) at 52% as against Telangana's 72% in their total annual revenue income. That means AP depends on Central devolution and grants to the extent of 48%, whereas Telanganas' dependence on it is 28%. This makes a big difference. In fact, Telangana gets much less amount of devolution than its contribution of central taxes to the Centre. AP collects less but gets more from the Centre.

Fiscal Prudence

The SOTR has a major significance in the Budget of a State. The average SOTR of States in the country is 46%. The top-performing States in the country have an SOTR of more than 65%. If we look at the RBI estimates from 2015-21 in this regard, only 8 States have more than 65% SOTR, including Telangana (75%), and these are the States leading the economic development of the country. (See infographics)

AP's high debt-to-GDP ratio, high quantum of freebies and off-budget borrowings etc are keeping it in the crosshairs of the Reserve Bank of India (RBI) for its financial risk, along with some other 10 States in the country. AP needs to work out its financial strategies to come out of that predicament of financial risk.

The Andhra elite must analyze those areas where the State is not doing good and bring it to the focus of the government so that the government takes suitable political actions to correct them. This outlandish dual State politics in Hyderabad will do no good, for themselves or the crossborder State they love. It is time they understood that what they were claiming all along with regard to Telangana is not correct. What Telangana people claimed in their 'udyamam' have become real.

It is deep pockets of government revenue and the prudential use of it that can make a State self-reliant in its Budget. It is time for the Andhra elite to come out of their hangover of false prestige and unfounded victimhood. They need to work hard to make their State financially sustainable.

59

CHANDRABABU NAIDU'S 'ANDHRA CHAUVINISM'!

(Telangana Today | 3 March, 2023)

N.Chandrababu Naidu is back in the game of narrating the old tales of his patronizing Telangana in the united Andhra Pradesh. His latest litany is that the people of Telangana ate rice for the first time only after the TDP came to power.

He said, "before the advent of TDP, the people ate only maize, ragi and bajra in Telangana. They had the privilege of consuming rice only after the TDP's rice scheme". He also said the TDP is the reason for wealth creation and good living standards in the region. It is a black lie.

Rice is grown in 'T' under thousands of MI tanks since ages.

TS' Contribution

Records show that Telangana had more than 40,000 minor irrigation tanks constructed from the medieval ages. Each village has one or two such tanks, under which, in kharif season, only rice can be cultivated in the wetland ayacut of the tanks and no other crop. People have been eating rice for as long as these tanks have come into existence. Other millet crops were grown in rain-fed dry lands and millets also formed a part of foodgrain as in the case of other parts of Andhra Pradesh. It is not like everybody was eating rice in Andhra and in Telangana, people started eating rice only after the advent of the TDP. It is a very ignorant and arrogant statement, reflecting the unbridled Andhra chauvinism of the TDP chief.

If he is referring to more rice production in the Andhra area, it was confined mostly to Godavari and Krishna delta areas in 3-4 districts. The rest of the areas in Rayalaseema, North Coastal and some upland areas of central coastal districts were as good or as bad as the agricultural lands of Telangana. Moreover, the delta lands produced coarse paddy like Akkullu and Hamsalu, which were poor in quality. Whereas, in Telangana, super fine rice varieties like Samabarlu/ Warangal rice (Hyderabad Rice-35) were grown for agro-climatic reasons. Even some semi-scented rice like Chitti mutyalu, Kakirekkalu (Kalabath) were also grown and eaten in Telangana. Even Andhras who wanted to eat fine rice had to mostly get it from the Telangana region.

Distorting Facts

If the TDP chief says that the rice scheme made the commodity affordable for the poor to eat, it could have made some sense. But saying that the whole of Telangana had the privilege of eating rice after the TDP's rice scheme is nothing but a cheap political statement. His claim that the TDP was the first to introduce the affordable rice scheme is also a lie as it was introduced by the Congress in Andhra Pradesh before them.

Anyway, what is the need for launching 'intintiki Telugu desham' programme in Hyderabad and crowing this false rice story in the separate Telangana State now after nine years of the State's demerger? Today, the TDP has no relevance in Telangana. The TDP led by Chandrababu Naidu had been the arch-enemy of the separate Telangana State. He was the reason for stopping, for around four-and-a-half years, the Telangana State declaration and causing the deaths of about 1,200 Telangana people. The people of Telangana rejected the TDP in 2014 and 2018 and the party is dying its natural death in the State.

Financial Strength

In the united state for 58 years from 1956 to 2014, the State budget was balanced without serious imbalance. But in 2015-16 after AP was demerged, residual Andhra Pradesh reported a big deficit of over Rs 11,000 crore whereas Telangana showed a Rs 238-crore surplus. Government statistics from 1956 to 2014-15 show that the per capita revenue of Andhra and Telangana was in the ratio of 1.00:1.43. The population of both regions are in the ratio of 5.0:3.5. If we analyze the Budgets of the two States from 2015-16 to 2020-21, for which the CAG audit is completed, the State own Tax Revenue (SOTR) of AP and TS is in the ratio of 1.00:1.60. Telangana's SOTR is around 73% while AP's only 51%. This shows the financial strength and difference in dependence of the two States on the Centre's devolution and grants.

That is broadly the configuration of the financial status of the two States. It all says that the Andhra region was not financially sustainable in its own State between 1953 and 1956 but was stable in the united state. After the demerger, Andhra State is again in the financial doldrums. Telangana is traveling comfortably with its balanced Budget, making rapid progress economically, like it was before the merger.

Thus, the Andhra politicians saying that they have taught lessons or provided things to Telangana makes a mockery of the truth. While politicians or self-centered people can say anything, what about the civil society or intelligentsia of Andhra which has a certain reputation to keep? People who judge the issue with objectivity based on verifiable facts are scarce. This chauvinism neither does justice to their State nor to themselves. A good example is Chandrababu Naidu himself who grew big because of the exploitation of Telangana and fell out because of its sabotage to it. He still cannot afford to leave it, yet denigrates it at will.

60

THE 'CROWN' OF TELANGANA

(Telangana Today | 28 April, 2023)

Telangana's struggle is like an independence war for the freedom of a nation. It went on for 58 years and about 1,500 people laid down their lives for it. Many new States were created/reorganized in India after independence. But none had to go through such a harrowing experience for such a long time. It needed a memorial commensurate with its sacrifice, struggle and pride. The new Secretariat and the Martyrs Memorial taking shape before it are to fulfill that great aspiration of the Telangana people.

Like always, the naysayers and the opposition parties lambasted the government on it. They said the old complex, which was good for the 23-district united state, was more than good for the new State which is less than half of it. But the government averred that the present complex was randomly built at different times and lacked infrastructural facilities like adequate parking, fire safety and modern features for a State secretariat.

The idea was mooted in 2016. The government alternatively contemplated finding a suitable place for the new complex elsewhere like at Chest Hospital grounds, Erram Manzil and Gymkhana grounds to avoid demolition of the present structures. But for various reasons, it did not materialize.

Laying Foundation

Because of its centrality in Hyderabad city and as the large part of the complex is old and required demolition, the government went back to the idea of building a brand-new integrated secretariat complex at the same site. A Cabinet decision to that effect was made on June 19, 2019. The foundation stone was laid on June 27. Meanwhile, a slew of public interest litigations was filed on the government decision in the High Court of Hyderabad.

A ministerial sub-committee and high-powered technical committees were constituted to study the state of the old complex to make suitable recommendations. The technical committee, in its report, found that it was not possible to make any changes to the conditions prevailing in the existing buildings.

There were eight blocks located in the congested lanes where fire service vehicles cannot enter and it was not feasible to have fire safety measures there. They observed that the secretariat complex had 10 blocks, with accommodation of 4.45 lakh square feet, of different ages ranging from more than 100 years to 20 years — varying from dilapidated condition to working condition. Except for two blocks, other blocks were reported to be in a rundown condition. The building blocks were disjointed and scattered over an area of 25.5 acres.

The repairs to the old buildings with the aged plumbing, electricity, etc, needed heavy expenditure. There were no adequate conference facilities, parking and a green area. The cost could be as good or even more than the new construction, if it was attempted to make the repairs and carry out renovation to create spaces and other suitable facilities, without demolition.

So, it was felt that it was better to demolish the existing structures and build an integrated building complex with modern facilities. The ministerial sub-committee concurred with it. The government took the decision. The proposed integrated building complex with seven floors was estimated to cost Rs 650 crore.

Various PILs

The main grounds of the PILs were: no need for demolition; not a priority; unilateral decision by the government and huge expenditure. The bench refused to interfere in the State government's decision saying it does not find any irregularity in the Cabinet decision. It dismissed the PILs filed separately between 2016 and 2019. Yet, the opposition to the new Secretariat continued. The Pradesh Congress Committee president of Telangana went to the National Green Tribunal (NGT) on the specious grounds of environmental damage. The NGT found no merit in the plaint and dismissed his plea.

Every State has a Secretariat or government building complex depicting the history, culture and ethos of its people. Karnataka has the grandest of them all, built in 1956. Karnataka was not short of buildings either in Bengaluru or Mysuru. Kerala, Himachal Pradesh and Tripura have beautiful Secretariat buildings. Even small States in the northeast region have beautiful government buildings depicting their architecture and culture. Ahmedabad and Naya Raipur Secretariats are modern examples of integrated Secretariat buildings.

There was nothing wrong if Telangana wanted to build a Secretariat depicting the architecture, culture and ethos of the State, in place of a drab and haphazard-looking agglomeration of old blocks. It is a new State and certainly needs to have its new identity. The Secretariat, the seat of power of the State government, is one of the embellishments of that identity. Even the Supreme Court concurred with the decision of the High Court.

Apart from the incongruity of the old structure, there was no need for a government to live in an unhappy place where the State's identity was ridden roughshod over for 58 long years. There was a need to have a complete break from the earlier feudal past and the later neo-colonial majoritarian rule in independent India to breathe a refreshing air of political freedom into the new State for Telangana, which they won so heroically.

Telangana's Quintessence

The new design depicts the Deccan-Kakatiya architecture and culture expressing Telangana's quintessence, with all the Indian Green Building Council norms, meeting the stipulations of fire safety, disaster management and other mandatory regulations. It has concrete structures on 2.4 acres of the 27.5-acre campus and the rest is dedicated to greenery, landscaping, footpaths, parking and other accouterments. If such a prestigious structure was coming up in place of an unorganized old structure at an affordable cost, there was no reason to oppose it.

When Andhra Pradesh is said to have spent about Rs 1,100 crore for a temporary Secretariat, what was the issue if Telangana builds a permanent integrated Secretariat complex with about a little more than half of it? Telangana needed a new government building complex, which could as well be like a memorial to all the sacrifices its people made in their long and arduous struggle for political freedom.

It has now materialized, constructed in just two years. The 120-ft height Ambedkar statue and the Martyrs Memorial in front of it are the fine embellishments to the new Telangana Secretariat building. And it is aptly named after Dr Babasaheb Ambedkar, the architect of Article 3 of the Constitution, which helped Telangana fulfill its long cherished dream of a separate State, overruling the cantankerous 'Andhra and Kendra' politics.

61

A DECADE OF DEEDS, FULFILLMENT

(Telangana Today | 13 June, 2023)

June 2 marked the ninth anniversary of Telangana State's formation and the State entered into its 10th year of existence. During this period, the State's forward march was very eventful and inspiring. For a region which was denied its Statehood for six decades, forced to be in the company of a domineering majority region and was fighting with its back to the wall for its rightful share of its own region's resources, it is commendable progress. A revelation of its denied potential and proving wrong skeptics and an avowed vindication of its ardent activists' hopes.

At the peril of repetition, we need to recount Telangana's outstanding progress in the union of States on its 10-year journey. It has risen to a position of above 5 in the larger States in terms of GSDP and number one in per capita GSDP. The erstwhile united State was hovering at the 15th-18th position before 2014. In most of the macroeconomic indicators too, it has secured its place at the top. Its Budget performance is acknowledged to be very prudential by the Reserve Bank of India. It has also made a mark in several innovative socioeconomic schemes in these years.

Against Odds

But the two national parties and other local parties in the State refuse to acknowledge it. The Congress does not talk about progress but indulges in personal and family invective without evidence. The BJP local leaders instead of trying to get the denied help from their recalcitrant ruling Centre, promote anarchy and disgruntlement for their own political benefit. Other local parties like the TJS simply indulge in knee-jerk reactions of rejection of everything the Telangana government does. They have lost the perspective of the new State and its essential reconstruction.

The media is a peculiar mixture, dominated by 'two Telugu States' (a euphemism for Andhra) media, both print and digital. There are some local anti-Telangana and some pro-Telangana outfits. The latter is dubbed as pro-government, blithely by the antagonists. Even if they report the official Central and State data and the ground-level situation as it is, it will be billed as pro-TS government. Yet, the Telangana media reporting dedicated news on the State's progress is doing a fine job. It has shown its merit and brought the real progress of the State to the fore.

The progress made by Telangana in these years needs to be reviewed against the backdrop of its formation. It is a demerger of two merged States, not a bifurcation of the original State. It was a conditional merger. The States Reorganization Commission (SRC) did not recommend it. The Centre forced it for political reasons. They did not gel like other linguistic States. There were vehement intermittent revolts against it with a lot of loss of human life.

Naysayers Abound

It was the misfortune of Telangana to have fallen for the wrong political calculations of the Centre, in its forcible merger with Andhra in 1956. The Centre had revised such decision in the case of Bombay-Gujarat and Punjab-Haryana and bifurcated them later. They flourished after separation. In 2000, three States were created which were not in the purview of the SRC and their struggle for separate States was not as intense as in Telangana. Despite all these examples, everybody who was somebody professed that the demerger of Telangana was wrong and would trigger many such divisions. But nothing of that sort happened, except providing a profound new lease of life to the suppressed Telangana State.

As if the 58-year ordeal is not enough, the BJP Central government from 2014 started its discrimination against Telangana. It has withheld central funds in a willful manner, employed a deliberate political squeeze on the State – did not provide flood relief to Hyderabad and buy rice from the State, jeopardised Telangana's irrigation projects with its draconian takeover of river water projects on Godavari and Krishna, did not sanction national institutes, medical colleges, Navodaya schools, etc.

It also made big political raids on the State to win the GHMC election and a few by-elections to corner the BRS. It denigrated the State's development with unsubstantiated allegations, personal attacks on the Chief Minister and his government, and treated Telangana in a very condescending manner. It is a very unsavoury attitude of a central government towards a newly formed State. Leave alone helping it, trying to squeeze financially to subjugate it politically is an undemocratic act.

Strength and Resilience

Despite all this, Telangana conceived, launched and implemented many infrastructure and welfare projects, commensurate with the needs of the new State, which have become the models for other States. Perhaps Telangana is the one State which has executed all its projects with speed and efficiency and brought them to full use. Examples are many – power projects, Mission Kakatiya, Mission Bhagiratha, Kaleshwaram Lift Irrigation project, the new Secretariat and new districts. Besides, a plethora of socio-economic schemes, which in combination with capital projects, put the State in the number one position in per capita income (2023) in the country.

This underscores the economic strength and resilience of the State. It has also proved beyond doubt that Andhra was dependent on Telangana in all the 58 years in the merged State, and not the other way round. Telangana has the highest State-owned Tax Revenue (SOTR) in the country – about

75% as against the 46% average of the States. AP has about 50% SOTR. For 2021-22, the SOTR of Telangana stood at 78.87% while AP was 46.49%. The debt to GDP ratio of Telangana is at 24.7% as against AP's 31.5%. AP is heavily dependent on the Centre for its deficit revenue dole-outs. As for central tax and grants devolution for 2021-22, Telangana got just Rs 27,330 crore as against AP's Rs 74,556 crore.

The media is a peculiar mixture, dominated by 'two Telugu States' (a euphemism for Andhra) media, both print and digital. There are some local anti-Telangana and some pro-Telangana outfits. The latter is dubbed as pro-government, blithely by the antagonists. Even if they report the official Central and State data and the ground-level situation as it is, it will be billed as pro-TS government. Yet, the Telangana media reporting dedicated news on the State's progress is doing a fine job. It has shown its merit and brought the real progress of the State to the fore.

The progress made by Telangana in these years needs to be reviewed against the backdrop of its formation. It is a demerger of two merged States, not a bifurcation of the original State. It was a conditional merger. The States Reorganization Commission (SRC) did not recommend it. The Centre forced it for political reasons. They did not gel like other linguistic States. There were vehement intermittent revolts against it with a lot of loss of human life.

The progress and achievements made by Telangana have vindicated in full the grievance, claim and aspiration of the people of the separate State. It is all because of the fine culmination of the State's inherent economic strengths and pragmatic political leadership, strategisation, bold conception and execution of projects by the BRS government. Chief Minister K Chandrashekhar Rao did his homework in detail, selected the right projects, chose the right people for the right work and monitored relentlessly to bring the projects to use at the earliest. The prudential management of the Budget proved to be the key. For the good fortune of Telangana, all these things have come into play in the right measure at the right time to make the desired progress.

That made us reclaim our 'Amar Sonar Telangana', which we had lost to Andhra domination in 1956 ingenuously.

62

A UNIQUE TRIBUTE TO MARTYRS

(Telangana Today | 4 July, 2023)

The unique Telangana Martyrs Memorial, inaugurated on June 22, is a culmination of the sacrifices of thousands of Telangana people in pursuit of freedom from the domination of others. The struggle occurred even before India's independence. Thousands laid their lives in the armed struggle for the liberation of Telangana from the feudal past and have found a place in world history.

Even after independence, Telangana was thrown into the travails of subordinate freedom and made to struggle for 58 years and had to sacrifice hundreds of lives to gain its full political freedom inside the Republic of India. That happened on 2 June 2014, a red-letter day in the history of Telangana.

Early Agitation

In 1952, there was an agitation against the 'non-mulkis'. Seven people died in police firing. In 1969, in the united Andhra Pradesh in the agitation for separate Telangana, 376 people were killed in police firing. In the final State struggle, about 1,200 people are reported to have committed suicide for the sake of Statehood. It was the most heart-rending part of the whole loss of human life.

Many new States were reorganised in the country after independence, but they did not see such a high number of deaths. Except in the case of the Maharashtra-Gujarat division where 170 people were killed in police firing. Unlike the reorganisation of other States, Hyderabad State was merged with Andhra against the will of its people and the recommendation of the States Reorganization Commission, 1956, in the name of one language.

All other reorganised States amalgamated easily. But in the case of Andhra Pradesh, it did not happen. There were big agitations in 1969 and 1972. There were several original and duplicate agreements and they were only implemented in the breach than in implementation. The Centre, which has to supervise the integration of the State and implementation of the agreements, always supported Andhra for political reasons.

Indifferent Centre

Despite almost continuous discord and exploitation of Telangana resources by the majority of Andhra, the Centre never considered the demerger demand of Telangana for almost six decades. Lands in Hyderabad city, Telangana's revenues and other resources were freely used by Andhras for their betterment, leaving the local people in the lurch. It caused despair in the minds of Telangana people.

Telangana needed to mobilise its entire population in agitations like Maha Garjana, Million March and Sakalajanula Samme to force the implementation of the decision to declare Statehood in Parliament. These tenuous circumstances made the minds of Telangana people, mostly the youth, vulnerable and they resorted to suicide. This happened mostly between 2009 and 2014 when the Centre was dilly-dallying on the decision.

Here, such a large number of suicides is a peculiar phenomenon. It happened because of the callous indifference of the central government for almost six decades and the insensitive dithering of the Congress government at the behest of Andhra politicians for four-and-a-half years. The UPA government almost aborted the Telangana State declaration in the face of 'samaikyanadhra' agitation as the Congress was pinning hope on more number of MP seats in AP than in Telangana for its 2014 election calculations.

But providence willed otherwise. The Congress lost almost all of its 36-38 byelections during that period in both the regions to then TRS (BRS) and the YSRCP, and was staring at a blank account in 2014 in both regions. In such circumstances, Sonia Gandhi took the decision to carve Telangana to salvage its political numbers at least in Telangana.

This long history of denial by the Centre, the four-and-a-half years of heartless playing for time and the unbearable majority Andhra jingoism in it made Telangana youth lose heart and resort to such incongruous suicides.

Healing Wounds

Generations of people have borne the brunt of the wounds of the heroic struggles and the sacrifices. The most vexatious pain is from the suicides of hundreds of youth. It created an unremitting angst in the hearts and minds of people in the new State of Telangana. Though the State has come into existence after it and is progressing well, the unusual demise of their own in such a hapless way created a feeling of guilt and remorse for not being able to prevent it. It needed to have a memorial to assuage that intense sorrow. The creation of this unique Martyrs Memorial, the 'Amara Deepam', is such an endeavour and is very well done.

Telangana Martyrs Memorial is the world's largest seamless stainless structure and is resistant to rusting and corrosion. It is a massive egg-shaped mirror-finished edifice. The main structure is built on an 85,000 sqft area while the total built-up area of the memorial's complex is 2,85,000 sqft. The structure also has a 'diya' designed by M Ramana Reddy, the renowned artist from Telangana.

The flame is made of low-carbon structural steel and turns golden yellow when illuminated with external warm lighting. The six-floor structure houses a museum, an audio-visual hall that has 80 seats on the first floor with a 170-inch LED screen, a 650-seater convention centre-cum-museum and a photo gallery on the second floor, a restaurant at the top floor along with open terrace seating. The 161-m tall building has come up on 3.29 acres.

"The shape of an oil lamp and golden flame on top are markers of respect and tribute to the martyrs who fought over the decades for Telangana. It will also help the future generations to notice the sacrifice made by them," Ramana Reddy said. The structure, in many ways, resembles the 'The

Bean'— formally titled 'Cloud Gate' — in Chicago's Millenium Park, 'The Bubble' in the western Chinese city of Karamay, and somewhat the Future Museum in Dubai.

It is a matter of pride that such a unique edifice was designed by a Telangana artist-cum-architect, and was built by local builders under the guidance of state engineers.

63

PRLI - SOUTH TELANGANA'S WELLSPRING

(Telangana Today | 1 September, 2023)

The Palamuru-Rangareddy Lift Irrigation (PRLI) project has got a new lease of life after the advent of its full environmental clearance in August. The project is a wellspring to south Telangana just as the Kaleshwaram Lift Irrigation Project (KLIP) is to North Telangana. KLIP is almost completed and has started giving its promised benefits. It is poised to play its preeminent role in the irrigation and agriculture productivity of Telangana.

PRLI with other related schemes like Jurala, Kalwakrthy, Nettempahad, Bhima and Koilsagar, forming a southern water grid, is expected to play the same role in south Telangana. Though KLIP is larger, PRLI is as important because of its more drought-prone command, difficult terrain and endless disputes with Andhra on the Krishna water.

The project was plagued by the litigation of Andhra State, the pandemic and the intransigence of the central government. The new anti-federal river water GO of the Center and the NGT stay on the environmental clearance had delayed the project by more than two years. A partial clearance for the drinking water part of the project was available earlier. Since the NGT has provided the full environmental clearance now, the Telangana government has resumed the work on the irrigation component of the project. The State government is concentrating on completing the project at the earliest.

The Project

PRLIS aims to provide irrigation to drought-prone upland areas of Mahabubnagar, Nagarkurnool, Nalgonda, Narayanpet, Ranga Reddy and Vikarabad districts for an ayacut of 12.3 lakh acres. Its ancillary benefits are drinking water to 1,226 villages in 70 mandals en route to GHMC, Hyderabad, and water for industrial use in districts. The project involves lifting 90 tmc of water in 60 days during the flood season from the foreshore of Srisailam reservoir located at Yellur (V), Kollapur (M) in Mahabubnagar district to KP Laxmidevipally (V), Kondurg (M) in

Ranga Reddy district which is the highest elevation point in the project command, with 5-stage lifting and then utilizing water by gravity.

The six reservoirs of the project have a combined storage capacity of 63.34 tmc. In addition to the balancing reservoirs on line, there are several offline reservoirs like Sivannagudem, Kistarampalli and Gottimukkala with varying storage capacities ranging from 0.5 tmc to 7 tmc and many MI tanks which will be filled by the project. The water use is 80 tmc for irrigation, 8 tmc for drinking water and 2 tmc for industrial use. In addition, there is a massive replenishment of groundwater, helping recoup the badly ailing borewell irrigation in these drought-prone districts.

Water Share

The all-important green nod for the project is a shot in the arm for the Telangana government, which is galvanising its effort to complete the works. It comes in handy to the government's plans to start impounding water in at least 3 to 4 balancing reservoirs of the project over the next two to three months. It is known that the works on different components of the project have been completed in the range of 45% to 91% so far.

The division of Krishna water in the united Andhra Pradesh to its three regions was felt to have been made arbitrarily without regard for the catchment and cultivable areas, and the population, which was supposed to be the basic criterion for such division. As if the injustice in the distribution of dependable water as estimated by the Tribunal was not enough, the AP government went into over-utilisation of the so-called surplus and floodwaters in the Andhra region with its Cabinet decisions and government orders. PRLIS aims to provide irrigation to drought-prone upland areas of Mahabubnagar, Nagarkurnool, Nalgonda, Narayanpet, Rangareddy and Vikarabad districts.

Legitimate Right

The Srisailam reservoir has become a backyard water trough for Rayalaseema, making manipulations in the drawdown levels in the hydel project in the name of drinking water to Chennai, a Telugu Ganga project, Srisailam Right Bank Canal and all kinds of 'srujala sravnthis' to take Krishna water to irrigate the old Tungabhadra ayacut and also all the way to Penna basin areas, which are outside the Krishna basin. Even before the water share of Telangana was used, Andhra and Rayalaseema utilized beyond their share, building reservoirs exceeding 200 tmc capacity to draw floodwaters from Srisailam via the ever-widening Pothireddypadu Regulator (PPR).

In the united State, it was an intra-State issue. The Telangana region did not have the right or opportunity to present its case in the Tribunal or to the Center. But even after Telangana came into existence, the manipulation has continued. The PPR, which was originally designed for 11,000 cusecs, was increased to 44,000 cusecs before the merger. It has now been increased to 88,000 cusecs discharge capacity, to take water from the lowest level of the Srisailam reservoir via its new controversial LI projects.

In addition to this, the water availability tangle of the project raised by the Central Water Commission and the ambiguous terms of reference to the Brijesh Kumar Tribunal in the matter are other sources of irritation to PRLI. The State government weathering all these impediments is fighting for its legitimate right in the share of Krishna water both in KRMB and the BK Tribunal, and also with the Center's irrigation ministry.

The matter is of utmost importance for south Telangana. It is such a serious matter that it is imminent for all political parties in Telangana to work together to foil the motivated efforts of the Andhra government and the tacit support of the central government to it. And thwart their attempt to deprive Telangana of its legitimate share of Krishna water.

Hope that with the determined efforts of the State government and the dedicated work put in by the irrigation and electricity departments and the legitimacy of Telangana's claim on the project, PRLI will be completed at the earliest and provide full benefits as envisaged.

www.ingramcontent.com/pod-product-compliance
Lightning Source LLC
LaVergne TN
LVHW091626070526
838199LV00044B/951